MANAGING COMMODITY RISK

Forthcoming Titles in the IIA Series

MANAGING CURRENCY RISK
John J. Stephens

MANAGING REPUTATIONAL RISK
Jenny Rayner

MANAGING COMMODITY RISK

using commodity futures and options

JOHN J STEPHENS

The Institute of Internal Auditors
UK and Ireland

JOHN WILEY & SONS, LTD.

Chichester • New York • Weinheim • Brisbane • Singapore • Toronto

Other Wiley Editorial Offices

John Wiley & Sons, Inc., 605 Third Avenue,
New York, NY 10158-0012, USA

WILEY-VCH Verlag GmbH, Pappelallee 3,
D-69469 Weinheim, Germany

Jacaranda Wiley Ltd, 33 Park Road, Milton,
Queensland 4064, Australia

John Wiley & Sons (Asia) Pte Ltd, 2 Clementi Loop #02-01,
Jin Xing Distripark, Singapore 129809

John Wiley & Sons (Canada) Ltd, 22 Worcester Road,
Rexdale, Ontario M9W 1L1, Canada

British Library Cataloguing in Publication Data

A catalogue record for this book is available from the British Library

ISBN 0-47 1-86625-3

Typeset in Times by Deerpark Publishing Services
Printed and bound in Great Britain by Biddles Ltd, Guildford and King's Lynn

This book is printed on acid-free paper responsibly manufactured from sustainable forestation, for which at least two trees are planted for each one used for paper production.

contents

CHAPTER 4: Mechanics of the Marketplace   81

CHAPTER 5: Hedging with Commodity Futures and Options – The User's Hedge   119

CHAPTER 6: Hedging with Commodity Futures and Options – The Producer's Hedge   161

CHAPTER 7: **Creative Commodity Risk Management**   197

tables

one

commodity risk, commodity futures and the management function

INTRODUCTION

Risk management has become one of the most fundamental managerial functions in modern business. This is not surprising since doing business and taking risk is basically the same thing. Risk is consequently not something that is to be avoided and eliminated at all cost. Rather, risk must be properly managed and effectively controlled. If you manage it successfully, your reward will be profit. If you do not, you will be rewarded by losses and failure.

As a direct consequence of the growing realisation of the importance of risk management, there has been a veritable explosion in material on the subject. Its study, analysis and techniques have developed into growth industries in themselves. The internal control function in business is becoming more and more directed towards managing risk in all its many forms and guises. Indeed, the Turnbull Report in the UK has unequivocally equated internal control with risk management.

Consequently, it has become well nigh impossible to deal with the total subject of risk management in one all encompassing work. The divergence and diversity of possible risks that need to be managed have blossomed in too many directions at once. The material on the subject deals thus with it in ever narrowing and compartmentalised categories. Such a fragmented approach has clear and definite disadvantages.

On the other hand, the subject of risk management is not necessarily relevant in its totality to every business. A fragmented approach does however allow the individual businessperson to selectively study only those aspects of the subject, which are relevant to that person's business. Alternatively, a particular person might be concerned with

1

certain limited risks and not the totality or plurality of possible risks in business. It is the intention of this book that it should fill exactly such a need for you in your business with regard to commodity risk.

The intense interest in and study of risk management as a discipline has resulted in it being divided and sub-divided into as many categories, sub-categories, types and sub-types as human ingenuity can devise. Nevertheless, it is a fascinating subject with many nooks and crannies. In this book it is proposed to investigate and to deal with managing that division of risk that may be termed 'commodity risk'. However, our particular interest lies in the manner in which such risks can be managed through the use of commodity futures. This approach no doubt requires some explanation.

THE PURPOSE OF THE BOOK

Virtually every business faces commodity risk in one way or another. The prime purpose of this book is to show ordinary businesspeople how they can use commodity futures to manage the price risk associated with commodities, in their businesses. The purpose is not to deal with the subject in a highly technical, academic or esoteric fashion. It is not necessary for every manager in business to have the knowledge, skill and understanding of a professional trader or portfolio manager.

This book is not primarily aimed at the professional portfolio manager or derivatives trader. However, there are many managers, owners and other responsible people in business who need to know how futures can be used for managing risk. They need to know and understand the commodity markets and their instruments. It is for them and for all those others, straining, training and aspiring to learn the music of the markets, that this book is written.

Risk management is not an ad hoc activity. Managing commodity risk will have different implications for different businesses. One thing is certain though, every business must take full cognisance of the incidence of commodity risk, its possible impact on the business and the best instruments and techniques for managing such risks.

Nevertheless, let it never be forgotten that people, quite unsophisticated in the rigors of finance, have used the futures markets extremely successfully for more than 150 years. They have used it mainly to hedge themselves against the risk of adverse price movement of agricultural products. The fact that the markets and their related contracts have become very much more sophisticated does not detract from the fact that the principles used so successfully for over one and a half centuries remain valid to this day.

Therefore, the first thing that every businessperson needs to realise is that yes, the futures markets are there for them also. They have to know what the markets can do for them, how the instruments work and how they should use them. They should have sufficient knowledge to give them the confidence to use the available facilities to their advantage.

There are scores of professional traders, analysts, brokers and consultants who are well able to deal with the technical detail of risk analysis and risk management. Their knowledge and skills are there at your disposal if and when you need to use them. The main thing that you need to know is when you require professional help and when you do not. Then you also need to know the purpose and the extent of your requirement.

In order to meet the special needs of businesspeople, this book sets out to deal with the subject of managing commodity risk through the use of commodity futures. Although commodity futures is not the only readily available risk management tool, it will often be the most accessible and appropriate tool for you in your business. The manner in which the subject will be dealt with is discussed below.

THE METHODOLOGY

In order to properly serve the purpose of the book a particular methodology and division of the material is adopted. Firstly, in order to facilitate understanding and to make the work as accessible as possible, each aspect of the subject is dealt with in such a way so as not to presume or rely upon any prior knowledge on the part of the reader.

Each chapter is devised as a stand-alone unit. Each one is divided into sections dealing with particular divisions and sub-divisions of the subject matter. This structure will enable the reader who may be familiar with certain aspects to ignore those sections and to focus only on material that is of particular interest or relevance to him or her.

Having said that, it must also be emphasised that the book is specifically designed as one that can be read through from the first page to the last. The sequence of subjects and topics has been selected to follow naturally from one to the other. Therefore, persons who have never seriously concerned themselves with the futures markets and how they are used in business should quite easily be able to become sufficiently informed on the subject by reading through the book. As was said a little earlier, the reader will not become a qualified expert on either the commodity or the commodity futures markets, but he or she will be fully armed with the necessary knowledge to use the markets and their instruments competently.

The rest of this present chapter is devoted to introducing the reader to the topics that will be discussed in greater detail later in this book. This overview should serve as a guide to what follows and will also give a general impression of the subject matter. It will serve to establish at least some familiarity with the contents and scope of the material that will be dealt with in the book.

THE COMMODITY MARKETS

The first course of action will be to familiarise the reader with the cash commodity markets. The cash commodity markets are those markets that deal directly with the commodity in question. It is the market on which crude oil, precious metals, fresh produce and such goods are bought and sold. It is imperative first to understand the commodity markets because the futures markets, where our eventual interest lies, are inextricably linked to the cash commodity markets.

Futures contracts are derivative instruments. That means that they derive their value from something else. They have no value in themselves. Their only value is the value that they derive from some other *merx*.

That 'something else' from which futures contracts derive their value is called 'the underlying'. The underlying is the commodity that forms the subject matter of the futures contract. Exactly how this works will be explained in detail in later chapters. The term 'commodity' in the sense it is used in the commodity futures markets, will also be discussed. The technical meaning of that term is not necessarily what might normally be understood.

Because futures contracts derive their value and their subject matter from 'physical things' or goods that trade on commodity markets, it is necessary to understand the working of those commodity markets. It also follows that the mechanics of at least one other derivative instrument, namely forwards will have to be investigated. Due to the focus on commodities, the forward contract that will be discussed is of the type usually described as cash forward agreements.

Forward contracting forms an important element in the cash commodity markets and futures contracts actually developed naturally from them. Forward contracts are valuable weapons in the risk management arsenal. However, they are only of concern insofar as they shed light on and promote understanding of futures contracts.

A thorough analysis and understanding of the mechanics of the cash, cash forward and commodity futures markets is a necessary foundation for every businessperson. Understanding how these markets are used in the day to day management of a business is then the next step. Without a properly grounded knowledge of how the business practice of managing risk with commodity futures works, a manager is much like the captain of a ship without a rudder. He or she is at the mercy of the tides, currents and storms of the markets and there is no way to steer out of trouble.

Whenever there are too many unknowns in any course of action, businesspeople will perceive that course of action as being too risky. Knowledge brings understanding; understanding adds value.

COMMODITY FUTURES

The second leg of the structure of the book discusses commodity futures. It is in fact part and parcel of the commodity market, but it does form a distinctive market within the wider commodity market.

The risks that will be dealt with are risks that originate in the commodity markets. The tool that will be used to manage that risk is commodity futures contracts. Therefore, having investigated how the commodity markets operate and how the risk that they engender affects our businesses, it is time to consider the working of the remedy.

This book does not intend to imply that futures are the only remedy. Many business managers will be aware of the multiplicity of derivatives that are available for managing business risk. Indeed, they are such flexible instruments that countless new ones are being devised and synthesised from existing ones as you read this. There is a tremendously liquid market in over the counter instruments (OTCs) such as swaps, forwards and options

It appears however, that the world of commodity futures largely remains terra incognita to most businesspeople. It is almost as if a leap of faith is required for the ordinary businessperson to actually go and buy or sell a futures contract. Nevertheless, the futures markets trade huge numbers of contracts daily. Many futures contracts are thus extremely liquid. If the sizes of contracts are taken into account, even greater quantities of commodities are traded on the futures markets than on the cash commodity markets. As will be demonstrated though, the futures markets do not really fulfil the role of acting as a conduit for the cash commodity. They are financial markets that play a financial role.

In many industries the use of futures contracts is all in a day's work. Certainly people involved in the agricultural industry are well versed in the use of futures. This is no doubt due to the fact that the first futures exchanges developed out of the needs of the agricultural sector. To this day most farmers, elevator operators, millers, grain merchants and the like use the futures markets on a daily basis. However, they are not the only, or even the main users of futures and options on futures.

who uses them?

These markets have far outgrown their agricultural roots. In fact, businesses throughout the foodstuffs industry make extensive use of futures products to manage the risks in their businesses. They are not alone. By far the greatest users of these instruments are probably portfolio managers in investment banks and financial houses. They use these markets extensively on a day to day basis to manage their risk. The financial gurus of the modern commercial world would not dream of operating without including futures and options on futures in their investment portfolios.

The reasons why the concept of futures is so successful will become clear as you become familiar with the material contained in this book. Suffice it to say at this stage that the majority of trades that are done on futures exchanges today have no connection with agriculture or foodstuffs, for that matter. They are traded for commodities other than agricultural ones, such as base and precious metals as well as energy products that include crude oil, gas and electricity. They are especially traded for their financial products that range from Treasury notes, interest rates and equity indices right through to bankruptcy rates and catastrophe insurance.

accessibility of the commodity futures markets

What may not be so generally known is that the futures markets are extremely accessible and can be utilised by virtually every business. They are often much more accessible than other derivatives, simply because they offer risk management possibilities for much smaller quantities. This opens the door to effective risk management even for the smaller business.

For example, the minimum amount of crude oil that you could get an energy cap or floor on is usually 1000 barrels of crude. By comparison, one oil futures contract on the International Petroleum Exchange (IPE) has a mere 100 barrels of crude as its underlying. Similarly, currency swaps are available in minimum amounts of $5 000 000 and £5 000 000. Against that, the Swiss franc futures contract trading on the Chicago Mercantile Exchange (CME) is for an amount of SF125 000. This translates into anything between $85 000 to $100 000 per contract, given recent exchange rates. There are even exchanges, such as the MIDAM, that exist only to trade smaller versions of futures contracts trading on other exchanges.

In addition to the greater accessibility, the range of available contracts and products has grown to the extent that businesses in virtually any commercial sector can make use of them. Consequently, the futures markets have become extremely liquid. Some contracts are liquid right up to 2 years and more into the future. High liquidity means that it becomes safer to enter futures positions, because you will always be able to find a willing buyer or seller at whatever moment you regard as opportune to liquidate your position.

what are commodity futures used for?

It is estimated that more than 80 percent of all trades transacted on futures exchanges are done for the purposes of hedging. It must be categorically stated that one must select the right instrument for the job that needs to be done. Therefore, there will often be other derivatives that will serve equally well or even better under particular circumstances. Nevertheless, futures and options on futures will always be one of the alternatives. It will often be the better and less risky alternative.

Although hedging is the most important use of futures contracts, their use is obviously not limited to that. They have all the uses that other derivatives have. They are there to take risk for profit. That is why speculators are drawn to the futures markets like bees to a honey jar. Speculators play a very important role in the whole market mechanism. They lend liquidity to the markets. The hedger will find that when a commodity futures contract is bought or sold, the other side of the trade is often not taken by another hedger, but by a speculator. The speculator will make trades depending on the view he has taken. The commodity risk manager will more likely be in the market to protect the business from risk or to limit one or other risk that the business is exposed to.

Commodity futures contracts are also used to diversify portfolios. It is not intended to go into great detail regarding the possibilities of such diversification in this book. The reason for that is that diversification of risk is most appropriate in managing the risk in a portfolio of risks. It would be difficult to convince a prudent businessperson to expose the business to other risks that have nothing to do with that business, just to diversify the risks that the business is exposed to in the normal course of things. That is not to say that ordinary businesses do not and should not diversify their risk. An example of diversification is used a little later in this chapter. Diversification would make more sense for a business if it diversified the actual business undertaking. That is a totally different situation however, from merely using commodity futures contracts to diversify existing business risk. The latter action does not make sense for businesses outside the financial sector.

Such techniques of risk diversification are far more appropriate to the activities and responsibilities of fund management, as well as to asset and investment management. Investment banks and financial institutions have made a business out of managing risk. They collect and assemble baskets of financial risk. Their needs and techniques are far more involved and sophisticated than other types of business will ever require.

OPTIONS ON FUTURES

These are very important instruments that should not be neglected. Although options on commodity futures are a relatively recent addition to the futures markets, they have already become irreplaceable adjuncts to futures contracts. They have been incorporated as valuable extensions and additions to the risk management techniques associated with commodity futures. In addition, they have developed into risk management instruments in their own right. Thus, they constitute a very important element in the toolkit of every manager of risk.

An option on futures is like many other options and option constructs that businesspeople know and use. Exactly what is involved will be made clear when options are dealt with later on in this book. What makes them different however, is that they are derivatives of derivatives.

If that sounds like double-Dutch, then do not be concerned. If you have never met these instruments before, you should be totally confused at this stage. If you are not confused, you probably do not understand what is going on. Either way, I suggest a nice, strong cup of coffee before you continue reading.

When commodity futures were discussed, you will recall that it was said that they are known as derivatives because they derive their value from something else. That 'something else' was thereupon identified as the underlying commodity, which forms the subject matter of the futures contract concerned. An option is also a contract. Its subject matter is a futures contract. The value of the option is derived from the value of the underlying futures contract. A commodity futures option is therefore a derivative of a futures contract.

The value of an option is therefore a derived value. As was stated above, it derives its value from an instrument that is in itself a derivative instrument. It is for this convoluted reason that options on futures are known as derivatives of derivatives. It makes for some interesting price relationships between the price of the underlying commodity, the price of the futures and the continuous value of the option on the futures. This is not a matter that needs to concern the business manager greatly. This is the interesting subject matter of some of the rocket science associated with the derivatives markets. Again, if it is not funds as such that are being managed, but commodity risks, the risk manager can take note of these matters and move on.

You will not be surprised to learn that to calculate the proper value of an option is a rather complicated mathematical modeling exercise. That sort of detail will not be included in this book. All the technical values ascribed to options will be dealt with however and how they should be utilised to our limited purposes will be fully discussed and demonstrated. There are fortunately many extremely good software packages around that will do all these fantastic calculations for us. Most of the time only the basic math that is required to manage our market positions will be dealt with. There are also extremely good textbooks available if you really aspire to these Olympian mathematical heights.

The gravamen of what needs to be said at this stage is that the easy access and availability of options add much more flexibility and scope to risk management with futures. In virtually every risk management situation there will be a choice of using futures contracts on their own, or options on their own, or of making use of futures combined with options, or even options combined with options.

The reason why they work so well in tandem with futures is of course, because they have futures contracts as their underlying assets. This means that during the life of an option, the holder has the right, but never the obligation, to exercise the option, thereby acquiring a position in a futures contract. The details of the whole process will be comprehensively covered when the subject of options is dealt with.

Upon exercise, the option holder will be in the position either of a person who has bought a futures contract or of a person who has sold a futures contract. The option holder will be assigned the futures position through the working of the exchange on which the option is traded. The assigned position that is then held in futures contracts will depend on whether the holder had originally bought a call option or a put option. All of this will also be explained in its proper place.

Nevertheless, at this stage you can see quite clearly why these two instruments, futures and options on futures, are used in combination. In tandem they become extremely flexible and very effective instruments that are used to deal with a great variety of situations. This does not derogate from the fact that either can be used independently of the other. It depends on what best suits the circumstances.

This is an exiting landscape that will be explored together with you, the reader. There is much to discover. There is a great deal more to learn about the subject than can be covered in this book. If the discussions and investigations in this book only serve to whet your appetite to learn more about this fascinating subject, it will have served its purpose admirably.

IDENTIFYING COMMODITY RISKS AND THEIR IMPACT

The third matter on the agenda is a discussion detailing and illustrating how commodity risks can be identified in a business, categorised and analysed. It is only once the nature and mechanics of the risk generating markets are properly understood that the risks inherent in them and the risks they present to a business enterprise can be fully appreciated.

In general terms, when the different risks that business faces are discussed, the category of risk that is dealt with in this book, namely commodity risk, will resort under market risk. Every business is subject to market risk in one way or another. When the commodity risk that a business is exposed to is focused upon, only a particular segment of the business' exposure to general market risk is being singled out for investigation and discussion.

It is thus necessary to properly understand how this particular segment of risk translates into risk for our business. Only then will meaningful management of it become possible.

In a later chapter exactly what is meant by commodity risk, thereby defining and identifying the beast to be pursued in our endeavours will be discussed. Then the influence of commodity risk on a business will be examined. How is this type of risk identified?

It will be appreciated that the purchase, sale use and possession of goods and commodities may entail all sorts of risks. Not the least of such risks being the risks of attrition through pilferage, other types of physical damage and spoilage. These are insurable risks related to commodities and they have the potential to cause serious financial loss. Nevertheless, let it be clear right from the outset that for the purposes of this book, those types of risk to commodities are not of any concern at all. The risks that are of concern, are those risks that are associated with loss due to the price movement of commodities. The problem of protecting our businesses from adverse price movements while trying to profit from favourable ones is the real concern here and it forms the subject matter of the book.

For a proper understanding and appreciation of this type of risk, our investigation must follow two avenues: firstly, the impact that particular risks will have on a business and secondly, the impact that managing that risk will have. This implies a careful consideration of all the risks that are faced in our businesses. Those risks that originate from the possible adverse price movements of commodities are the ones that will obviously occupy our attention in this book. Then an evaluation of the significance of any such adverse price move for the business must follow. Thereafter, a proper analysis of what measures are required to manage the risk must be undertaken.

The purpose of the initial risk management exercise in any firm is primarily to determine whether it is worth the cost and effort to manage any particular risk or not. It may well be that the impact that a particular commodity's price fluctuation can have on a particular business is too small to be significant. If such is the case, the risk can be accepted. That is always the risk manager's first option. Nevertheless, the identification and evaluation of every risk is important for the company. Its identification and impact evaluation must be recorded. It should thereafter be monitored on a regular basis. Just because the impact of a particular risk is not very significant at one particular point in time, it does not follow that it will remain so.

The Turnbull Report on Internal Control already evidences the importance of such a course of action. The report serves as guidance for directors of listed companies incorporated in the UK, on the Combined Code of the Committee on Corporate Governance. The report 'is based on the adoption by a company's board of a risk-based approach to establishing a sound system of internal control and reviewing its effectiveness.' (Internal Control – Guidance for Directors on the Combined Code, ICAEW 1999, p. 4). Although the report deals with listed companies, the principles enunciated are applicable to all businesses. What constitutes sound business practice for listed companies remains principally sound, no matter the type or size of the business concerned.

Clause 17 of the report sets out the factors that the board of a company should consider in judging a sound system of internal control. These are:

- the nature and extent of the risks facing the company;
- the extent and categories of risk which it regards as acceptable for the company to bear;
- the likelihood of the risks concerned materialising;
- the company's ability to reduce the incidence and impact on the business of risks that do materialise; and
- the costs of operating particular controls relative to the benefits thereby obtained in managing the related risks.

It is precisely these considerations that are addressed in this book. It will be stressed throughout that a company is limited in what it can achieve in managing commodity risk by, inter alia, the cost/benefit ratio of particular risk management instruments and techniques.

When the impact of certain commodity price fluctuations are considered, account must be taken of a number of factors. Firstly, the impact that the risk may have on the bottom line of the business must be considered. It is only natural that this will be the risk manager's first consideration. However, there are also other considerations. Commodity risk will impact differently on different aspects of the business. All aspects will have to be considered. Risk management itself will impact on the overhead costs of a business. Although costs might be the most immediate impact, there may well be other implications for the business as well.

When the impact of the risk is considered against the impact of what may be involved in managing that risk, the only prudent course open to a reasonable businessperson is being followed. Some of the implications of commodity risk and its management are discussed below.

the impact on profits and value

The first and most immediate impact of commodity risk is of course, on profits. Adverse movements in the cost of raw materials and other overheads impact negatively on profits. However, not only profits are affected. Adverse commodity price movement may have a negative effect on company asset value and even on its market penetration. Market penetration may suffer due to the impact that commodity prices may have on the demand for the firm's product or service.

The latter situation was clearly evident in the oil crises of the early 1970s. The price of oil was driven up to such heights by the OPEC cartel, that it not only seriously threatened the profits of those companies that use oil and oil products, it actually shrunk the oil market. Demand for oil decreased even though there was no serious alternative energy source immediately available. This is an extreme example.

There are always ups and downs in commodity prices. A company's profits and competitive market position will normally be threatened by these movements long before the total market for a product or service is. A firm that has a well-organised, pro-active risk management policy in place will always be better able to survive adverse market conditions and to take advantage of favourable ones than a company that does not.

the impact on the organisation

In many businesses, managing commodity risk will have implications for the structure of the organisation as well as for its human resource function. As an example of the latter, consider a factory that practices 'just-in-time' (JIT) inventory control. Virtually every manufacturer practices this system today, because it has proven its worth.

The whole system of JIT inventory control means that the price of raw materials, energy and money play no role in deciding either the timing or the quantity of inventory orders. Notwithstanding its clear and proven superiority over other forms of inventory control, JIT exposes a manufacturing concern to naked price risk. Nevertheless, this risk can and must be managed. When JIT is combined with effective commodity risk management, it becomes an even more advantageous inventory control system. Although there are numerous ways of approaching the management of the commodity risk in this instance, one of the most effective ways will be to make use of futures and options.

The question that arises for a company is on whom the responsibility for managing the risk will fall? How must the company structure be amended (if at all) to accommodate the function of managing that price risk? It is surely not a job for the orders clerk, the warehouse manager, or the factory manager. Yet somebody must be responsible. There is of course never one easy answer. It will never be a case of one size fits all. But the problem will need to be addressed and solved. These are the sort of questions that will be examined when the impact of commodity risk on company structure and procedures are dealt with.

MANAGING THE RISK

Managing the risk is what this book is eventually about. Through the use of numerous examples it will be attempted to illustrate exactly how futures and options on futures are used to manage commodity risk in everyday business situations.

As the discussion progresses through the detail of how these instruments and their markets work, what the safeguards are and what their use can mean to you in your business, you will come to appreciate their potential. The idea is to introduce you, the reader, to a range of business situations and to demonstrate through numbers of examples how the risks are dealt with.

Once the mechanics of the markets are properly understood and the commodity risks faced in your business have been identified, the necessary measures to manage that risk can be introduced. In this regard, there is no better way to sum up the purpose of risk management, which coincides with the purpose of this book, than to quote the concluding sentence of clause 13 of the previously mentioned Turnbull Report:

> ''Since profits are the reward for successful risk-taking in business, the purpose of internal control is to help manage and control risk appropriately rather than to eliminate it.''

What is said in this quote is true of every business on this planet, not only of businesses in the UK or of companies listed on the stock exchange. What is stated as being the purpose of internal control is equally true of the purpose of risk management. That also is the underlying philosophy of this book. It is in the light of this conviction that the subject of managing commodity risk through the use of commodity futures and options will be approached and dealt with.

In any business, those risks that will likely result in profit will be welcomed and sought out, while those risks that can only generate losses will be avoided. More often than not, the risks that are sought are inseparable from those ones that are better avoided. Certain risks come with the business. For instance, if you are in the business of selling cars, the basic risk that you face is that people will stop buying cars. No great risk you might say. However, the real risk might well be that people stop buying the cars that you have an agency for. Even if that does not happen, people might for many possible reasons, stop buying cars in the area where your car lot is located. One can carry on narrowing down the risk factors, thereby discovering more and more such risks in every business. The basic risks cannot be avoided, but there are ways of managing them.

the five ways of dealing with risk

There are basically five ways of dealing with risk: the first is to avoid it; the second is to accept it; the third is to leverage it; the fourth is to diversify it and the fifth action is to hedge it.

◻ EXAMPLE I-I: DEMONSTRATING THE FIVE BASIC WAYS

At this stage it will probably more illuminating to sketch a scenario that will serve as an example. Once the following working example has been sketched out, each of the five ways will be applied to the scenario to demonstrate how it affects the business concerned.

the scenario Consider a factory, Brassy Class, that manufactures brass furniture. It is obviously prepared to accept all the basic risks of competition and the risk that people would wish to buy such furniture, etc. It is in business exactly because it believes it can deal with those risks very well through its special knowledge and expertise in the industry.

With this particular business, as with most businesses, comes the risk that the prices of their basic materials may change adversely. If the company invests in a large inventory of its required raw materials, they will be able to factor that cost of material into their production costs for some time into the future. They will thus be less susceptible to a rise in the price of their raw materials. In fact, they have only changed the direction of the risk they are exposed to. Sitting with a large inventory of raw materials that they bought at a certain price, they are now susceptible to a drop in the price of raw materials. A drop in price would not only serve to lower the value of their inventory, but it will make it difficult for the company to compete with companies that now buy their raw materials at the lower price. It looks like a lose–lose situation.

In addition, they will have to tie up a lot of capital in inventory, which will also probably hold a number of disadvantages for the business. Also, the company will incur carrying cost. Carrying cost includes interest on the capital invested in inventory, the cost of warehousing it, insurance and so on.

Since purchasing large stocks is obviously not a good option, the question arises as to what the best method might be of managing this particular risk, namely that of an adverse change in the price of raw material. This question will be discussed under each of the five possibilities, all of which will definitely not be applicable or appropriate, but will nevertheless serve to illustrate the point. You will also notice that more than one method might be suitable. The real answer will depend on a number of other factors in the business, which will become obvious as each option is discussed.

avoiding risk This sounds like a rather straightforward option, but it is not. It does not matter how Brassy Class operates, it will always face the risk of adverse moves in the price of its raw materials. The risk is therefore unavoidable in principle. However, it is not unavoidable over specific periods of time.

Most commodity risk that you would deal with in your business, would be much like the risk that Brassy Class faces: although it is a risk you would rather not have, it is a natural concomitant of the business you are in. You therefore cannot avoid it in the first instance, but you can avoid it by contracting out of the risk for a period.

The first option is to avoid the risk by investing in a large quantity of inventory. The disadvantages of this option have been discussed. It does not really avoid the risk of adverse price movement at all. It merely changes the risk that the company is exposed to from the risk of a rise in price to the risk of a drop in price. As a risk avoidance strategy it is thus illusory.

That is not to say that it cannot be used as a strategy however. There may be times when management is so totally convinced that the price of the raw material is going to rise that the risk of a fall in price is purely theoretical. The expected quantitative rise in price must then be sufficiently great so that the increase in cost occasioned by holding the inventory is justified.

Forward contracting is another way of avoiding the risk. A forward contract is an agreement whereby one party undertakes to purchase some *merx* from the other party at an agreed time in the future for an agreed purchase price. Payment of the purchase price will be made against delivery of the goods.

If Brassy Class opted for this course of action it would be in a better position than if it had purchased the inventory beforehand. It will not be subject to an adverse increase in price because it has contracted at a fixed price. It will still, however be at risk of a drop in price as in the previous suggestion. However, the same considerations and counter considerations will apply as in the previous strategy.

The strategy of forward contracting has the advantage that it will not tie up the firm's capital in inventory and it will not incur any carrying charges directly. However, the forward purchase price it will have agreed to pay, will be a greater price than the spot price at the time of entering the contract. The carrying charges will have to be compared to the price difference in order to make a valid comparison of the advantages of one strategy over the other. Nevertheless, the advantage of not tying up capital in inventory is a major one that goes beyond the consideration of interest.

accepting the risk   The next option that brassy Class has is to just accept the risk. It may just carry on, purchasing its inventory as and when required, probably on a JIT basis. It takes no action to protect itself from the risk of an adverse price move of its raw materials.

A responsible company can only adopt this course of action after careful consideration of a number of factors. The first and most important consideration is the impact that an adverse price move might have on the total cost of production.

Let us say that in Brassy Class's case, the accounting people get together and they determine that the cost of raw materials, ordered on the JIT basis, only contributes 5 percent to the total cost of the finished article. They then take into account the worst probable rise in the next 12 months together with the proven annual volatility of the market. They come to the conclusion that, based on those calculations, the worst possible price rise over the next 12 months would be a 50 percent increase on present price levels.

The worst case scenario would therefore entail a 2.5 percent increase on the present overall cost. Given their gross mark-up and net profit margins, they might decide that they could easily absorb such an increase, should it take place. Alternatively, they might decide that, given their competitive position in the market, they could pass on the increase to the consumer without any notable buying resistance.

If the above considerations apply, the company may very well agree to accept the risk. A word of caution is required however. Before the considerations discussed above can be truly valid, the company would have to investigate the cost and advantages of utilising any of the other four methods of risk management.

The cost of implementing another strategy might be negligible and it may have advantages other than merely dampening or neutralising the possible 2.5 percent cost increase. Firstly, the company might consider what the net cost advantage, gained by using an appropriate risk management technique, could mean to shareholders in the form of dividends. It may decide that the effect on dividends is even more negligible, thus discounting that consideration.

However, the company might also consider whether another course of action would allow them to maintain prices, perhaps even lower them, while their competitors, who merely accepted the risk, will be forced to raise their prices or take a knock on profit. The worst possibility to consider is that the competition adopts another cost effective course of action. Brassy Class may well find itself in a very vulnerable situation. It may be forced to lower prices in order not to lose market share to the competition, while at the same time absorbing the additional cost. The implications for the company might then become quite serious.

leveraging the risk   To leverage the risk means in fact to increase it, to support it and to make it greater. This clearly could not be a viable option in the case of Brassy Class. One would only leverage risk if it were a risk from which you intended to make a profit. Whenever you leverage a risk, you should at the same time take appropriate measures to hedge it or at least to diversify it in order to prevent a devastating impact when an adverse price move occurs.

For the purposes of this example however, the principle of leverage can still be illustrated by using the Brassy Class scenario. The major price element in brass, is the price of copper. The board of Brassy Class is so certain that the price of copper is going to drop over the next 6 months, that they decide to make some additional profit from this expectation. They consequently sell a certain quantity of copper futures contracts. They do not have the copper and they do not wish to buy it. By taking this action the company will have leveraged their risk position as far as copper is concerned.

They are now in double jeopardy. If the price of copper rises instead of taking the expected fall, the price of brass will also rise, increasing the company's cost of production. Additionally, they will face a loss on their futures contracts. This course of action is therefore potentially disastrous.

Should the price of copper, by some fluke, actually decline as expected, the director who suggested the leveraging proposal will probably be hailed as a hero, immediately promoted to CEO and given a bonus. This is not risk management. It is pure gambling. It is utterly astonishing to see that companies actually indulge in this sort of thing.

diversifying the risk   It was stated earlier on that risk diversification would normally be more appropriate to portfolio management than to risk management in a business, especially in a business that does not involve managing baskets of financial risks. However, as mentioned at the time, such a course of action is not totally out of the question, even for Brassy Class.

In order to illustrate this option, some very different assumptions will have to be made. Firstly, an assumption will have to be made that the contribution of raw materials to total cost of production is much higher than 5 percent. For the purposes of the example, it will also have to be assumed that the view that the board takes on the future price of the raw materials is such that it sees the growth of the company, or its market penetration threatened thereby.

As would be the case with most businesses, it would be impossible in Brassy Class' case to diversify only the risk on raw material. The raw materials required are absolutely dictated by the product manufactured. Diversification would therefore have to involve a diversification of the business itself. The board may decide that with the present equipment and human resources it might be quite feasible to diversify into the manufacture of aluminium furniture. The price of aluminium and the price of copper are not correlated. This means that exposure to the price of aluminium will tend to dampen the risk that results from being exposed to the price of copper and vice versa.

Indeed, the markets for the finished articles could be targeted in such a way that they will not be correlated either. So on the market side they will also have diversified and therefore dampened their risk. A word of caution needs to be sounded here.

If the company diversifies into aluminium furniture manufacturing through additional investment rather than by scaling down the manufacture of brass furniture, the company may not be diversifying at all. Indeed, in terms of risk exposure to the furniture market as such, the company may be leveraging the present risk. A true diversification would be engineered by converting the excess brass furniture manufacturing capacity, obtained through a downscaling, into an aluminium furniture manufacturing capacity.

hedging the risk   Hedging the risk may be Brassy Class's easiest and cheapest option under normal circumstances. If the board is satisfied that the present cost projections will ensure adequate profits for the company and a suitably competitive position in the market with good growth prospects, its first consideration should be to try to preserve the status quo as far as material cost is concerned.

Hedging is not the same as avoiding risk. Hedging is the purposeful taking on of another risk that is negatively correlated with the risk being hedged. Negative correlation means that the two risks move exactly oppositely to one another: if the one variable gains £1 sterling in 1 day, the other variable will lose £1 sterling during the same day. The loss on the one is made up by the gain on the other. Risk is thus not avoided, but rather, it is neutralised.

The easiest way to do that is to buy a futures contract as a substitute for a spot market purchase. It acts as a 'place-holder' for a future purchase of the physical commodity. This whole concept will also be explained in detail later on. You will learn how simple it is to assume a negatively correlated risk by means of a futures contract.

The advantage is that this course of action does not involve any immediate investment of capital. That places it on a par with avoiding risk. However, it has a few advantages over risk avoidance as described above. The futures contract does not irrevocably compel the company to buy the quantity of raw materials on the future date. The company may decide to buy more, less or none at all when delivery day arrives. This is due to the facility of 'setting-off' that is part and parcel of the futures markets.

This facility will allow the company to continue its JIT program, since it is not obliged to buy the quantity of raw material at the time of delivery stipulated in the futures contract. This is unlike the situation with risk avoidance. If the material is bought forward, the advantages of JIT will probably be lost. Whenever the company has to place an order for raw materials, and it finds that the price of the raw materials has moved adversely, it can use the profit on the futures at that stage, to offset the additional cost of the materials.

Again, there is the danger of the previously mentioned basis risk. There is a difference between the spot price of a commodity and the futures price. The price difference is referred to as the basis. The spot price of a commodity and the futures price of that commodity will not track each other perfectly. In other words, the basis (the price difference) may widen or it may narrow.

It is very difficult, but mostly impossible, to hedge against basis risk. However, basis risk presents much less of a danger than 'naked' commodity risk. Also, so much is known about the movement of basis, that it is not a totally uncalculated risk. The mechanics of the market and the factoring in of basis moves will be investigated and discussed in some considerable detail. For the moment, the assurance can be given that, although it is a factor that must be given due consideration in every futures transaction, it is not a factor that need deter us from using the futures markets.

Apart from using a futures contract to hedge the risk, the company may decide to make use of options on futures. This involves a cost, because there is a premium to be paid on an option. Brassy Class might also lose some flexibility in the interim period, but the company will be compensated for that slight inflexibility, inasmuch as they will be able to take advantage of a decline in the price of the raw material. In purchasing an option, the risk of the company will be limited to losing the premium paid for it. If prices fall, the option the company would have purchased in order to protect them against a rise in price, will experience a decline in value. The company will then merely abandon the option, or sell it back into the market and purchase the material at the lower spot price. By being able to sell the option back into the market, albeit at a lower price than was paid for it, the company will at least be able to limit the cost of the hedge. This facility would not be available if the position were hedged with futures or by a forward purchase.

CONCLUSION

It must be apparent at this stage that there are many avenues open to the risk manager. Circumstances and the situation of his company will dictate a lot of the possible choices and options. Some of the options may simply be a matter of preference or due to the company's degree of risk aversion.

The discussion up to this point must also have revealed another important fact: not all risk management options can be availed of by using futures and options. In the commodity markets, futures and options can be used very successfully to leverage risk and to hedge risk. As discussed above, in managing commodity risk, risk diversification cannot be readily achieved merely by employing commodity futures. The only feasible way to diversify commodity risk would be to diversify the business of the company into other commodities.

The chapters on managing commodity risk will therefore mainly deal with how the risk management technique of hedging can be successfully and advantageously applied through the use of commodity futures and options on futures.

CHECKLIST FOR THE REVIEW OF CHAPTER 1

General overview: the overall control objectives of the material dealt with in this chapter are to gain a basic understanding of how commodity risk can be identified and managed

	Key Issues	Illustrative Scope or Approach
1.1	Has the business identified those commodities that may place it at financial risk?	These include all such physical goods as are owned, used, held, consumed and/or produced by the business;
1.2	Has the impact of adverse price moves in each commodity been appraised?	• Adverse moves in the prices of commodities can impact on the profits of a business by directly increasing overheads or by decreasing the selling prices of goods produced; • Adverse moves in the prices of commodities can impact on the value of a business by decreasing the value of physical assets or of inventory held;
1.3	Has the impact of managing the risk of each commodity been assessed?	Generally speaking, managing risk has an impact on the organisation in terms of staff training, creating a risk management culture and can even increase the head count. Managing the risk inherent in using any particular commodity must be assessed in terms of the direct trading costs of the derivatives used, resources required against the benefits to be gained;
1.4	Does the business repeat the steps outlined in 1.1, 1.2 and 1.3 above on a continuous basis?	Businesses and the commodity markets are constantly in a state of flux. What may not be a substantial risk today, may be a crucial risk tomorrow. On the commodity futures markets new contracts are offered continuously. What may not be an economically viable risk management prospect today, may be one tomorrow.

continued

Key Issues	Illustrative Scope or Approach
1.5 Does the business, with respect to each commodity involved, consider the five possible ways of dealing with risk?	Many factors influence the commodities used by a business. New product specifications, customer requirements and advances in technology may bring new commodity risks and thus require new assessments to be made regularly; ● Avoiding the risk – if the risk is not a necessary concomitant of the nature of the normal business; ● Accepting the risk – if the impact of accepting the risk does not have substantial financial consequences for the business and if the cost of managing the risk is not warranted by the advantage gained; ● Leveraging the risk – when the risk is so beneficial to the business and the outcome so certain that the risk can be increased by assuming a further positively correlated risk; ● Diversifying the risk – when it is possible to decrease the exposure to one risk and to replace the decrease with another risk that is not correlated with the first risk; ● Hedging the risk – when another risk that is negatively correlated with the first risk can be assumed so that the two risks neutralise each other.

two

the commodity markets and their instruments

INTRODUCTION

All trade takes place in a market or 'the' market, depending on the context. The various and numerous ways that the word 'market' is used is apt to cause confusion. There are daily references to the Asian market, the European market, the cash market, the futures market and the energy market to mention but a few.

In fact, there is only one giant global marketplace. Every possible commercial good and service is traded, bartered and exchanged on this one giant market. In the past, lack of communication segmented the market into these different locations, allowing each location to be seen as a separate self-contained market. As the global village shrinks, the single, global marketplace is becoming more apparent and more accessible.

Nevertheless, markets and the dynamic mechanisms that operate in them can be viewed from so many perspectives and analysed for so many purposes, that the confusing uses of the word 'market' will inevitably remain. This should not act as a deterrent to reaching a proper understanding of what is meant by the different uses of the term. Each use does have an underlying ratio that helps us categorise and analyse the markets. Without these aids to understand and evaluate particular aspects of the overall market, comprehension of market dynamics may very well be lost.

CATEGORISING THE MARKETPLACE

Because of the foregoing considerations, it is advisable to start the investigation into the commodity markets with a discussion of some of the different ways in which the term 'market' is used.

When it is averred that there is a market for something, it is usually meant that there is demand for that product. Using the term 'market' in this fashion is extremely misleading. A market is so much more than mere demand. One could imagine substantial demand potential for fresh dinosaur droppings, but for obvious reasons, there will never be such a market. Demand on its own can thus never constitute more than a potential market.

Before there can be said to be a market for any particular good or service, there must be both demand for and supply of that good or service. Additionally, as a necessary precondition for the existence of any real market, at least some operating mechanism allowing demand and supply to meet and interact is required. In an active market, buyers represent demand and suppliers represent supply. There are as many ways in which buyers and sellers can get together and communicate as human ingenuity can contrive. They can meet at a particular place or places, or through some other medium, such as printed matter, telegraphs and telephones or on the Internet.

It follows that there are innumerable ways that markets can be categorised. They can be categorised by meeting place, by the goods traded on it and so forth. Only some of the more important categories that are relevant to the purpose of our subject will be dealt with in this discussion.

Obviously, only goods that have commercial value will trade on a market. Anything tangible or intangible that has commercial value is referred to as a *merx*. One could therefore be forgiven for assuming that the term commodity is synonymous with the term 'physical goods'. However, this is not quite so. The word 'commodity' is a term that is often used loosely, probably because its proper meaning is difficult to pin down. Its definition for the purposes of this book will be fully investigated when the identification of commodity risk is discussed in a following chapter.

In all the discussions in this chapter, markets that trade physical goods will generally be dealt with, unless the context implies differently. The mechanics of markets tend to be exactly the same whatever is being traded. Commercial principles are valid for all markets.

the global market

Commodities are traded all over the world. Because of the globalisation of the market, the price in one place in the world will influence the price in other places. Even as far as supply and demand is concerned, it is of more value to look at global supply and demand than to fixate on any local condition. Local inventory of a commodity will obviously influence the local price, while the leads and lags in logistics will also play a role in fixing a particular price in a particular place.

Many managers are often in danger of losing sight of the global supply/demand situation of a commodity in formulating their market expectations. Of course, certain commodities are by definition local, such as damage insurance premiums, or Western Gas in the US. Nevertheless, by far the majority of commodities are available globally.

Consider the example of a local soybean crop failure. This will undoubtedly cause a local shortage and a rise in the local price. Many farmers and merchants have from time to time cultivated exceedingly high price expectations under such conditions. The question really is: how high can the price go? Actually, the price can only go as high as import parity.

Import parity is the price at which sufficient supplies can be imported and delivered to a particular locality to meet local demand at that locality. This implies that there is not an import parity price for a country as a whole. There can be an import parity price for delivery at a particular port. The import parity price at any particular locality will thereafter increase directly proportional to the distance of that locality from the port of importation. The only factor that influences this price is the cost of inland transport. It is in fact a very straightforward calculation to make.

the cash market

The cash market is the physical goods or commodity market in which everybody normally trades. It is not an institution or even necessarily a place. It refers to that amorphous, but ubiquitous global 'market' that is so often the subject of economic analysis. However, the term denotes the market where the physical, the real, or the actual commodity, as opposed to any derivative or financial instrument is bought, sold or exchanged.

There are many places all over the world that are specifically built or set aside for the buying, selling and bartering of physical goods. However, it is not to such places that reference is made when speaking of the cash market. All such 'marketplaces' are only local and specific manifestations of the much wider and universal commodities market. In fact, the cash commodities market is a sub-division of the global market. When the term 'cash market' is used, the word 'cash' is intended to indicate the nature of the *merx* traded on the market – the *merx* being 'cash'.

Cash in this sense refers neither to the method of payment, nor to the time of payment. It simply refers to the fact that it is a trade, the subject matter of which is the actual or physical thing, whatever 'thing' it might be. The cash market is therefore the market where, for instance, the actual gold, copper, corn, or whatever commodity people happen to be dealing with, will be bought and sold. It follows that the word 'cash', as used in the marketplace is synonymous with the physical product, or commodity. A farmer might say 'I sold some cash corn into the market today', as opposed to saying 'I sold corn futures into the market today'.

the primary market

A commodity, as it will be defined somewhat later on, is per se a primary instrument. It is a thing of commercial value that derives such value from the markets in which it is traded. Its value is purely a factor of the supply and the demand for that *merx* itself. In other words, the value of the *merx* is whatever market participants are willing to pay for it.

It is clear that metals, corn, and stocks are primary instruments. Even Treasury bonds are primary instruments. Notwithstanding the fact that the price of a bond can be derived from the prevailing rates, its value is not a derived value. This is because the rates are in fact calculated from the prices of Treasury bonds in the first place. The value of a Treasury bond is determined in the open market by discovering what people are willing to pay for them. What people are willing to pay for them is influenced by the cost of money, which is the interest rate. Therefore, the price of a Treasury bond reflects both the value of the bond and the prevailing rate. The one can be derived from the other, but the Treasury bond remains a primary instrument because it has primary value.

the derivative markets

The derivative markets are those markets on which derivative instruments are bought and sold. Derivatives form a whole class of financial instruments. Futures contracts and options on them, being two of the instruments that fall into this class of financial instruments, are accordingly part of the general derivatives markets.

A derivative instrument is a financial instrument that derives its value from the value of some other *merx*. The *merx* from which it derives its value is the primary instrument, which trades on the primary market. It is also referred to as the underlying of the derivative instrument.

There are a number of other derivative instruments, apart from futures contracts. Each derivative instrument has its own niche in the practice of risk management. A responsible manager must at least be conversant with the basic characteristics of all of them.

The most important derivative instruments are swaps, forwards, over the counter (OTC) options, exchange traded options, commodity futures and options on futures. All swaps and forwards are over the counter instruments. Over the counter options, or OTCs, are so called because they are not traded on an exchange. They are usually, although not invariably, bought and sold through banks and other financial institutions.

It may be a bit of an overstatement to say that they can actually be bought over the counter, but the appellation is not entirely inappropriate. Pre-packaged derivative instruments are available with standard conditions and in 'popular' quantities. Any client can walk into a bank and, subject to certain conditions, walk out with any of these pre-packaged instruments. However, they are by their nature instruments that can be structured on an individual basis to suit the needs of a client. For the most part, OTC instruments are negotiated and carefully structured to meet a client's risk management needs.

The subject of derivatives as such need not detain the discussion. As stated previously, each derivative has its niche. The object of this book is to concentrate on the multifarious uses of futures instruments.

the spot market

The spot market is sometimes confused with the cash market. There is in fact a clear distinction in the terminology. Whereas, as has been demonstrated elsewhere, the word 'cash' in the cash market refers to the subject matter of the trade, the word 'spot' in 'spot market', refers to the terms of delivery. Nothing precludes a spot transaction from being a credit transaction or a transaction on account. 'Spot' does not refer to the terms of payment. The term is so frequently encountered that it deserves some further discussion.

A spot transaction is a cash market transaction. A cash commodity is bought against immediate delivery in a spot transaction. The meaning of the term 'immediate delivery' varies from commodity to commodity. Immediate delivery does not necessarily mean right now. Spot delivery could range anywhere from right now, to same-day delivery to delivery in a week or even a month's time. The defining factor is that delivery is not contractually deferred in any way, but takes place as soon as is reasonably possible. This feature distinguishes spot transactions from cash forward and futures transactions. In the latter two transactions, delivery of the underlier will occur at an agreed to, specified date in the future.

Not surprisingly, the price charged for a commodity in a spot transaction is called the spot price. Market price reports often quote the spot price of a commodity in addition to the forward or futures price. All commodities have spot prices. Most loans are made at the spot interest rate. The interest rate that is charged on a spot loan is called the spot interest rate. The exchange rate on spot foreign exchange purchases is similarly referred to as the spot exchange rate.

PRICE DISCOVERY IN THE MARKETPLACE

No matter what category of market is being referred to, the same basic activity is taking place. One might say the basic activity in any market must be the buying and selling of some *merx*. That of course, is true. However, the matter is not quite that simple. The functions of markets are rather more complex. Because buyers and sellers 'meet' each other in the market, the market functions as a price discovery mechanism. In other words, both buyers and sellers may go to market, each with his or her own idea of what the price is that he or she is prepared to pay for, or sell a particular commodity at. However, it is only when they meet each other that they will discover what the price is that both parties will be prepared to settle for. This fact has some far-reaching implications for defining successful markets, as will be seen later on.

the market as an auction

The prices of commodities, as is the case with everything else, are determined by supply and demand. Such prices are 'discovered' in the marketplace. Price discovery is probably the most important function of a market. Although prices are discovered in many different ways in different markets, the process is best understood as an auction. By one means or another, all markets 'auction' off whatever commodities are brought to it. Through the auction process buyers and sellers, come together, the former offering commodities for sale, while the latter bid money thereon in competition with one another.

This transparent process of 'bid' and 'offer' is the fairest method of price discovery yet devised. The more all interested parties are represented in the market, the better the market price reflects all the diverse factors and elements that go into determining a fair price for a particular commodity at a particular time. Larger markets accordingly tend to be more successful than smaller markets. As previously explained, the price established for a particular cash commodity on a particular market on a particular day for immediate delivery is known as the spot price for cash.

The same principle and process of price discovery applies to futures markets. As will be fully discussed later, futures trading is restricted to tightly controlled exchanges, whereas spot transactions mostly take place 'over the counter'. The term 'over the counter' refers not only to the countless numbers of spot commodity transactions on the open market. It refers also to the millions of private commodity and derivative instrument transactions that take place daily and that are not necessarily reported per transaction. Only products that are readily available or financial instruments that can be created by agreement between parties, can be the subjects of over the counter trades. When the advantages of organised exchanges are dealt with, the importance of the distinction between 'over the counter' instruments and 'exchange-traded' instruments will become apparent.

Of course, there are thousands upon thousands of open and public markets where trading in cash commodities take place every day. Just imagine for a moment all the fresh produce markets, fish market, meat markets, the metals exchanges, the livestock auctions, crude oil exchanges and many others. The publicly quoted spot prices of commodities are usually prices that have been discovered on such open and organised commodity markets. On such markets, transactions are usually properly reported and processed.

MARKET PARTICIPANTS

buyers and sellers

The two most basic market participants are of course, buyers and sellers. In the modern world, buyers and sellers will seldom act personally in the handling of their transactions in the marketplace. More often than not, agents, also known as brokers will represent them. Agents and brokers usually act for a commission, charged as a percentage of the price realised on the transaction. The charge is usually referred to either as commission or as brokerage.

speculators

Speculators might be buyers or sellers of the cash and they are very important participants in every market. They buy and sell the commodity with the sole purpose of profiting from price disparities and movements. They neither produce, nor use the commodity in any way. Their role in the market is complex, but generally, they lend liquidity to the market. By assisting in realising market forces that are prevalent in the larger economy, they play an important part in price discovery. Additionally, by moving goods between areas with price differentials they may actually assist in spreading the physical availability of commodities more evenly. The latter action results in generally lower and more stable prices.

MARKET POSITIONS

Buyers and sellers in the markets are said to have a market position. In the cash market a participant will have a cash position, while in the futures market, a person will have a futures position. The 'position' will usually be 'long' or 'short'. This terminology will become clearer as the present discussion progresses.

When a person comes to market, he usually does so in order to obtain some cash position. He may already have a cash position that he wishes to change in the market, or he has no cash position, but he wishes to adopt one.

a long cash position

A person who owns or possesses something is said to be 'long' that thing, whatever it might be. His position in the cash market will be 'long'. There are two ways that a person can obtain a long position: either he can buy the *merx*, or he can produce it. It is immaterial whether he produces by means of manufacture or agriculture. A person, who holds a long position in any *merx*, is often referred to as a 'long'.

Buyers come to the market with the intention of purchasing the commodity. Usually, they would be users of the product in some way, or they might be speculators. They do not necessarily have any cash position; i.e. they neither possess, nor owe anybody the cash commodity. Their intention is solely to go long cash. Once a buyer has made his purchase, his position is long cash. It is immaterial whether he has taken delivery or possession of the cash; once he has bought, he is long. This certainly is the situation of the buyer who lacks any cash position when he comes to market.

a short cash position

A person who has sold something without owning or possessing it is said to be short that thing, whatever it might be. His position in the market is 'short'. He is often simply referred to as a 'short'.

The short is of course, obliged at some point in the future to deliver the *merx* that he sold. A short is therefore another type of buyer that comes to market. The short comes to market with an established position in the market, most likely with the intention of changing that established position.

going long the market or shorting the market

When the short comes to market and goes long the commodity by buying it, his two opposite market positions naturally cancel one another out. Once the 'short' has gone 'long', he has no cash position any longer.

For this situation to prevail however, it is an absolute condition that he buys the identical commodity in grade, quality and quantity that he is obligated to deliver. If he does not buy exactly the commodity that his short position requires, he will still be short that commodity to a greater or lesser extent, depending on by how much his long position cancels out his short position. In addition he will be long the commodity that he actually bought.

If he buys more of the identical commodity than his short position requires, he will no longer be short, but he will be long cash for the residue. Conversely, if he buys too little of the commodity, his net position will be short cash for the shortfall.

The seller of a commodity usually, but not always, owns, or possesses, or is in some way entitled to dispose of such cash commodity. The seller might be the producer of the commodity, or a speculator. As has been mentioned, a person who has bought, or who owns or possesses the cash commodity is said to be 'long cash'. Sellers, usually therefore, are usually long cash and go into the market to 'short cash', i.e. to sell the cash. The seller who has sold his goods has no cash position – certainly, as far as the goods he brought to market are concerned. When he came to market he was long cash, then he shorted cash. Selling is also termed 'shorting'. Again, being simultaneously long the cash and short the same cash commodity results in the two positions cancelling one another out. Consequently, no cash position is held at all.

determining the market position

From the discussion so far, it should be reasonably straightforward to determine what the market position of a particular person at a given moment is. However, it may not always be so obvious when dealing with intangibles.

Consider a woman who owns equity in a company listed on the stock exchange. It is clear that she is long the equity. Say, however, she owns an equity portfolio with a profile much like the Dow Jones Industrial Average. This means that her portfolio will react to market movements much like the Dow reacts. She is clearly long the equities she holds, but what is her position relative to the Dow? As it happens, she will also be long the Dow. The following discussion will clarify this.

Probably the simplest way to determine whether a person is long or short, is to determine what the price risk is that the person faces. A person owning or possessing a thing, has an asset. Any person holding an asset wishes that asset at least to keep and not lose its value. From this general statement, it can confidently be stated that a person, who is long an asset, is a person who would lose if the asset loses value. The shorthand statement would be to say that a long risks a fall in price.

It follows that the short risks a rise in price – but why? The short, as has been explained, is a person who is under an obligation to deliver a *merx* in the future which he does not yet possess. This situation necessarily implies that he will be required, at some time in the future, to acquire that *merx* – whatever it may be. If the price of the *merx* rises before he acquires it, the cost of acquiring it will obviously increase. A person in that (short) position would naturally benefit if the price of the *merx* were to fall rather than rise.

cash positions in intangibles

The special case of stock indices has already enjoyed some discussion. One or two others may also be helpful to illustrate the principle. Consider the situation of a person who has borrowed money. What would be the borrower's position regarding interest rates?

Applying the risk test, a rise in interest rates would clearly be detrimental to a borrower. Let us not, for this purpose, consider the fact that a borrower may have entered into a fixed rate agreement with the lender. That fact does not influence his market position. It does influence the risk in that particular case, but not the market position. He has neutralised the natural risk of a borrower, against which he has given up the opportunity of gain, should interest rates drop. Such a borrower has in fact hedged his risk by agreement.

Since a borrower would naturally lose when rates increase and gain when they drop, it follows that the borrower's market position must be short interest rates. Once a market position has been hedged, the original position, short or long remains. Keep in mind that the original position is only neutralised by taking an equal and opposite position in the same commodity. The hedge neutralises the risk of the original position and does not neutralise the position itself.

Now consider the situation of the lender. A lender would normally be vulnerable to a fall in interest rates, since the return on capital would be diminished. A long is vulnerable to a fall in price and therefore the lender is long interest rates. However, what is her position if she has entered into a fixed rate loan? As is the case with the borrower, that stipulation does not alter the fact that she is long. It means that the opportunity of a rise in interest rates has been sacrificed in order to eliminate the risk of a drop in rates. Her position too, is hedged by agreement.

Next, consider the position of a company that runs a fleet of vehicles and takes out short term insurance with an underwriter. The fleet owner's premiums would be determined by a number of factors, but most profoundly by the general short term insurance rates applicable to his type of business in his area of operations. The usual term for such insurance is 1 year. Usually short term insurance rates are not amended during the currency of the term of an underwriting agreement, although there are notable exceptions. Whatever the situation, be it during the term of the agreement or at renewal, the fleet owner is vulnerable to a rise in insurance rates. It follows that the fleet owner is short insurance rates.

One might be tempted to argue that the underwriter, on the other hand, would not really lose should rates decrease. This is due to the fact that insurance rates are determined actuarially to compensate for risk. If claims risk decreases, insurance premiums decrease and vice versa. Therefore, if premiums decrease the underwriter's compensation is that it faces less claims risk. However, do not be misled by such considerations. The fact of the matter is that the total income of the underwriter will decrease if rates decrease. The underwriter must tailor its risk/reward profile so that it gains greater opportunity for profit when facing greater risk. Consequently, when the risk it faces decreases, the underwriter's opportunity for improved profit also decreases. Whichever way one looks at it, the underwriter is long insurance rates. Furthermore, since one party is short cash, the party holding the opposite position in the agreement must of necessity hold the opposite position in cash – long, in this case.

The final example that will be examined here, is the case of the factory that uses many units of electricity in its production process. Clearly, a rise in the unit price of electricity will increase the cost of production of the factory. It follows that the factory is short electricity rates. The power company is therefore long electricity rates. Again, the argument that a decrease in the rate charged for electricity is a concomitant of the cost of production and increased demand cannot be credited. For the same considerations spelled out in the previous example, the cash position of the power supply company is long.

CASH FORWARD CONTRACTING

Since ancient times, the commercial necessity for being able to make an agreement in the present time for rights and obligations that lie in the future has been recognised. Forward contracting was thus a well-established part of Roman law by the time of Justinian's codification of the law around 500 AD. It is still a valuable and integral part of the modern market mechanism.

Forward contracts are usually merely referred to as forwards. They are mainly used to trade stocks, commodities and currencies. A special instrument has been developed by banks for use in the interest rate markets. They are known as forward rate agreements (FRA's), but they are often also referred to as interest rate insurance.

The basic elements of the standard forward agreement are that it is an agreement between a buyer and a seller for delivery of a specified quantity and quality of the cash commodity at an agreed upon place and date in the future, in return for payment of an agreed upon price. The forward agreement is of interest to us only because it is the forerunner of the modern commodity futures contract.

Forward contracts are by their very nature over the counter instruments. That means that they are not exchange traded and can be tailor-made to suit both parties. This feature distinguishes them from futures contracts, which are standardised contracts traded on an exchange. However, in the commodities markets forward contracts do have certain disadvantages.

The first and foremost disadvantage is that they involve credit risk to both parties. The buyer in a forward agreement is exposed to the risk that the seller will be able to perform its obligation to deliver the subject matter of the agreement. The seller on the other hand, is exposed to the risk that the buyer will be unable to pay the purchase price against delivery of the underlying commodity. Credit risk is a disadvantage it shares with all other OTC instruments. There are of course, ways and means to live with this disadvantage. It is done every day.

Credit risk was not the only disadvantage of cash forward agreements. Price discovery was extremely difficult as deals were generally struck in private. These problems were especially harsh in the agricultural sector. Communication was complicated by distance and production is seasonal by definition. It is not necessary for the purposes of this book to detail all the disadvantages that lead to the development of the futures contract.

However, before that development is dealt with, let it immediately be said that the disadvantages of the forward contract did not lead to its demise. On the contrary, forward contracting is alive and well to this day. It forms as important a function in modern commerce as it did in ancient times, if not more so. The disadvantages only served to indicate that there were still lacunae in the market. There was room for additional financial instruments and structures. Futures developed to fill this lacuna and not to substitute forwards.

THE COMMODITY FUTURES CONTRACT

Having dealt with the cash commodity markets, a discussion of futures contracts, which are directly derived from them, can be attempted. Although futures contracts are part of the commodity markets, they are not part of the cash market. Although the underlying is the cash commodity, the subject matter of trades on the futures exchanges are futures contracts and not the physical cash commodity.

development of the contract

Due to the previously mentioned number of problems that faced the agricultural industry of the American mid-west in the last century, futures contracts were developed.

The first futures exchange was the Chicago Board of Trade (CBOT). The success of this market resulted in the Chicago Egg and Butter Board becoming the second futures exchange in the world. This latter exchange is known today as the Chicago Mercantile Exchange (CME). They were soon followed by the Kansas City Board of Trade (KCBT) with a futures contract on hard-red winter wheat.

Today futures exchanges flourish world-wide. It is estimated that one new futures exchange is founded every year, somewhere in the world. The major contracts are not concerned with agriculture, but with a great variety of commodities, interest rates, currencies and innumerable indices that vary from equities to bankruptcy rates.

essence of the agreement

A futures contract is an agreement entered into on the floor of an exchange, of which all the terms and conditions, excluding the price, are standardised and prescribed by that exchange. In terms of the agreement, the buyer undertakes to purchase from the seller a predetermined quantity of a standardised commodity. Delivery of the commodity will be made by the seller and accepted by the buyer at a predetermined future time and place. Both the time and the place of delivery are prescribed by the exchange and form part of the standardised terms and conditions of a futures contract.

buyer's obligations

The buyer's obligations all lie in the future. He has two obligations. The first obligation is to take delivery of the commodity purchased. The second obligation is to pay the purchase price.

The buyer has the right, through the facility of the process of the offsetting, to eliminate all his obligations. Offsetting is a unique feature of futures contracts. It is this feature which gives to futures contracts their flexibility and vitality.

seller's obligations

All the seller's obligations lie in the future. The seller's only obligation is to deliver that quantity and quality of the underlying commodity for which he contracted. Against delivery, he will be paid the agreed purchase price.

Like the buyer, the seller can rid himself of his obligations through the process of offsetting. This is a matter that will be discussed in detail in due course.

structure of the contract

The commodity futures contract came into being as a result of three innovations on the cash forward agreement. The first innovation was to standardise all the terms and conditions of the contract so that the parties need only agree on the price to be paid for the underlying commodity. The second innovation was to trade contracts on a specially created public exchange. The trading took the form of an open outcry auction. The third innovation was to make the contract freely on-sellable to third parties.

Futures contracts are designed by futures exchanges and offered by them for trading on the floor of that exchange. The basic standardised terms of a futures contract are at least the following:

- The underlying commodity is specified. Only commodities that lend themselves to standardisation and gradability can form the subject matter of a futures contract. This is because both the buyer and the seller must have complete certainty as to what they are buying and selling, respectively.
- The basis grade of the commodity is specified. The basis grade is the standard grade of the commodity that may be delivered on a futures contract. It is determined by the exchange on which the contract trades. An example of a basis grade is Yellow Corn No.2. 'Yellow Corn' identifies the underlying commodity. 'No.2' identifies the basis grade of the commodity.
- The size of the contract is a basic feature of standardisation. The contract size refers to the quantity of the commodity that is traded per contract. For instance, one CBOT corn futures contract is for the purchase of 5000 bushels of corn.

Futures contracts cannot be traded in fractions. In other words, one can only buy or sell say, corn on the futures market in multiples of 5000 bushels. Similarly, you can only buy or sell pound sterling against the US dollar in multiples of £62,500 sterling.

This factor influences risk management since it may not be possible to take up a futures position that is quantitatively equal to the risk being managed. As will be shown later, a quantitative mismatch of this nature can either ameliorate or exacerbate a movement in the basis. This matter will also be discussed in detail at a later stage.

- Certain warehouses or depositories are indicated by an exchange as 'regular for delivery'. For each futures contract the exchange will specify the point to which and from which delivery will be made.
- In order to facilitate trading on the floor of the exchange, a number of price related regulations are prescribed. The exchange will specify the price quote. This refers to the way in which the price of the futures contract is structured. The exchange will specify the price unit per unit of the underlying commodity. For example, the gold futures contract on the COMEX trades in US dollars per fine ounce. CBOT corn trades in cents per bushel and US Treasury bonds trade in US dollars per point.
- The exchange also prescribes minimum price movements, known as 'ticks'. This means that a bid or an offer must be higher or lower than the previous one by at least one 'tick'. The result is that the price of the futures will always be multiples of a 'tick'. The minimum price fluctuation (one tick) for a CBOT wheat contract is 0.25 cents per bushel. This translates into a 'tick' being $12.50 per contract (5000 bushels × $0.0025).
- The delivery month of the contract will be specified. Futures exchanges offer contracts with specific underlying commodities for a series of delivery months. For instance, the CME offers futures on French francs with delivery dates in March, June, September and December.

the delivery process

The delivery process plays a very important part in the futures market mechanism. Most trades on the futures markets are not done with the purpose of either taking or making delivery of the underlying commodity. However, the possibility of being able to deliver the underlying commodity on a futures contract is extremely important. Without the facility of making delivery of the underlying commodity, the price mechanism of the futures markets would not be linked to the cash commodity's market price. Therefore, the delivery process acts as a link between the cash market and the futures market. This link will be examined in detail in a later chapter.

Delivery of the underlying cash commodity can only be made during the delivery month specified by the exchange. For example, on February 15, a trader sells a December French francs contract on the CME. He would not be able to deliver the French francs until December. Delivery of the underlying commodity can only be made when the clearing house of the exchange directs the seller to deliver it to the buyer.

But for one notable exception, the buyer has no say in the delivery process. Delivery is initiated by the seller. The seller who intends to deliver the cash commodity will notify his broker of his intention to deliver. His broker will send a notice of intention to deliver to the clearing house. The notice that the broker delivers to the clearing house will specify the details of the intended delivery.

The one notable exception to the rule that the seller determines the details of delivery is on trades of currency futures on the CME. In this case, the buyer determines the location from where settlement will be made. Settlement of currency contracts is thus at the option of the buyer. The settlement will be made from a bank in the country of issuance. For example, on a contract involving the French franc, the buyer determines from which bank in France settlement will be made.

the basis grade

The fact that the basis grade is one of the important standard conditions of a futures contract has already been mentioned. On many futures contracts that are offered, the exchange will allow the seller to deliver a substitute grade that is lower in quality than the basis grade. The price that he receives will be discounted to compensate for the lower grade.

The exchange may also allow a seller to deliver a higher grade of the commodity than is specified as the basis grade. In that case, he will receive a premium on the price. This latitude is not allowed in every contract. The lower and higher grades of the commodity that may be delivered form part of the futures contract specifications.

Allowing the delivery of substitute grades serves a very important purpose in the overall market mechanism. The purpose it is to allow for an increase in the supply of the deliverable commodity. The possibility of 'corners' is thereby minimised.

A corner is also known as a 'squeeze'. It is established when an individual or group of individuals acting in concert accumulates all or most of the available supply of a commodity. The people who hold the corner can then dictate the price of the commodity. Since they control the supply of the cash commodity, they can control the price of the commodity on the cash and on the futures markets.

OFFSETTING FUTURES POSITIONS

The third innovation of futures contracts that was mentioned previously, is the facility of offsetting. It is a facility created by the fact that the futures exchange interposes itself between the contracting parties after the deal has been entered into on the floor of the exchange. The exact mechanism will be explained in the following chapter. At this stage of the discussion, it is merely necessary to take note that the clearing house of a futures exchange acts as a seller to all buyers and as a buyer to all sellers.

Offsetting is a facility that allows a futures contract to be freely on-sellable to third parties. Under normal circumstances, one party to an agreement cannot substitute someone else in his stead, without the consent of the other party to the agreement. In the case of a futures contract, it is possible. This is because the clearing house in fact acts as the counter party to every party involved in a futures contract.

In a futures contract any party can offset his position by taking an opposite and equal position in the futures market to the position already held. In order to make an offsetting trade, it must be done on the same exchange and in the same delivery month in which the original position was taken.

Assume that a trader buys ten December gold futures contracts on the COMEX. He buys the ten contracts because he believes that the price of gold will rise. When the gold price has risen, thereby meeting his expectation, he wishes to offset his position, realising his accrued profit in the process.

In market terminology, the trader would be said to be long ten December gold futures. In order to offset his position he would have to go short ten December gold futures on the COMEX. Had he shorted only nine December gold contracts, he would not completely have offset his position. He would still be long one December gold contract. Had he shorted ten December gold contracts on the CBOT, he would not have offset his position at all. This latter action would have increased his holding of gold futures contracts. His total position now would be long ten December COMEX gold futures and short ten December CBOT gold futures contracts. This holding of futures positions would be termed a spread position.

The result of the interposition of the clearing house between the parties to a futures contract therefore is that a person who takes a position in futures is not concerned with the identity of the opposite party. Although both parties are theoretically obligated to each other to perform their respective obligations in terms of the futures contract, both of them are also aware of the fact that they can get rid of their obligations by means of offsetting. Both of them are also aware that all obligations are guaranteed by the clearing house of the exchange. Neither one of them is therefore concerned with the creditworthiness of the other. Credit risk, which is a concomitant of all over the counter derivatives, is thus practically eliminated from futures transactions.

OPTIONS ON COMMODITY FUTURES

Options are one of the oldest derivatives in the world. They are known to have existed and to have been used since ancient times. Some thousand or so years BC, a Greek philosopher from Miletus was confronted with the age-old challenge: 'If you're so clever, why aren't you rich?'

He decided to accept the challenge. Using his knowledge of agriculture and the weather, he foresaw that there would be a bumper olive crop. He therefore travelled throughout the region, taking out options on the use of every olive press that he could find. When the olive harvest was garnered, it proved to be a bumper crop as the philosopher had predicted. The farmers soon realised that there were no olive presses for them to use, since only the philosopher had the right to use them. Consequently, they were forced to pay the philosopher for the right to use the olive presses. After this commercial exercise, the philosopher was acknowledged to be both clever and rich.

The nature of an option may now profitably be investigated. An option is an agreement which gives the buyer (holder) thereof the right, but not the obligation, to require the seller (or writer) of the option to perform according to the agreed provisions of the contract. The discussion will be restricted to the topic of options on futures. However, much of what is applicable to options on futures, is obviously also applicable to options in general.

AN EXCHANGE TRADED AGREEMENT

It stands to reason that if the underlying asset of an option, in this case a futures contract, is exchange traded, then the option itself must also be traded on the same exchange. Like a futures contract, an option is an agreement. In order for any agreement to be exchange tradable, it needs to be standardised. The option contract on futures is therefore a standardised agreement. The only term on which the parties have to agree is the price.

option premium

As can be inferred from the previous paragraph, there is a price to be paid for an option. An option gives its holder certain rights. Those rights have a value. The value of those rights will depend on a number of factors. These factors and how they interact will be discussed later in this chapter.

The value of an option is reflected by its price. The price of an option is referred to as its premium. The buyer of an option pays the premium, while the seller, who is often also referred to as the writer of the option, receives the premium.

the assumed risk

Since the main concern of this book is the management of risk, the primary focus will always be on the risks that are intentionally assumed when a particular derivative instrument is traded. Keep in mind that managing risk is generally achieved by assuming other, correlated risks.

The first concern is therefore to know what the voluntary, intentional risks are that are assumed when a particular instrument is traded, not the subtle or concomitant risks, which are of secondary importance. It does not mean that the subtle or unintended risk, such as basis risk, legal risk and so forth are not important – they are. However, they can be dealt with. They are not the risks with which risk is managed. They represent risks that will be managed in their turn. These latter risks will thus be dealt with separately.

An long option presents a lower risk than a futures contract. The maximum loss that a buyer of an option can suffer is the loss of the premium. There is no limit, in principle, to the amount of profit that can be made on an option. In fact of course, profit is limited to what the market will allow.

To the seller or the writer of the option, a different risk profile presents itself. The seller of the option receives the premium and he gets to keep that premium, no matter what. The premium represents the sole and total profit that the option writer can make. If the price moves away from the option, the holder of the option will allow it to lapse and the seller keeps the premium. However, should the market move in the option holder's favour, he will exercise it and the writer of the option will make a net loss equal to the net profit of the holder. This in effect means that the option writer's possible loss is unlimited, while the profit is capped at the premium of the option.

expiration of the option and its futures contract

The futures contract that underlies a particular option will be prescribed by the exchange. The option will not have the same expiry date as its underlying futures contract. The option's expiration date will precede the delivery date of the underlying futures contract. Since the underlying asset of the option is a futures contract, it follows that the option must expire before its underlying asset does. Keep in mind that a particular futures contract will have a particular delivery month, and it ceases to exist after its delivery date.

When an option expires or is exercised, both the holder and the writer of the option will be assigned positions in a futures contract. The respective futures positions that will be assigned depend on the type of option that was held or written. Firstly therefore, the two types of option that are available will be discussed.

TYPES OF OPTIONS

There are only two types of options, namely calls and puts. This is true of options generally and not only of options on futures. The definitions of the two types of options discussed below are essentially applicable to all options, whether exchange traded or not. However, since our concern is specifically with options on futures, no special effort will be made to point out those features of options that are universally applicable against those features that are particular to options on futures.

call options

A call option is an agreement that confers upon the buyer the right, but not the obligation, against payment of the premium, to buy a commodity futures contract from the seller at an agreed price.

The agreed price of the futures contract is called the strike price of the option. However, it will be convenient to first define put options before the terminology is discussed.

put options

A put option is an agreement that confers upon the buyer, against payment of the premium, the right, but not the obligation, to sell a commodity futures contract at an agreed price, to the seller of the option.

Notice that the two types of options are really two sides of the same coin. The put option gives the holder the right to sell the futures, while the call option gives the holder the right to buy futures. In both instances, the seller takes the opposite position to that of the holder of the option, except that the option cannot be exercised at the instance of the writer. The writer is thus assigned the opposite futures position to the holder, but does not have opposite rights. The writer in fact has no more rights, only potential obligations.

OPTION TERMINOLOGY

Option premiums have already been discussed. The premium is the price that must be paid for the option itself. The term 'strike price' and the term 'writer' of the option will also require some consideration.

When the fact that options confer on their holder the right either to purchase or to sell a futures contract at a specific price is considered, it becomes apparent that that price is an extremely important element of an option. That agreed price, at which the underlying futures contract may be bought or sold, is referred to as the strike price of the option or alternatively, as the option strike.

There is a further alternative term. The strike price of an option is also referred to as its exercise price. This appellation is due to the fact that it is the price at which the underlying futures contract position will be assigned to the holder of the option, if the option is exercised.

Option maturation is a further term that requires some discussion. It refers to the expiration date of the option. It can also be said that an option matures on its expiry date. Every option is granted only for a period. The life of an option is therefore the period between the time when the agreement is entered into and the agreed time on the last day that the option can be exercised. After the passing of this last moment, the agreement is terminated, all rights and obligations cease and the option is thus extinguished.

Market usage thus has it that the option expires or matures. An option on commodity futures has an expiration date assigned by the exchange on which it trades. The first day, on which a particular option may trade, represents the start of the life of the option. An option's 'period to maturation' is the time period that is left to the expiration date of the option.

CLASSIFICATION OF OPTIONS

There are three categories into which options are classified: the type of option, the class of the option and the series of the option. There are also two exercise styles of options. Each of these categories and styles will be dealt with consecutively.

The type of option refers to whether the option contract is a put or a call. This is the broadest possible categorisation of options.

The second category is the class of an option. It refers to all the option contracts of the same *type* that cover the same *underlying futures contract*. This categorisation ignores the strike price and expiration date of the option as well as that of the underlying futures contract. An example of a second category classification is 'CME Canadian dollar puts'.

The *option series* is the third category and is the fullest possible description of an option. The option series identifies an option specifically. It refers to all option contracts of the same *class* with the same *exercise price* and the same *expiration date*. An example of the description of an option series is a 'CME Australian dollar June $0.775 call'.

the option series

In principle, there can obviously never be only one option in a series. It may be a fact at a certain point in time, that only one option of a particular series has actually come into being by having been traded. In other words, the open interest on that option series equals one. However, the number of options that might be in the series is unlimited. There are as many options available as there are buyers and sellers that can agree to a premium.

Notice that in the full description of an option the exchange on which the option is traded is the first element mentioned. It is essential to get the option classification correct. If you do not get the series correct when you place an order with your broker, great confusion will result. The confusion may not be the greatest problem. The confusion may result in serious and substantial financial loss.

The second element specified in the series is the underlying futures contract. The month that follows the mention of the futures contract is the third element. Notice that this third element refers to the delivery month of the futures contract and not to the expiration date of the option. To find the possible expiration date of the option reference must be made to the contract specifications issued by the exchange. For instance, the April futures contract on the Australian dollar on the CME has quarterly, serial months and weekly expiration for options.

This means that you have a wide variety of option expirations to choose from, while all the time trading the April Australian dollar futures contract. You will find this kind of diversity of option expirations on most heavily traded futures contracts.

Before the two styles of option exercise, relating to the conditions under which options may be exercised, are dealt with, the effect of the difference in the strike of an option and the price of its underlying must be investigated. This will be done in the next section.

OPTIONS AND THE MONEY

Apart from being classified in a particular way, options are also described in terms of the difference between their strike price and the price of the underlying. Thus, options are said either to be in-the-money, at-the-money or out-of-the-money. This terminology will be explained presently.

example 2-1: scenarios illustrating a call option

Taking an example from ordinary life: assume that you wish to purchase a second-hand motor vehicle. You go to a motor dealer and find a car that you like. You are however, not quite sure that his asking price is fair market value for the vehicle.

On the one hand you do not wish to pay too much for the car, but on the other hand you would not like to lose the deal if it is a fair price. You therefore take an option from the dealer to purchase the car. This is obviously a call option. The strike price of the option is the price that the dealer is charging you for the car. The expiration of the option will be a date and time agreed upon between yourselves, which will be negotiated so as to give you a fair opportunity of researching the price. In this type of deal the motor dealer would most probably not charge a premium for the option. However, he will probably also not give you a long time to make up your mind. The expiration of the option will therefore be within a relatively short period of time. There are now three possible scenarios that arise.

☐   AN OPTION IN-THE-MONEY (ITM)

In the first scenario, it may be assumed that you do your research and find that the dealer's price is in fact lower than the fair market value (I didn't promise to make it realistic, did I?). In this case, the market value of the car is higher than the strike price. This means that you could actually purchase the vehicle from the dealer and immediately sell it down the road for a profit.

Assume for the sake of the example that the strike price of your option was £4000. Your investigation revealed that the value of the car was £4500. The call option that the dealer gave you is 'in-the-money' by £500.

☐   AN OPTION AT-THE-MONEY (ATM)

In the second scenario, imagine that your research reveals that the price the dealer wants for the vehicle is a fair one. This means that the market price of the car is equal to the strike price of your option. In market terminology, your option is said to be 'at-the-money'.

☐   AN OPTION OUT-OF-THE-MONEY (OTM)

For the third scenario, a more realistic circumstance might be envisaged. Your investigation reveals that the dealer is asking too much for the car. He gave you an option to purchase the vehicle for £4500, but you've established that you can purchase exactly the same vehicle for £4000 at another dealer down the road. Consequently, your call option is out-of-the-money by £500.

example 2-2: scenarios illustrating a put option

For the next example, circumstances very like those imagined in the first example may be used. The difference this time is that it is assumed that you want to sell your car, rather than buy one. The first second-hand motor dealer that you walk into offers you £4500 for your car. You think this might be a good price, but you would like to see if you could do better. Nevertheless, you would hate to pass up his offer, were he offering as good a price as you could get.

You negotiate with the dealer and get him to keep his offer open for a certain period of time. 'Keeping his offer open' is in fact the same thing as giving you an option to sell your car to him at a particular price, within a certain period of time. This is a put option. Having obtained that option from him, you now take your car to go and do some 'market research'. Again, three possible scenarios present themselves: the option might be ITM, ATM or OTM. These scenarios will now be discussed.

❐ THE OPTION IS ITM

Assume your investigation shows that the dealer, who gave you the put option, is offering a better price than you can find elsewhere. The best price you could find for your car at another dealer was £4000. In this case, the market price of the vehicle is lower than the strike price of your option. Because it is a put option, it thus follows that the option is in-the-money by £500.

If the situation in the scenario is compared with the situation in the first scenario described in Example 2-1, it will be apparent that the two situations are opposites. In the first example, the call option was in-the-money when the market price was higher than the strike price. The reverse is true in the example of a put option.

❐ THE OPTION IS ATM

In the second scenario, imagine that through your investigation you find that £4500 is the price that most dealers offer you on your car. A number of dealers offer you the same amount and a few offer you slightly less. It would therefore be said to say that the first dealer offered you the true market price on your vehicle. Your put option is at-the-money.

In this case, there is no difference between the situation in this scenario and the situation in the same scenario in Example 2-1. Both a call option and a put option are at-the-money when the market price of the underlying and the strike price of the option equal one another.

❐ THE OPTION IS OTM

In this scenario it is assumed that your investigation reveals that virtually all the other dealers are prepared to offer you £5000 for your car. It appears therefore, that the market price of your car is higher than the strike price of your option. Since your option has a strike price of £4500, your put option is out-of-the-money by £500.

Once again, if the situation in this scenario is compared with the situation in the same scenario in Example 2-1, it will be discovered that they are opposites. A put option is out-of-the-money when the market price of the underlying asset is higher than the strike price of the option. A call option is out-of-the-money when the market price of the underlying asset is lower than the strike price of the option.

THE EXERCISE STYLES OF OPTIONS

The two different option exercise styles that are available can now be discussed. The two exercise styles are respectively known as American-style options and European style options. The difference in style refers solely to the conditions under which the option may be exercised.

Both styles of options require that an option must be in-the-money in order to be exercised. This is a sensible requirement. Why would anyone wish to exercise an option that is out-of-the-money? By definition, an out-of-the-money option is an option whose strike price is 'worse' than the market price. In other words, the holder of the option would be better off by abandoning it in favour of trading in the spot market. Similarly, if the option is at-the-money it serves no purpose. For the same price one might as well buy or sell in the market where the underlying asset trades.

Since both exercise styles determine that only in-the-money options can be exercised, the real difference between them lies in the time of their exercise.

European style options can only be exercised on maturation on condition that they are in-the-money at that date. This is the style of option mostly used in over-the-counter options. They do not provide continuous risk, because there is no possibility of continuous exercise.

American exercise style options on the other hand, provide that the option may be exercised at any time that it is in-the-money. Since they provide continuous exercise opportunity and therefore greater risk, their premiums are higher than those of European exercise style options. The options offered on commodity futures are all American-style options.

EXERCISING COMMODITY OPTIONS

When an option is exercised it is cancelled. Because it is cancelled it has no value. It is therefore pointless to speak of the value of an option at exercise or at expiration – its value is zero. There is however, obviously a profit to be realised from an option upon exercise. This is necessarily so, since the option can only be exercised if it is in-the-money. If it is in-the-money, there must be a profit.

example 2-3: exercising call options

Assume a meat packer bought CME boneless beef August $0.62 calls. The boneless beef August futures contract is now trading at $0.68. The meat packer's call options are in-the-money by $0.06 per lb. The underlying of each option is one boneless beef futures contract with a size of 20 000 lbs. of beef. The meat packer decides to exercise his options.

He telephones his broker and instructs the broker to exercise his call options and simultaneously to short the same number of futures contracts. Assume the meat packer held six call options. By exercising his options, the meat packer is now long six CME boneless beef August futures contracts. At the same time, he is short six CME boneless beef August futures contracts. As was detailed in the previous discussion on futures contracts, the above situation where long and short positions in the same contract in the same delivery month are held, they will cancel each other out.

The broker reports back that the six futures were shorted at a price of $0.69 per lb. The order to exercise the options was also successfully executed. The situation of the meat packer is now that he had been assigned six futures contracts at a price of $0.62 per lb., which he then sold for $0.69 per lb. He has thus made a profit of $0.07 per lb. This gives him a total profit of $8400 ($0.07 × 20 000 lbs. × six contracts).

It is important to note from the example that in order to realise the profits on the exercise of options, an offsetting position in the futures must be taken simultaneously with the exercise of the options.

There is of course another choice. The option holder can exercise the option and then hold the futures position in the expectation of more profit. However, a pure futures position carries more risk than an options position. Once you have paid a premium to gain the lesser risk of an option, it is a poor trade to exchange that for a position of higher risk, while the same result can be achieved by holding on to the option in the first place.

example 2-4: exercising put options

For the purpose of this example, consider a producer of natural gas situated in Texas. The company's treasurer notices that a prolonged cold snap has prompted higher natural gas prices. The firm produces a monthly output of 200 000 MMBtu.

On the one hand the firm is concerned that if the weather warms up, prices will drop. On the other hand, should the cold weather worsen, they would not like to miss out on the higher prices that would result. The firm's dilemma is therefore that while they want to ensure present prices, they want to preserve the opportunity for profit should prices rise.

The treasurer contacts the firm's broker and establishes that the KCBT Western natural gas futures contract is then currently trading at $1.87 per MMBt. Consequently, the treasurer of the firm instructs their broker to buy 10 KCBT Western natural gas May

$1.85 puts. This will fix the price of half their May output at $1.85 per MMBt, of course, less the premium they will have to pay on the options.

The broker reports back later the same day that the order was filled at a premium of 12 cents per MMBt. The net price at which the firm has thus fixed half of its May production is $1.73 per MMBt ($1.85 strike price – $0.12 option premium).

As the firm had feared, the cold snap quickly passes. The May options contract on the KCBT expires on the 23rd of April. On the 22nd of April, the treasurer notices that the May futures contract is trading at $1.45 per MMBt. His put options are thus in-the-money. He immediately phones the firm's broker and instructs him to exercise the ten put options. He also instructs the broker to buy ten KCBT Western natural gas futures at the market. (The term 'at the market' means that the broker must buy the contracts at the ruling market price when the order goes to the trading floor of the exchange.)

The broker later reports back that the order to buy the ten futures contracts was filled $1.44 per MMBt.. The net futures position of the firm is now long ten contracts at $1.44 and short ten contracts at $1.85. This results in a gross profit of $0.41 per MMBt. ($1.85 – $1.44). From this profit, the premium of $0.12 has to be deducted, giving the firm a net profit of $0.29. Calculating this per unit profit out to the total amount of profit, a sum of $29 000 ($0.29 × 10 000 MMBt per contract × ten contracts) is arrived at.

The $29 000 profit that the firm made on their options trade can now be used to offset the lower market price at which they will have to sell their May gas production.

OPTION VALUES

Through the discussion thus far, it has been established that at expiration and at exercise, an option has no value. It has also been established however, that options do have value during their lifetime. The value of an option is reflected in its premium.

The market of course determines option premiums. Supply and demand in the market-place determines the value of all options. There are two elements in the value of an option. The first element is intrinsic value and the second element is time value.

intrinsic value

The intrinsic value of an option is the amount by which the option is in-the-money. A full discussion of when an option is in the money has already been completed. An option that is in-the-money will have a premium that is greater than the amount by which the option is in-the-money.

This follows from the fact that the option holder can immediately exercise an in the money option and realise the intrinsic profit. This has been amply demonstrated previously. Surely, nobody would sell a right that can immediately be converted into hard cash, for less than the amount of hard cash that it can be converted into. Although, having met a number of politicians in my time, perhaps that question should read: 'very few people…etc.'

time value

It is an observable fact that options with no intrinsic value are still valuable. Also, the value of options that have intrinsic value is greater than the intrinsic value. Time value accounts for this state of affairs.

· Time value is based on the probability that a particular option may gain intrinsic value, if it has none. If an option already has intrinsic value, then there is a probability that it may gain in value. There are obviously a large number of factors that influence this probability. The question that really bothered market analysts for a long time, was what the weight was that had to be assigned to each of these factors. Some of these factors will now briefly be looked at.

price of the underlying

The closer the price of the underlying asset comes to the strike price of the option, the more valuable the option becomes. This is due to the fact that the price move that would be required to put the option in-the-money becomes smaller, and the likelihood that the option will gain intrinsic value becomes greater.

A call option would therefore become more valuable as the price of the underlying futures contract moves up towards the strike price of the call. A put option will become more valuable as the price of the futures contract drops down and towards the strike price of the put option.

market volatility

Volatility is a measure of risk. It is a measure of how much the value of a variable diverges from a mean value over a period of time. The greater the divergence, the greater the volatility. Obviously, the more a price 'jumps' around, the greater the chances that the price of the futures contract will hit the strike price of any option on the contract.

It is therefore not surprising to find that the value of all options increases when the volatility in the underlying futures market increases. When market volatility subsides, the premiums of all options decline.

time to maturity

Its time to maturity plays a major role in the value of an option. It is apparent that the longer the period left to an option's expiration, the more opportunity there will be for the price of the underlying futures contract to move favourably for the option holder. Again, it is apparent that the basic factor that drives option values, is the probability that the option will move into the money. The longer the period to expiration, the greater that probability and therefore the greater the time value of the option. The less time there is to expiration, the less the probability of moving into the money and therefore the value of the option is less.

The time to maturity factor does not cause a linear depreciation of the option. At the start of the life of the option, time decay works very slowly. Later its effect on the value of the option becomes greater as its time to expiration draws near. However, do not expect to see the action of time decay with every passing day on the value of an option. The other factors that influence the value of an option often have a very much more immediate and dramatic effect on its value than time decay has. Nevertheless, time decay is always there, eating its way slowly through the value of an option and its value will be zero at expiration. Time decay always wins out in the end.

current interest rates

Since time influences the value of an option, it is not surprising that the time value of money also has a role in influencing its value. The interest rate that is factored into option values is the current risk-free interest rate.

PRICING OPTIONS

Using options in the financial markets only became viable after Messrs. Black and Scholes developed the first option-pricing model in the early 1970s. Although options have always been in use, the difficulty in the financial markets has always been their pricing. Until the Black–Scholes model was developed, it was not really feasible to determine the fair value of an option. When that calculation became possible, the financial option markets were born. A lot of research has since been done in attempts to improve the model. All later systems of price modelling are still based on the original Black and Scholes model.

A number of inputs are required for any option-pricing model in order for it to calculate the option premium. Each one of the inputs are in themselves a variable, except for the strike price of the option. Each variable changes in a particular way in response either to what is happening in the market or due to the passage of time. The related ways in which each of these variables changes, have been named and are collectively known as the Greeks.

Each of the Greeks will be quite superficially dealt with, since there are extremely good option pricing software packages available that will do the calculations if required. Therefore, unless you particularly want to indulge in the high-end of mathematics, it is more important to know what the Greeks can tell you than to know how to calculate them. The four most important Greeks are known as delta, gamma, theta and vega. They will now be dealt with consecutively.

- Delta is the amount of change in the option premium for every one unit of price change of the underlying. This is the most important variable that will be used in commodity risk management. The other variables are obviously used as well, but it all depends on how involved you want to become with exact pricing of options. For risk management outside of banks and finance houses, it would be an unnecessary burden.
- Gamma is the rate of change of delta for every unit of price change of the underlying.

At the start of the section, it was mentioned that each of the Greeks was a variable. Therefore the delta of an option will change, as the price of the underlying changes. Gamma tells us by how much it will change for every unit that the price of the underlying changes.

- Theta is the price change in the option premium for a given change in the period to option expiration. This is usually measured in units of 1 day. Theta is the value that tells us exactly how much time value is lost on an option from day-to-day. It is therefore the measure of time decay.
- Vega is the price change in the option premium for every 1 percent of change in market volatility. The option premium increases directly as volatility increases. The relationship between the change in premium and the change in the volatility of the underlying market is linear. However, Vega's relationship to anything Greek is entirely fictional and imaginary.

CHECKLIST FOR THE REVIEW OF CHAPTER 2

General overview: the overall control objectives of the material dealt with in this chapter are to familiarise the reader with the qualities and uses of commodity markets and the derivative instruments of commodity futures and options.

	Key Issues	Illustrative Scope or Approach
2.1	Does the business carefully distinguish its cash market position relative to each commodity that is employed in the normal course in some way?	There are two market positions • A long cash position – it is held when the cash commodity is owned, possessed or produced. It is also held when the cash has been bought for delivery at a future date • A short cash position – it is held when the cash has been sold and there is consequently an obligation to deliver, whilst the cash is not owned or possessed
2.2	Does the business assess and equate its market position in terms of risk directionality?	Risk directionality is a tool used to distinguish market position in intangible commodities, or when risk management techniques require risk exposure to be equated to market position • If the business faces the risk of a decline in the price, the position equates to a long cash position • If the business faces the risk of a rise in the price, the position equates to a short cash position

continued

Key Issues	Illustrative Scope or Approach
2.3 Does the business use the commodity markets to their full potential?	Two categories of commodity markets are usually distinguished: The cash market and the futures market • The cash market is the normal market where the cash commodity is traded. The spot market is where goods are traded for immediate delivery and cash forwards are used to buy and sell commodities for future delivery • The futures markets are run by commodity futures exchanges where forward positions in commodities are traded, mainly for the purposes of hedging
2.4 How does the business protect its financial position from commodity risk?	Using financial derivatives to hedge the risk is the most powerful protection from commodity risk, they are: • Cash forward agreements • Financial swaps • OTC and exchange traded options • Commodity futures contracts • Options on commodity futures
2.5 What risks will the business face if it uses commodity futures contracts?	• Due to price movement of the underlying commodity, the possible gains and losses are unlimited • The business faces only the risk of loss or gain through the widening or narrowing of the hedge basis, when futures are used in a hedge • If the contract is not offset before delivery day, the company faces the risk of having to accept or give delivery of the underlying physical commodity
2.6 What risks will the business face if it uses options on commodity futures?	• The maximum loss that can be suffered on purchasing an option is equal to the premium paid • The maximum profit on a long option is unlimited • The maximum loss that can be incurred by selling an option is unlimited • The maximum profit that can be realised on the selling of an option is the premium that is received

continued

	Key Issues	Illustrative Scope or Approach
2.7	What factors determine the value of an option?	The value of an option is determined by: • The time value of money – the higher general interest rates, the higher the value of an option. The relationship is not linear • The time to maturity of the option – time decay will cause the option to lose value • The price of the underlying futures contract relative to the strike price of the option – the closer the price of the underlying to the strike price of the option, the higher the value of the option • The volatility of the underlying market – the higher the volatility of the market, the higher the price of the option. The relationship is not linear
2.8	How will the changing values of commodity options affect the financial position of a business?	The value of an option will always be in a state of flux during its currency. The option will not have a value upon expiry or earlier exercise. At option expiry in the money, or on earlier exercise the futures position gained as a result of the option will realise a profit

three

commodity futures exchanges

INTRODUCTION

All commodity futures exchanges are associations of their members. They do not buy or sell commodities, or commodity futures, neither do they determine prices for commodities, nor for commodity futures. The basic service they render is to act as a marketplace for their members, offering certain commodity future contacts to be traded on that marketplace. They charge fees for their services, but since the exchanges are associations not for profit, the fees are low – calculated merely to cover costs.

The public at large gain access to the facilities offered by the exchanges through the exchange members. Exchange members may deal with the public directly or through introducing brokers. Fees are payable for their services. As will be seen from the discussion that follows, there is strict control in all developed countries over the whole futures industry. The purpose of control is to protect the public so that the facilities of trading commodity futures can be used with confidence.

membership of exchanges

In the US, only individuals may own memberships on commodity futures exchanges. In order for a firm to be a member firm, it needs to be associated with at least one individual member. This rule differs from one country to the next, depending on the legislation and controls that are in place in a particular country. However, it is a rule in all countries that only members of a particular exchange may trade on the trading floor of that exchange.

There are different forms of membership that confer different trading privileges. The

51

details of this need not detain us; suffice it to say that members of the public can have their orders executed on an exchange only through having an account with a member. In the US these members are known as futures commission merchants (FCMs). Many FCMs in the US are members of a number of exchanges, thus affording persons who have accounts with them the facility of trading on multiple exchanges. More often than not an introducing broker (IB) will act as go-between in the opening of an account with an FCM.

control of the futures industry

It may be as well to note, at this stage, that the futures industry is strictly controlled and policed in most countries. In no country is this truer than in the US. There the industry is regulated by an independent Federal agency, styled the Commodity Futures Trading Commission (CFTC). It has extensive powers to protect the public and participants in the futures markets. The National Futures Association (NFA), which is the recognised self-regulatory organisation of the futures industry, assists them. NFA membership is compulsory for FCMs, IBs, commodity pool operators (CPOs) and commodity trading advisors (CTAs) who are empowered to decide on trades or place orders for customers.

The exchanges have established rules to ensure that trading complies in all aspects with the regulation of the CFTC. However, it is the exchange that is responsible for establishing the rules that govern the conduct of its members. It is also responsible for the enforcement of its own rules on its members. Additionally, each exchange settles and arbitrates disputes between members and between members and the public through permanent committees established by it. All parties must agree to arbitration before the appropriate exchange committee will arbitrate in a dispute.

However, it is still the responsibility of the CFTC to supervise the trading in commodity futures as a whole. They have established certain rules that are binding upon anyone who wishes to trade in commodity futures. Subject to the CFTCs power of review, they allow the exchanges to regulate themselves.

TYPES OF EXCHANGES

There are basically two types of exchanges: open outcry and electronic. The original exchanges were all of the open outcry type. The electronic exchange is a recent innovation that is proving to be extremely successful and popular. Most modern exchanges have both electronic and open outcry sessions. They run the two systems in tandem, thereby effectively allowing trading to take place 24 h a day.

the open outcry exchange

In Chapter 1, price discovery in the futures markets was likened to an auction. This is exactly what happens on an open outcry exchange. Open outcry exchanges are equipped with large trading floors. The trading floors have trading pits, or rings. They are called pits because they are round or hexagonal shaped steps that descend down from the general level of the trading floor. In each pit, only one particular contract is traded. In many contracts, each step of the pit represents a particular trading month. A trader thus indicates the contract month in which he wants to trade, by standing on that step.

Brokers must announce their bids and offers in a clearly audible manner so that any other broker in the pit can hear. The announcing of bids and offers in a loud voice gave rise to the term 'open outcry'. As can be imagined, the system results in a confusing cacophony of sound. Certain standardised hand signs are also employed, resulting in much gesticulation, waving and pointing to augment the vocal bids and offers. The overall result is one of controlled chaos that requires a trained ear, sharp eyes and a quick mind to make sense of what is happening in the trading pit.

In the USA, open outcry exchanges are preferred. It is considered that it is the only really reliable way of price discovery. Since a marketplace is a competitive environment, a lot of emotion goes along with the process of price discovery, as it does in an auction. Emotion is an important factor in any market and it is feared that the 'feel' of the marketplace will disappear should open outcry be done away with. Yet, the electronic exchange has some definite advantages.

electronic exchanges

In an electronic exchange, all transactions are done on open line computers. Only members can trade by means of the computer link. Transactions are visible to anybody who has access to the link. The visibility of transactions improves surveillance and control; this feature further inhibits and prevents malpractice.

Since there is no trading floor, a geographical spread of participants is possible. This allows exchange members to be situated closer to the community they serve, while at the same time all brokers are electronically linked with the whole community of brokers as if they are all in one place.

Open outcry exchanges need large, expensive buildings to house the trading floor and a myriad of support facilities. Broker members always require their offices to be as close to the trading floor as possible and they are generally accommodated in the exchange building. By contrast, an electronic exchange has no need for these facilities. They are consequently much cheaper to set up and to run. The cost saving can then be passed on to the public, significantly reducing the cost of trading.

A further important advantage is that, due to modern technology, trading effectiveness is increased with less paperwork and no transcription errors. A full transaction trail is always available. Of even greater importance for the users of the exchange is the fact that market information is available immediately. Decisions can be made as trades are made, contemporaneous with emerging trends, thereby avoiding the risks resulting from the inevitable time delays inherent in traditional exchanges.

As mentioned earlier, the result of this advance in technology has been that all major exchanges that started off as open outcry exchanges have now changed to being mixed exchanges. They accomplish this by having different trading sessions. Usually the morning and afternoon sessions will take place on the trading floor as open outcry sessions. The evening and overnight sessions are done electronically. The net result of these dramatic technological advances has been to create 24 h trading on all major exchanges. This dramatic extension of trading hours has created tremendous opportunities and advantages to all users of futures markets. It has in fact opened and made accessible world markets that could not easily have been accessed only a few years ago. These are some of the opportunities of which risk managers must avail themselves continuously.

SUCCESSFUL COMMODITY FUTURES EXCHANGES

There are a few essential elements that will determine the success or otherwise of an exchange. The first, and probably the most important element, is that there must be plenty of commercial activity. This requires large numbers of participants. It cannot be over-emphasised that a market must be liquid in order to afford the trading public the facility of opening and covering their positions at exactly the required time. A liquid market trades large volumes and is called an efficient market, but is also called a continuous market. The opposite type of market condition is known as a 'thin' or illiquid market.

market liquidity

Buying and selling is a competitive activity. When large numbers of buyers and sellers actively compete with one another, the price difference between bids and offers will be small. The price difference is referred to as the 'bid/offer spread'. From the fact of the resulting small bid/offer spread, it follows that the price difference between one trade and the next will also be small. Consequently, an efficient market will be a low volatility market.

Conversely, in a thin market, you will often find a wide bid/offer spread. The price difference between subsequent trades will then be wide and the market will be very volatile. The market may easily go 'limit-up', or 'limit-down' and it may be impossible to enter or to liquidate a position.

an unregulated economic environment

A second point to consider is that a successful market can only function under free economic conditions. Government regulation and interference with production and prices are anathema to proper price discovery. The price of a commodity must be free to find its own natural level as determined by market conditions at any particular time. When these conditions do not prevail, the market will not be properly responsive to changes in supply and demand. Neither buyers nor sellers will be enthusiastic about entering such a market. Speculators will not even venture close.

appropriate commodities for futures trading

Thirdly, the underlying cash commodity must be appropriate for trading on a futures market. This means that the commodity must be readily standardised and gradable. Since delivery must be possible against a futures position, buyers must be certain of the actual cash commodity they will receive, without the necessity of having to inspect each consignment. With such a restriction a futures market will be impossible. All these factors limit the commodities that can form the underlying cash of a futures contract.

THE CLEARING HOUSE

It would be impossible for a commodity futures exchange to operate without a clearing house. Every exchange either has its own clearing house, or it is affiliated to one. The role and effective operation of the clearing house is essential to an exchange.

clearing trades

Firstly, the clearing house clears all trades transacted on the exchange. Members report all trades that they transacted during a trading session to the clearing house. The clearing house then determines the margin requirements for that broker member in accordance with its own rules. This will be explained under the heading of margin.

The following step is to match buyers and sellers on each of the trades. For each trade, there must be both a buyer and a seller. When the selling broker and the buying broker report trades to the clearing house, it performs the vital function of acting as a buyer to all sellers and a seller to all buyers. As previously discussed, it is precisely because of this function that the facility of offsetting is made possible.

When a person enters into a futures position he neither knows nor cares who has taken the opposite position. Although he is theoretically bound to the other party in terms of the obligations he assumed under the futures contract, the clearing house actually steps in between the parties and acts as the opposite party to each of them. When it clears transactions, it makes sure that there is a seller and a buyer for each transaction. However, it will allow either party to offset their position unilaterally. The parties will be able to do that without having recourse to, and without the consent of the other party, because it (the clearing house) will ensure another counter party to substitute for the party who has offset his position. Offsetting merely means that one takes the opposite position in a contract to the position one already has.

For instance, a certain Mr. C. Kent is long 5000 bu December corn on the CBOT. Unbeknown to him, in the books of the clearing house the opposite position, namely short 5000 bu December CBOT corn, is held by Ms. L. Lane. When Mr. Kent wishes to offset his position he will do so by going short 5000 bu December CBOT corn. Once he has done so, it means that someone else has taken a long position of 5000 by December CBOT corn. Mr, Kent is now out of the market – he was long 5000 bu and now he is short the same 5000 bu. The opposite positions he holds naturally cancel one another out. But, someone else is now long the 5000-bu December corn. Since 'long 5000 bu December CBOT corn' was the original position held by Mr. Kent, it is obvious that the new long has taken the place of Mr. Kent. The position of Ms. Lane is unchanged. There is still a full contract in place because there is a seller – Ms. Lane. There is also a buyer – the new long who took Mr. Kent's place. Although the original transaction between Mr. Kent and Ms. Lane was done at a different price from the transaction between Mr. Kent and the new long, it does not affect the matter. Precisely because the clearing house interposes itself between the parties and acts as buyer to Ms. Lane and as seller to the new long, the two transactions can be at different prices.

Indeed, the matter can be taken further. Ms. Lane can offset her position by going long 5000 bu December CBOT corn. When she has accomplished that, the person who bought from her is the new short who takes her place in the contract where Mr. Kent's replacement already holds the long position. The latter is of course totally unaware and unaffected by this change. The new net position is that the original parties to the contract, namely Mr. Kent and Ms. Lane, have both now exited the market. Yet, the open position they originally established still exists, albeit with two new parties, each of who entered their respective positions independently of the other, at different times and at different prices.

From the foregoing it must be clear that an offsetting trade can only be made in the same contract, for the same delivery month and on the same exchange as the original trade was made. The exact interaction that takes place to allow for the establishment of new open contracts, the establishment of open interest and the effect that has on the market will be discussed in a later chapter.

price settlement

Secondly, the clearing house settles the end-of-day price for each contract traded on the exchange. Whenever you look at commodity futures market prices, you will see at least four, but probably five prices given for a trading session: a price at the open, the highest price achieved, the lowest price reached and the closing price. The fifth price will be the settlement price. These prices will be quoted as the open, high, low, close and settlement prices.

In the markets outside of North America, the settlement price may be called the 'marked to market' price. It is so called because it is the price that is used to calculate the client's equity position at the end of the trading day. That is the calculation which determines whether the client has made money or lost money since the previous day, or since the futures positions were taken in. This calculation of each client's account at the end of the day is called marking the account to market. This will become clear when the subject of margin is dealt with.

The settlement price is where the price was 'settled' by the clearing house or the end of the trading session. The price is settled at the end of each day's trading session. This price is not merely the price at which the last trade was done. The clearing house designates the last portion of the trading period, e.g. the last half hour of trading, as 'the closing period'.

A mathematical formula is employed to determine the settlement price, which will usually be a weighted average of the prices at which transactions were done during the closing period. The settlement price plays a rather important role in the scheme of things, especially because margin adjustments are made based on the settlement price at the end of the day trading session. This will be explained presently when the subject of margin is dealt with.

SOME ADVANTAGES OFFERED BY FUTURES EXCHANGES

The principal benefit of an exchange is that it allows the producers and users of cash commodities to reduce the risk associated with price fluctuations substantially, through hedging. A hedge is established by taking a position in futures that is opposite to the cash position.

Hence, a mining firm who is long gold in the cash market will take a short gold position in the futures market. The futures transaction is in fact a temporary substitute for a cash market transaction that will be entered into some time in the future. Because prices in the cash and futures markets are linked, they will move in the same direction. A fall in the price of gold in the cash market will be followed or even preceded by a downward move in the futures market. The mining company will now face a loss in the cash market due to the deteriorating price of gold, but it will be compensated for that loss by the profit shown in futures on their short gold position.

It must be stated categorically that the price move in the spot market will not be quantitatively matched by the price move in the futures market. Although the prices in the two markets are linked, they are not duplicated. It follows that in the above example of the mining house, its profit on the futures may be slightly greater or smaller than its loss in the cash market. This will be the result of a basis move. The basis between the futures and the spot prices will change. This is a subject that is discussed fully elsewhere in this book.

Conversely, an exporter who is short cash wheat will take a long wheat position in futures. Should the cash price of wheat rise, the exporter will face a loss on the cash market. This loss will be closely matched by a profit in the futures position, where the rise in prices has appreciated the value of his long position.

The trading public further benefits by having well-structured exchanges to trade on. Futures exchanges draw speculators and focus their risk capital. The risk manager gains by having a market with greater liquidity in which to trade. When the risk manager wishes to establish a hedge, or wants to lift it, there must be someone to take the opposite position to the one the risk manager wants to take. You never want to find yourself in a situation where you are locked into a futures position and you cannot get out because the market is illiquid. It bears repeating that the larger the number of participants in the futures market, the more successful the market.

Before you ever venture into a particular futures market, ensure that it is a liquid market. This refers not merely to an exchange where lots of trades are done on a daily basis, but the specific futures contract that you wish to use must be a contract that consistently shows a high volume of trades. If you are unsure of this fact from the available information, then ask your broker before you enter into any futures position in a particular contract.

A further and often-overlooked advantage of hedging is that the businessperson who is hedged gains creditworthiness. This is because banks and other lenders recognise that a hedged position carries less risk than an unhedged one. Obviously, the less risk a client is exposed to, the more creditworthy the client. A fully hedged business can consequently negotiate credit readily and at more favourable rates than it would if it were not hedged.

THE MARGIN REQUIREMENT

Margin is an essential element of the working of futures exchanges. Trading in futures may only be done on a margin account. Margin refers to an amount of money that must be deposited when a futures position is established and maintained. This deposit can be regarded as a security deposit or bond, to be held against the later performance of contractual obligations.

Keep in mind that both sellers' and buyers' obligations to, respectively, deliver and pay lie in the future. So a person who now 'buys' a futures contract is really only recorded as the buyer on a contract which requires him to perform his obligations in the future. He pays nothing when he enters into the transaction. The same holds true for the seller who delivers nothing and receives nothing when he enters into the agreement. It therefore does not matter whether one assumes a long or a short position, the margin requirement is exactly the same.

A dichotomy thus exists between market usage and reality. In market usage, a person is said to buy futures contracts, or to go long the futures. In fact, he does not buy contracts at all. Unlike an option contract, a futures contract has no value in itself. There is no price to pay for the contract. The contract as such is therefore never bought or sold. The buyer of futures is merely recorded as the buyer in a contract in which he 'buys' the underlying commodity for delivery at a future date. 'Buying' is therefore somewhat of a misnomer. The buyer pays nothing for the contract, but he will pay the agreed price for the under-lying commodity, if he does not offset his position before the delivery date of the futures contract. Market usage again, is to refer to the price of the futures for a particular delivery month. The so-called price of the futures is merely the price of the underlying commodity on which the parties agreed when they entered into the futures contract. It is really the price of the commodity projected into the future as far as the delivery month.

Similarly, a person who sells or goes short the futures does not actually sell a contract. That person again, is merely recorded as the seller of the underlying commodity in a contract that requires delivery at a future date. The short will however, be obliged to make delivery of the underlying commodity of the futures contract, unless he offsets his position before delivery date.

The margin process starts between the clearing house and the broker member. From time to time, the board of directors of an exchange determines the margin for each contract. Remember that every contact has a standard size, i.e. quantity of the underlying cash commodity. This allows the margin to be standardised per contract. It follows that the amount of margin that is required for a particular contract will change over time. The mechanics of this process will be examined presently.

determining the margin required

The determination of the margin requirement on any contract is directly related to the historic volatility of that commodity. The more volatile the price of a commodity, the higher the risk and consequently, the higher the margin required. As previously mentioned, the clearing house deals only with broker members and never with the public. It will therefore look to the member for all margin requirements. It is the member who, in turn, must look to his client for margin.

It is thus not surprising to find that one of the most important operating departments of a member firm is the margin department. They calculate and report every client's equity position to him on a daily basis. Using the exchange's settlement price for the day, they calculate the client's position against that price to determine the net equity in his account. When this matter was raised at the start of this discussion, it was this process that was described as marking the account to market. If any additional margin is required, they will make a margin call on the client, which must be met promptly. It is essential to understand how this process works, since one of the lesser known aggravations of futures trading is trying to figure out what your first few broker accounts are trying to tell you.

THE MARGIN MECHANISM

There are basically three types of margin: initial margin, maintenance margin and variation margin. Each type of margin will be dealt with separately.

initial margin

Initial margin is also known as original margin. Initial margin is that amount of money that has to be in a margin account before a person is allowed to take in a futures position. Margin can be met either by a deposit of cash, or by the giving of security. The security given will have to be to the satisfaction of the broker. On the CBOT, US Treasury bonds or notes with a maturity of greater than 3 years, may be considered as margin. In the latter case, only 80 percent of the market value of the bonds or notes will be taken into consideration as margin.

hedger margin

Hedger manager margin is a lower amount of initial margin that is required of hedgers. On most exchanges, the margin requirements for hedgers are usually lower than for speculators and other users of the markets. For the purposes of this rule, the hedger has to be properly registered with the clearing house as a user of the underlying commodity.

It was mentioned at the beginning of this discussion, that margin is a security deposit. The amount of money that is required as margin is therefore directly related to the risk of loss. Because the hedger has a cash position that is opposite to the futures position held, the hedger is in a financially stronger position than his speculator counterpart. He is in a financially stronger position because any decrease in equity on his futures position will most likely be made up by an increase in value on his cash position. The whole concept of hedging is linked to this inverse relationship of profit and loss.

The hedger also presents a lesser risk to the market because he will be in a far better position to perform on the cash contact than the speculator. If the registered hedger were to buy a futures contract, he would do so in order to protect himself against either a rise or a fall in the price of the underlying commodity. He will in any event be active in the cash market of the underlying commodity. Were he to hold a long futures position until delivery day, he would be quite capable of handling receipt of the physical commodity, in the event that he might be obliged to take delivery thereof. Similarly, were he to sell futures, he would do so in order to protect himself against a fall in the price of the underlying commodity. If he held his short futures contracts until delivery day, he will be able to deliver the cash commodity.

The third reason why hedgers are preferred by having lower margin requirements is that they are usually businesses or companies. This means that the exchange member, through whom the hedger firm deals on the market, will be in a better position to ascertain its financial condition. The exchange member's ability to ascertain the financial condition of a speculator will usually be severely limited.

maintenance margin

Maintenance margin is the minimum amount of margin that is required to be held in the margin account relative to the futures position presently held. In other words, when a futures position is taken in, there must be initial margin in the client's margin account. If the client maintains his futures position overnight, the margin requirement becomes less. This lesser amount of margin is what is referred to as maintenance margin. It is the margin required to maintain a futures position overnight and longer.

variation margin

Both parties to a futures transaction must deposit initial margin. When the price of the futures contract is settled at the end of each trading day, one of the parties will have gained on the futures position, while the other party will have lost. This change of fortunes will have an effect on the margin required of the parties. The effect will be that one party will receive variation margin, whereas the other party will have to pay variation margin.

As will have become apparent from this exposition, variation margin is the amount of money that will be received or paid as a result of the movement of the futures price. In order to facilitate the explanation, an example will be used to illustrate the point.

Assume that a jeweller buys one March gold futures contract at $300 per fine ounce. When he buys the contact, the appropriate amount of initial margin is already in his margin account. At the end of the first day, the March gold futures price settles at $310 per fine ounce. The gold contract on the COMEX is for a quantity of 100 fine ounces of gold. Therefore, the jeweller has shown a profit of $1000 on the contract. An amount of $1000 will be paid into his margin account as variation margin.

The question that arises is from where does the $1000 come. The answer is that it comes from the margin account of the other party to the trade. The party that took the opposite position to that of the jeweller obviously sold the March gold futures contract. On the price movement of that day, that party lost $1000.

a favourable price move

The margin account of the jeweller will be investigated first. His margin account has the initial margin plus $1000 in it. However, because he is maintaining his futures position, his initial margin requirement has lessened to the variation margin requirement. Then net effect of this is that the jeweller has equity of more than $1000 in his account (the initial margin less the variation margin plus $1000).

He will not be allowed to withdraw this excess amount of money from his account. He will however, be able to withdraw the $1000. If he does not withdraw his profits, then he will be able to use the accumulated profit plus the excess of initial margin over maintenance margin that is already in his account, as margin for further futures positions. The lowering of the margin requirement therefore has the effect of allowing the user to 'pyramid' his futures positions.

The above example also illustrates another point. The jeweller took a long position in futures. A rise in the price was therefore a favourable move from his point of view. However, had the price declined by the same amount, he would have 'lost' $1000 on the day. In this event, he would have received a margin call. That is to say, his broker would have called upon him to pay in the amount of $1000 before trading started on the next trading day.

In summary, it can thus be said that a person holding a long position will receive variation margin when the price rises and will have to pay in margin when the price falls. The margin is transferred from the 'loser's' account to the 'winner's' account. The futures market, like all other markets, is a zero sum market.

an adverse price move

The state of the counter party's margin account can now be investigated. For the purpose of the example it will be assumed that the counter party is a speculator, who believes that the gold market will fall. The speculator is not necessarily concerned about the price rise on the first day. She may well be expecting a fall in price over the next week or two.

However, at the end of the first day the gold futures price has moved against her. Her margin account has now been debited with $1000 as a result of the move. Because she is maintaining her futures position, her margin requirement has also diminished to the variation margin level. One would therefore tend to assume that she does not need not pay the full amount of $1000. However, this is not so. She will be required to pay the full amount of $1000 into her margin account. She will have to pay the amount into the account before trading commences on the following trading day. This is because she is required to top up her margin account to the initial margin level after an adverse price move.

The converse also follows from the example. Had the price declined instead of risen by the same amount, the speculator would have received $1000 as variation margin, rather than having had to pay it. The situation can therefore be summarised by saying that a person who holds a short position in futures will receive variation margin when the price declines and will have to pay in margin when the price rises.

margin on spread positions

A spread position involves assuming both a long and a short position in the same or a related commodity futures contract. If the spread is a recognised spread by the exchange, lower margin will be required. With the exception of certain specific spreads, spreading is generally a speculative trade. Nevertheless, there may be occasions where spreads can be used by risk managers.

Lower margin is required if a spread position is taken because of the lower risk involved. Both legs of the spread must be entered at the same time to qualify for lower margin. That is to say, the related long and short positions must be taken simultaneously. There is lower risk involved in a spread position because the fluctuation in the difference between the two positions is generally less than the price fluctuations on either a net long or a net short position.

The difference between the price of the short position and the price of the long position is referred to as 'the spread'. When the price difference shrinks, the spread is said to narrow, while the spread widens when the difference between the two prices becomes greater.

increased margin requirements

The fact that the amount of margin required is linked to the historic volatility of the futures contract is a matter that was mentioned before. It naturally follows that the margin required is different for every futures contract. That is to say, the margin on one corn contract will be different from the margin required on one contact of gold. There will be no difference in the margin required on the same contract in different delivery months.

Of course, the difference in margin required stems in the first instance from the fact that the total value of one contract of corn is much less than the total value of one contact of gold. However, the difference in the margin required will not be proportional to the difference in the value of the contracts. The margin on any futures contract will not be varied by the exchange because the price of the underlying goes either up or down. As previously stated, margin is related to market volatility and the risk involved and not to price movement as such.

It thus becomes apparent that the variation of margin requirements will depend on a combination of all the factors mentioned above. Exchanges try to keep margin requirements as stable as possible. Nevertheless, when a market is volatile and the price of the contract is high, an exchange would inevitably have to increase the margin required on the contract concerned.

A futures commission merchant has the right to require higher margin from its customers than the amount of margin required by the exchange. This applies to both original and maintenance margin, but not to variation margin.

CREDIT RISK IN FUTURES

Whereas credit risk is a very real one in derivatives trading, it has all but been eliminated in futures trading. As is apparent from the above discussion, the margin mechanism in the futures markets serves virtually to eliminate credit risk. This is one of the features that make futures trading an attractive risk management tool to most businesspeople.

As was discussed in a previous chapter, whoever ventures to trade on the futures markets need not concern themselves with the creditworthiness of the counter party to the trade. Of course, the creditworthiness of the clearing house of the exchange is relevant to the risk. If you are not a member of an exchange, you will have to work through an intermediary, as most people do. The creditworthiness of the intermediary will also be relevant to the risk you run.

As was discussed at the beginning of this chapter, government controls and regulation of the futures industry in the Western world is very strict. The training and qualifications of every employee of an intermediary are supervised and subject to control. The ethics and financial stability of all intermediaries are constantly monitored. One can therefore be reasonably certain that when you trade on the futures markets, you are not incurring any additional or subsidiary risks.

Nevertheless, you should be careful in selecting an introducing broker or a futures commission merchant before you trade on the futures markets. Be sure to choose a firm and a person in that firm in whom you have confidence and with whom you will be able to work comfortably.

ORDERS AND ORDER STRATEGIES IN THE FUTURES MARKETS

Every market develops its own dialect. This development is inevitable as the requirements of markets differ. In the hurley-burley of the marketplace, it is necessary to have shorthand speech that everybody understands and that eliminates misunderstandings.

Misunderstandings in the giving and taking of orders for futures and options can have major financial implications. It is therefore necessary that every risk manager should know and understand this special language. It is not sufficient merely to be able to calculate exactly what position in futures the company wishes to take in order to manage its risk. That requirement must be communicated to the firm's broker in the language of the markets. In that way the company protects itself against the potentially devastating effects of placing wrong orders and suffering serious financial harm.

Knowing how orders works in the futures markets thus forms part of a company's risk management strategy. Do not suppose for one moment, that the company will be able to get away with talking ordinary English with a broker and leaving the market jargon to him. Both the customer and a broker must make sure that they understand each other correctly. The only way that this can be done, is by using the language of the markets as they should be used, for the purposes that they are supposed to be used for.

The purpose of this section is therefore to outline a number of the most important orders that customers may place for trading commodities on the commodity futures exchanges. There are wide varieties of orders, some of which are the same as orders in the securities markets. Others again, have no counterpart in the securities markets. Still others have the same name as orders used in the securities markets, but the effect of the orders in the futures markets differ slightly from their effect in securities markets.

the function of orders

The function of an order is to tell your broker or agent succinctly and clearly, exactly what it is that you want him or her to do. In order to facilitate this process, certain standard types of orders have been developed. At first blush it seems quite simple, since all you have to do is to tell the broker that you either want to buy or to sell a certain number of a particular futures contract. This is certainly part of an order, but it is insufficiently exact to avoid misunderstandings.

Most types of orders have developed around the strategy that you want the broker to follow and to be bound to follow, regarding the price at which the purchase or sale is made. The main difference between the different types of orders are thus to be found in that element of the order which tells the broker how he must approach the subject of price when he executes a trade on your behalf.

Consequently, the first element of all orders and of all types of orders is exactly the same. The first part of the order says 'buy' or it says 'sell'. The next element of the order is to tell the broker exactly what it is that he must buy or sell. This is done firstly, by specifying the number of contracts required, then secondly, by specifying the exchange on which the contract trades. The futures contract itself then follows in the order, described by means of the delivery month required and followed by the mention of the underlying commodity. An example of such an order would be: 'Buy (or Sell) 5 CME December Random-Length Lumber'. There can be no doubt as to the action required of the broker up to this point. However, nothing has yet been said about the price at which the order should be executed or 'filled', as the successful execution of an order is known in the futures markets.

This last element of the order is the only part that can become slightly involved, but the knowledge is essential to following a successful trading strategy on the futures markets. The major types of orders and the strategies for which they are used will now be discussed.

market orders

This is the simplest and most straightforward of all types of order. With this type of order, the broker is told to execute the trade at whatever the best price is that he can find in the market at the time that he executes the order. Taking the example of the order used in the previous paragraph, it would be written as follows, if it were a market order:

Buy 5 CME December Random-Length Lumber at MKT

Having received this order, the floor broker on the CME will buy five contracts of random-length lumber for December delivery at the lowest offer prevailing at the time that he reaches the pit. If the order were to be given verbally, the correct way to give it would be as it is written, except that after random-length lumber you would add words 'at the market'. To make sure that he has heard correctly, the broker may ask a question such as 'shall I take it to the market?' You can reply by saying 'take it to the market'. An alternative way that the broker might ask the question would be to ask 'do you want me to price it at the market?' Your reply could be 'yes, price it at the market'.

When one gives an order priced at the market, as in the above example, you can always be sure that it will be filled. When limits are placed on the price that the trade can be executed at, it is not always certain that success will be had in the finding of a counter-party at the indicated price. In this case therefore, you can therefore never be sure that you will receive a 'fill'.

limit orders

This is the basic order that is used to put a price tag on an intended futures transaction. It is also known as a resting order. The order is used to bind the broker not to pay more or sell for lower than the indicated limit price. A very important matter to keep in mind when placing any order, except a market order, is that there are definite rules as to where you must place the order. Some orders must be placed above the then current market price, while other orders must be placed below that market price. The broker cannot accept or execute the order if it is incorrectly placed in terms of the current market price.

In written form, the buy limit order is as follows:

Buy 10 NYMEX February Heating Oil at 0.6479 Limit

A price for the underlying is added to the previous order; having received such an order, the floor broker on the NYMEX will buy heating oil at 0.6479 or lower, if at all possible. He will not pay more than 0.6479. If he can only partly fill the order, say by buying four contracts at the limit price, he will buy only those four contracts. The balance of the order will be held over for possible execution later in the trading session.

The oral version of the above order will be exactly the same as the written version. The broker might ask a question like 'do you want to price it at 0.6479?' You might answer 'yes price it at 0.6479.'

The buy limit order must be put in with a limit price that is below the current market price. The order in the example would be a valid order if the February heating oil futures contract was trading at a price higher than 0.6479. From the rule it follows that, the buy limit order will be used to buy in a downtrending market. The buyer who put in the order expects that the price of the futures will fall down to the level of his order. The order will then be executed at that price or lower, never higher.

Normally one would not expect anybody to want to take in a long position in a descending market. A long position in a descending market would be a sure loser. However, there are two scenarios that can be postulated as giving rise to the need for a buy limit order. The two most common reasons would be firstly, that the buyer wishes to take a long position at that price, because he believes that that is a bargain price for the commodity and that it can only improve thereafter. Consequently, he wants to come into the futures as near to the bottom curve of the price as possible. The second possibility is that the order will be placed by a short position holder, who is prepared to cover his short position at that price, presumably because it gives him the profit he envisaged.

If the order in the example had been an order to sell ten NYMEX February heating oil contracts at the stated limit, rather than to buy them, the floor broker on the NYMEX would sell the oil at 0.6479 or higher, if possible. Again, if he could not to fill the whole order at the limit price or higher, he would partially fill it and hold the balance over for possible later execution.

A sell limit order, like the above example, must be placed above the market. That means that the price of February heating oil on the NYMEX must be trading under 0.6479 at the time that the order is placed. The order placed in the example therefore expects that the heating oil price will trade up to the price of the limit order, because the order will only be executed at that price or higher.

Taking in a short futures position on an ascending market is like buying a steerage ticket on the Titanic. However, unlike tickets on the Titanic, there are definitely situations where it makes sense to take short futures positions in a rising market. The first person who will want to do that, is the long position holder who wishes to offset that long position when the futures price reaches the limit set in the order. In this way he will realise the calculated profit he has accumulated. The second possibility is again the speculator, who might believe that if heating oil price reaches that limit price, the market will be overbought and will be due for a deep correction. He is thus trying to get a short position as near to the top of the trend as he can manage.

stop orders

Stop orders are adjuncts to market and limit orders. They are always used to qualify a market or a limit order further. They are used by traders to limit a loss or to protect a profit. The first stop order that will be investigated is the buy stop order.

The written buy stop order is as follows:

Buy 5 IPE March Brent crude at $23.14 stop

A buy stop order must be placed above the market. In other words, when the order in the example is placed, Brent crude must be trading on the IPE at less than $23.14. Upon receipt of this order therefore, the broker will enter the ring and observe the trading in Brent crude. The broker will take no action until the March Brent crude contract trades at or above $23.14, or if it is bid at or above that stop price.

As soon as any one of the above conditions is met, the broker will buy the five contracts at the best available price. A stop order therefore has the effect of forcing the broker to wait for the price of the underlying to trade up to the stop price and once that has been reached, the order is treated as a market order. Unlike the situation in a limit order, the broker is not bound to trade at a maximum or at any particular price, but he executes it as a market order, once the stop price is reached.

The verbal version of the order will be given exactly as it is in writing. The broker might read the order back to you as 'buy 5 IPE March Brent crude at $23.14 on a stop', or the broker might ask 'do you want me to put a stop on that?' You might then reply by saying 'yes, put a stop on that'.

There are three main purposes for which stop orders are used. They are used in the first instance to enter into a new futures position. The trader and hedger would enter the futures markets by buying a futures contract, only when they are certain that the market is in an up trend. The purchaser would therefore try to pitch his order at a slightly higher price level than the present market price. He will thereby be making sure that the price will have to trade up first, before he enters the futures markets on his order. A speculator might argue that if the futures price breaks through a specific resistance level, the contract would then rise sharply. He therefore places his order at one tick above the resistance level in question.

In the second instance, the buy stop order would be used in order to place a limit on a loss on a short position. A trader might hold a short position in the contract, believing that the price will go down. If the price rises, the short position will show a loss. The trader will accept a loss up to a certain point, but beyond that point the loss might be too great for him to accept or he will then accept that he has called the market incorrectly. He therefore places a buy stop order above the market so that should the price rise to that level, his futures position will be closed out at a controlled loss.

In the third instance, the buy stop order would be used to protect a profit. Consider the situation of a trader who has a short futures position. Assume that he originally shorted the futures at $25.30 and that futures are now trading at $22.10. The trader has already made a profit of $3.20 and he wishes to protect most of that, should there be an upturn in the market. He therefore places a buy stop order in the market at $23.14. This is a buy stop that is placed above the present market, as it should be. Should the price trend turn around and rise to $23.14, the trader's short position will be closed out with a profit of $2.16. He has thus protected most of his accumulated profit.

The sell stop order these written as follows:

Sell 5 IPE March Brent crude at $23.14 stop

The verbal order will be given exactly the same way, or the words 'on a stop' may be added after $23.14. The sell stop order must be placed below the market. In other words, when the order in the example is placed, March Brent futures must be trading at a price higher than the $23.14.

As in the case of the buy stop order, the sell stop order becomes a market order if the contract trades at or below, or is offered at or below the stop price. The floor broker on the IPE, who receives the order, will now go to the ring and observe the trading in Brent crude. If a contract trades at or below $23.14, or if there is an offer from another broker at or below $23.14, the floor broker will sell the five contracts at the market. He will accept the highest bid that is available at that time. Again, the broker is forced to wait for the price to trade down to the level of the stop, before he can take any action. This ensures that the sell order is executed in a down trending market.

The sell stop order will firstly be used by a person seeking to enter a new short futures position. The idea will probably be that since it is a short position that is to be taken, the person wishes to be sure that the position is taken in a market that is actually trending down. The ratio would usually be the opposite of that mentioned in the buy stop situation. In this case, the trader might be of the opinion that if the price of the commodity falls through a certain support level, the price will really take a dive. His trading strategy is to date a short position as soon as he is certain that a major price decline has begun.

As is the case with a buy stop order, the sell stop order would also be used by a person seeking to limit a loss. This would be useful for a person who has taken in a long futures position. His fear is that the price might not rise as he expects. He is prepared to take a certain loss, thereby accepting that he has called the market incorrectly. This is the point where he selects the price level where he pitches his sell stop order. This would give him some loss protection. Should the price drop to the level that he selected for his sell stop, his long futures position would be closed out and he would suffer no further loss.

The third use of the sell stop order would be to protect a profit. Consider the situation of a user of Brent crude oil that originally took long March futures positions at $20.16. March futures is presently trading at $25.30. The user of the Brent crude has an unrealised profit of $5.14. The Brent crude user's fear is that the price of Brent crude will drop, wiping out the unrealised profit. A sell stop order is therefore placed at the level of $23.14, which is pitched at a lower level than the present market price, as it should be. Should the price of March Brent crude oil futures drop down to a level of $23.14, the sell stop order will be executed and a profit of $2.98 per barrel will be realised.

If you are used to dealing on the equities markets, please note that the buy and sell stop orders are not identical in the two markets. Whereas a stop order on stock in the equities markets would become a market order only when there is a trade at the stop price, a stop order in the commodity futures markets becomes a market order when there is either a trade or a bid/offer at the stop price.

stop limit orders

Stop limit orders combine the provisions of stop orders with those of limit orders. The major noteworthy element of this type of order is that it becomes a limit order when the stop price is hit. This is in contrast to the ordinary rule explained in the previous section, namely that a stop order becomes a market order when the stop price is hit.

Consequently, it is an essential element of stop limit orders that prices are quoted in the order: a stop price and a limit price. Since the stop limit order becomes a limit order once the stop price is hit, the stop price must be given and the limit price must also be given. As in the case of pure stop orders, the stop price is hit either because the contract trades at that price or because there is a bid or an offer at that price.

The sell stop limit order is written as follows:

Sell 10 IPE March Brent crude at $23.14, limit $22.38

The sell stop limit order is placed below the market like any other stop order. The nature of the order is that of a stop order with a limit added to it. If it were a limit order, it would have been placed above the market, where a sell limit order must be placed.

The sell stop limit order, in the example above, tells the floor broker that he must sell the oil once the price and goes down to $23.14. He may however, not sell the oil for less than $22.38. The broker will thus attempt to sell the oil at a price of $22.38 or higher after the stop price has been hit. From the structure of the order discussed thus far, it is apparent that the limit price included in the order cannot be higher than the stop price. It must necessarily be so because it is an order that will be executed in a downtrending market. It is to be expected that the closer the limit price is placed to the stop price, the more difficult, and therefore the less likely it becomes that the broker will be able to execute the order.

If the broker is unable to find traders that are willing to pay the limit price or higher, he will hold the order over for possible execution later in the trading section. An order that is not filled on the trading day on which it is given, will lapse automatically unless contrary instructions are given.

The sell stop limit order is used with the same strategies as a normal stop order. In other words, it can be used in order to take up a new futures position, or to limit a loss or to protect a profit.

The buy stop limit order will be written as follows:

Buy 10 IPE March Brent crude at $23.14 stop limit $23.14

In this case, the order instructs the broker that if the futures contract trades up to or higher than $23.14, or if it is bid at or above $23.14 he must buy ten March contracts. He may not pay a greater price than $23.14. This is then an example of an order where the stop price and the limit prices are the same.

a board order

This type of order is closely related to the limit order, in so far as the sell order is placed above the market, just as is done with a limit order. Similarly, the buy order is placed below the market. In another respect however, it more closely resembles a stop order, since it becomes a market order the moment the prescribed price is hit. For that reason, this order is also known as a 'market if touched' or MIT order.

The written form of the buy MIT order appears as follows:

Buy 10 KCBT March Western Natural Gas at $1.75 MIT

In the verbal order, the words 'market if touched' would be added after the price. The MIT order would be used for the same purposes and under the same circumstances as a limit order. The only difference is that when an MIT order is used, the trader would be more certain of receiving a fill, than he would be if a pure limit order was used.

The sell MIT order appears in writing as follows:

Sell 10 KCBT March Western Natural Gas at $1.75 MIT

Assume that March Western Natural Gas is trading at $1.66 when the order in our example is placed. When the market and a trade takes place at or above $1.75, or if it is bid at or above $1.75, the floor broker on the KCBT would sell ten contracts of March Western Natural Gas at the best available price thereafter. When the indicated price of $1.75 was hit, or 'touched', the order became a market order and a broker would therefore trade at the best available price. He would not be bound in any way by the indicated $1.75 price of the order.

As previously indicated, the real difference between a limit order and a MIT order is that when the indicated price is elected, the limit order must be executed at the limit price or better. Against that, the MIT order becomes a market order once the indicated price is hit and may then be executed at any price.

contingent orders

This type of order is also known as a basis order. It is an order that is used in conjunction with any other order. It is actually an additional instruction that is added on to any other order. The purpose of this adjunct is to make the main order contingent upon some occurrence in another commodity or in another delivery month of the same commodity that is the subject matter of the order.

For example, consider the producer of natural gas, who wishes to take in a short futures position in KCBT September Western Natural Gas, but only if the Cinergy Electricity futures contract trades at $33.00. This trading decision is obviously based on the particular knowledge that the producer has of the trading relationship between Western Natural Gas and Cinergy Electricity.

The contingent order would then be written as follows:

If NYMEX September Cinergy Electricity trades at $33.00 or lower, sell 50 KCBT Western Natural Gas at $ 2.30 stop

The order in the example is quite apparently an ordinary stop order. Since it is a sell stop order, it must be placed below the current market price. It will become a market order if the stop price is hit. However, the floor broker on the KCBT Western Natural Gas trading pit will not execute the order, even if the stop price is hit, unless the September Cinergy Electricity contract on the NYMEX has traded at $33.00 or lower.

discretionary orders

The trading public will often face a dilemma. They do not wish to enter the futures market at any price that may be available in the market. They would therefore prefer to buy or to sell at a particular price, which they believe is the correct price for their purposes. This means that they would have to use a limit or a stop limit order. As has been mentioned previously, the problem with a limit order is that one can never be sure that the order will actually be executed. Since the order can only be executed at the limit price, it all depends whether there is a counterparty available at that particular price. The public's experience will thus be that with limit orders they will often find that they have not entered or exited the market when they had wished to do so. This can in fact be a dangerous development should one wish to exit a position in order to stop losses or to protect a profit. If the order is not filled, the losses will continue and the profit may disappear.

The discretionary order was thus developed as some sort of response to this dilemma. The order that is given is thus a buy or sell the limit order, but the broker is given a certain amount of leeway, which is defined in the order. An example of the discretionary order may be written as follows:

Buy 5 NYMEX April Platinum at $402.90 with 50 points discretion

The order in the example instructs the broker to buy April platinum, but not to pay more than $402.90 per fine ounce for the metal. This is the ordinary content of a limit order. On a buy limit order, the broker is always free to pay less than the limit. The discretion given in the discretionary order thus empowers the broker to pay more for the contract than the limit. In the order given in the example, the broker, in his discretion, will be able to pay up to $403.40 per fine ounce for the April platinum contract.

It follows that a discretionary sell limit order will empower the broker to sell at a lower price than the limit price. A limit order always allows the broker to sell at higher price than the limit price. Keep in mind that the sell limit order is placed above the market and that the purpose of the limit element of the order is thus to instruct the broken not to sell for less than that limit. The discretionary order therefore relaxes that limit, should the broker not be able to execute the transaction at the limit price, which would usually be because the price did not actually reach that limit on the day.

not held orders

Another solution to the previously discussed dilemma of limit orders is the not held order. Since it is designed to overcome the same problem as the discretionary order, it is very similar to that order. The not held order also gives the floor broker discretion in the handling of the order. In this case however, he is given a much wider discretion. The not held order gives the discretion to the broker as to whether or not to take the position at all. This is almost like placing the trading decision in his hands.

The not held order is written as follows:

Buy 5 NYMEX April Platinum at $402.90 not held

Again, this is a buy limit order and it would thus be placed below the market. Ordinarily the order would instruct the broken to buy the platinum and to pay no more for it than $402.90. The order in the example instructs the broker to buy five NYMEX April platinum contracts at $402.90 if he determines that taking such a position is warranted under the circumstances reigning in the market. In this case, the broker might enter the pit and observe the market. Assume that the April contract is trading at $402.90 and there are no better offers. If it were plain limit order, the broker would be obliged to execute the order at $402.90.

With the order in the above example, the broker would however have discretion. He may be of the opinion that the price will decline to below $402.90, if he waits a while. He therefore does not execute the order, but waits for an opportunity to buy the platinum at an even lower price. If the price does not go lower as he expects and as a result, the broker is unable to execute the order, the customer may not hold the broker to an execution.

It is apparent then that a not held order gives the broker discretion whether or not to execute the order at the limit price, when that price is hit. It however does not give him any discretion to buy at a higher price or to sell at a lower price than the limit. In this case, the broker's discretion is absolute. He determines whether the position should be or should not be taken and he acts accordingly. He cannot be held responsible for any action he takes or fails to take in terms of this order.

opening orders

This type of order will be given when the trader wishes to take the position at the beginning of the trading day, in other words during the opening period of the market. The order does not instruct the broker to trade at the opening price, but rather at a particular price during the opening period of the day's trading session. The opening period is a specific period designated by the exchange. All transactions made during this designated opening period are deemed to have been made 'at the opening'.

The reform of the opening order is as follows:

Buy 10 NYMEX February Propane Gas at $ 0.3880 opening only

This is clearly a buy limit order that must be placed below the market. For the purposes of the opening of the market, the previous day's closing price would be the market price. The order in the example would thus have a limit price that is lower than the previous trading day's closing price. The trader obviously expects the contract to open under its previous close.

If at any time during the designated opening period, the price is below this limit, the floor broker will buy the propane gas. If the opening price is higher, he will cancel the order. Similarly, if the order cannot be executed within the opening range, it will be cancelled. This means that even if the price should decline during the rest of the trading day, trading down to or even lower than the limit price given in the order, it will not be executed. That is because the order was a opening order and it was thus cancelled when it could not be executed within the time of opening.

closing orders

This type of order is exactly the same as the previous order, but its full execution is during the period of the close of the market. It is, in other words, an order to buy or sell at price that is within the closing range. Like the opening range, the closing range is a specific period of time designated as such buy an exchange and comes at the end of the trading session. During the designated closing range all transactions are considered made 'at the close'.

limit or market on close orders

This is another variation of the limit order and represents a further attempted solution to the problem of uncertainty of execution with a pure limit order. In this variation, a limit order is given to the broker. If he cannot execute the order at the limit during the trading day, he is automatically instructed to execute the trade at the market price reigning at the close of the market. The written form of the order looks as follows:

Buy 5 NYMEX February Propane Gas at $0.3880 or market on close

As it is a buy limit order, the price of $0.3880 is under the market when the order is given. It may be that the market is in a strong upward trend and that the price never actually drops down to $0.3880. The broker will therefore be unable to execute trade. This situation would obviously not suit the trader who gave the order. His attitude is that he wants to take a long futures position in the February propane contract. He would prefer to do so at $0.3880, but if that proves not to be possible, he is willing to enter the market at any available price, rather than to stay out of the market altogether. Since no opportunity presented itself to buy the contract at the limit price during the day, the broker will buy the propane at the close, regardless of the price.

fill or kill orders

By means of this order, the broker is instructed to take the order to the pit. When he reaches the pit, he must immediately announce the order. If the order is not immediately filled upon his announcement of it, the broker must cancel the order. If only part of the order is filled, the broker may execute it for that part, but for any part that is not filled immediately, it is cancelled forthwith. The written form of the fill or kill order is as follows:

Buy 5 KCBT September Western Natural Gas at $1.65 FOK

With this order the floor broker at the KCBT will enter the ring and announce his order. If he is able to buy only one, two or more contracts at that price, he will do so and immediately cancel the balance of the order. If he is unable to fill any part of the order, he immediately cancels the whole order.

one cancels the other orders (oco)

This type of order actually consists of two orders. Two orders are given simultaneously and if one is successfully executed, the other is automatically cancelled. The customer is actually instructing the broker to do one of two alternative orders. Whichever one he executes first will automatically cancel the other order. The order is written as follows:

Buy 5 KCBT September Western Natural Gas at $1.65 or buy 5 KCBT September Western Natural Gas at $1.75 stop

The order will usually straddle the current price of the contract. The order in the example consists of a buy limit order combined with a buy stop order. Assume that a producer of natural gas, who feeds his product into the Western natural gas hub, originally sold five contracts of KCBT September Western Natural Gas at $1.80. The contract is now trading at $1.70. The treasurer of the gas producer is of the opinion that the price will fall further and the buy limit order is thus placed below the market at $1.65. At that price, the firm's short position will be covered and a profit of $0.15 per MMBtu will be realised. However, should the opinion of the treasurer prove to be wrong, she has covered herself with a buy stop order just above the market at $1.75. Should the price of September natural gas rise from its present level of $1.70, the firm will still cover its short position, realising a profit of $0.05 per MMBtu.

Note that neither the words 'one cancels the other' nor the acronym OCO appears in the order. It is the only order in which two orders are joined by the word 'or'. This type of order instructs the broker to watch the market and act in either case, on whichever one of the two prices that happens first. He is not given discretion in this matter. It is not a discretionary order. Once the broker acts of course, the gas-producing firm will no longer have a futures position and the other part of the order is cancelled.

scale orders

This is a single order that instructs the broker to enter multiple futures positions on behalf of the client. The number of contracts that may be involved in the trade can vary from one to any other number that position limits of the exchange will allow, but there is only one trade at one price.

Through a scale order, a broker is instructed to buy or sell a contract and after completing the initial trade, he is be expected to buy or sell additional contracts at specified price differentials thereafter. The order for the initial trade can be either a limit or a market order. In writing, the order would appear as follows:

Buy 1 NYMEX April Entergy Electricity at $25.00 and buy 5 additional contracts each at 20 points lower

The order in the example instructs the broker to buy one contract of April Entergy electricity at $25.00 or less. Once the first part of the order has been executed, the broker is to purchase an additional contract at $23.00. If he succeeds in doing this, he must purchase another contract at $21 and so on until he has bought six contracts in all. If he succeeds, the last contract will be bought and $15.00. If the price does not fall that far, the broker obviously stops buying when the next price down is not reached. The rest of the order is just abandoned.

The ratio of a person who uses this order would most probably be that he expects a reversal in the current downtrend of the market. He is using a buy limit as his primary order, thus entering long positions into a descending market. By purchasing a contract every 20 points from $25.00 on down, he is bringing down the average price of his futures contracts with every purchase. When the price rises again, he will have the advantage of a low average price for his basket of long futures positions.

switch orders

This order is used to switch a presently held futures position to another futures position. The situation may be that a futures position is held in a contract that has an upcoming delivery date. The futures position holder does not want to deliver or take delivery of the underlying commodity and therefore has to cover the first position and the second position in the following delivery month.

A switch order is not really a type of order at all. It is simply two orders given at the same time. As it happens, the first order will close out an existing position, while the second order will establish a new one. In reality, it is an action that does not really require a name at all. A written example of what might be termed a switch order, will look as follows:

Sell 1 NYMEX April Henry Hub Natural Gas at $2.305Buy 1 NYMEX May Henry Hub Natural Gas at $2.322

Assume for the purposes the above example, that a factory that intends to use natural gas from the Henry Hub bought one April natural gas futures. It is now April and the factory must either offset the futures position by selling the contract, or they must be prepared to accept delivery. Since they are not yet ready to accept delivery of the gas, they decide to offset the futures position, while immediately going long the same futures contract in a more distant delivery month.

cancel former order (CFO)

Only an order that has not yet been executed can be cancelled. Before any attempt is made to cancel a former order, it must be established from the broker that the order has not been executed and that it can still be cancelled. The CFO order is a facility that allows a new order to replace a former order.

The form of the order requires that the new order is given first and the order that is to be cancelled is mentioned last. A CFO order is written as follows:

> Sell 1 NYMEX May Henry Hub Natural Gas at $2.322 CFO buy 5 KCBT May Western Natural Gas at $2.15

As is apparent from the above example, the new order and the cancelled former order need not be connected in any way. This is just a form of order that allows the trader to change his mind, and to substitute another order in place of the former one.

good till cancelled orders (GTC orders)

It has been mentioned earlier on that all orders are day orders, unless there is a contrary indication. This means that when any order is given before the close of trading on a particular day, the order will be valid for execution only up to the close of trading on that day. If an order has not been executed by the close of trading on the day it was given, it automatically lapses.

Some care is thus required from a person intent on taking a position in the futures. If you are busy preparing an order that you wish to give for execution on the following day, you must not communicate that order before the close of trading on that day. An order that is given after the close of trading on a particular day will be valid for execution on the following trading day. If it cannot be executed on that following trading day, it will lapse.

There may sometimes be orders that a trader wishes to keep alive for longer than 1 day. A speculator will often be unsure of how the market will break out of a 'squeeze'. He may be unsure whether the price will break up or break down and he is also unsure as to when the break out will occur. He knows however, that if the price breaks through a certain resistance level, it will continue with a substantial uptrend. On the other hand, if the price should fall through a certain support level, he knows that a continued downtrend will follow.

He therefore places an OCO order with his broker, pitching one leg of the order slightly above the resistance level and the other leg of the order slightly below the support level. This situation is unlike the example that was used in the earlier discussion on OCO orders. There one leg was a buy limit order and the other leg was a buy stop order. In this case, the speculator would use a buy stop order at the resistance level and a sell stop order at the support level. In the verbal form of the order, the speculator would add the words 'good till cancelled' at the end of the OCO order. The written version might look as follows:

Buy 1 KCBT September Western Natural Gas at $2.15 or sell 1 KCBT September Western Natural Gas at $1.95 GTC

For the purposes of the above example, assume that the gas is presently trading at $2.00. In the example, the broker is instructed to keep this order alive until it is either executed or specifically cancelled by the speculator. At some time, the price will break-through either upward or downward. Because it is an OCO order, the sell leg will automatically be cancelled if the order is executed at $2.15. Similarly, the buy leg will automatically be cancelled if the order is executed at $1.95.

exchange for physicals orders (EFPs)

This type of order is also known as an 'against actuals' order. It is an order that is executed outside the trading pit. It is thus an exception to the rule that all trading must be done in the pit of an open outcry exchange. However, this type of exception is recognised on virtually all futures exchanges.

The purpose of this type of trading is to circumvent the exchange's delivery procedure. The exchange's delivery procedure may be circuitous due to geography and location of certain hedgers. Through their respective brokers, an exchange of physicals will be pre-arranged. The two parties will then exchange the cash and futures positions.

Exchanging the cash and futures positions means that the party who is long the cash commodity (and therefore holds a short futures position), will deliver the cash commodity on an agreed basis to the other party. The other party is short cash and thus holds a long futures position. At the same time, the two parties will exchange their futures positions at the ruling price. The significant means of the short position will buy the contract from a long position holder at the ruling price. In this way, both parties will have offset the futures positions and the physical commodity will have changed hands.

Many futures exchanges report the volumes of the EFP trades on a daily basis. This is valuable market information for those traders who monitor certified stock of the commodity. The IPE for example, includes this information on its daily futures report. It reports the EFPs for the previous business day.

orders for options

Exactly the same type of orders are available for options trading as for futures. Therefore, all buying and selling strategies are available when trading options. The only difference is that all options transactions are either opening or closing transactions. This is an element that must be added to every order for options.

An opening transaction is one in which a new options position is established or in which an existing options position is increased. Conversely, a closing transaction is one that decreases an existing options holding or that eliminates an existing options position.

For instance, consider the situation of a hedger who has no options position. The hedger decides to purchase a call option. The order that he writes can be a market order, or a limit order, or a stop order, or anyone of the many other types of order. Whatever order strategy he employs, he will have to indicate in the wording of the order that it is an opening transaction. Similarly, when he closes out his position by selling that call option, his order to sell must indicate in its wording that it is a closing transaction.

CHECKLIST FOR THE REVIEW OF CHAPTER 3

General overview: the overall control objectives of the material dealt with in this chapter are to acquaint the business with commodity futures exchanges, their mechanisms and how they can be used most effectively.

	Key Issues	Illustrative Scope or Approach
3.1	How will the business interact with the clearing house of the exchange in a trade involving futures contracts and options?	The clearing house acts as a buyer to all sellers and a seller to all buyers of commodity futures contract and options thereon
3.2	What will be the credit risk faced by the company when using futures and options?	● The credit risk in a trade involving futures and options is limited to the credit risk presented by the clearing house itself ● A risk posed by the broker firm used by the business
3.3	How does the business ensure that it will not become locked into a futures trade without being able to offset its position when it deems fit?	Trading must be done only in successful exchanges with contracts that have good to extremely high liquidity
3.4	How will the business be affected by the margin requirement of trading in futures contracts?	The margin requirement is a security deposit. It virtually eliminates credit risk from futures trading. The implications for a business are: ● Initial margin – the amount of money that must be in the margin account of the business when the futures position is entered. It is the benchmark for topping up with variation margin after adverse price moves ● Hedger margin – a lesser amount of initial margin required from businesses that are recognised by the clearing house as users of the underlying commodity

continued

Key Issues	Illustrative Scope or Approach
	• Variation margin – the margin to be paid into the margin account after an adverse price move or to be received after a favourable price move. It will equal the amount of the price move Margin requirements can be changed by a futures exchange depending on the volatility in the market
3.5 Does management ensure that an appropriate order strategy is followed when executing futures trading strategies?	The order strategy is as important as the price strategy itself. The various types of orders have been developed over years in order to meet the multiple needs of the trading public Management must ensure that the guidelines it lays down incorporate the correct and appropriate order placing strategies to be used in conjunction with particular hedging strategies

four

mechanics of the marketplace

UNDERSTANDING THE MARKETPLACE

All the elements of commerce come together in the marketplace. It is here that the interaction takes place between all the factors required for the commercial trading of goods and commodities. That interaction creates such a chaotic jumble of activity, seemingly heading in all directions at once, that the information received often seems only to be market noise. With a bit of understanding, that market noise becomes the music of the markets. However, hearing the music of the markets should not be confused with anticipating the next bar. Only the composer knows how the melody continues. But if the music can be heard and the rhythm understood, it can be danced to.

In commodity markets, as in all markets, there are basically two conditions that can prevail: normal and inverse. The first market condition is called normal because, not surprisingly, it is the usual market condition. This condition is also variously known as a carrying charge market or a premium market.

In a normal market the price of a commodity will increase the further into the future delivery is required. The precise conditions and reasons for this will be explained in this chapter. A normal market is also called a 'premium' market because the further into the future the delivery lies, the higher the premium on the price. The appellation 'carrying charge market' is used because the amount of the premium on the price as the date of delivery moves into the future, is directly related to the carrying charge of the commodity. The factor of carrying charges, also called carrying costs, will be dealt with presently.

The second market condition that will be dealt with is the inverse market. When inverse market conditions prevail, it is also said that the market is in backwardation.

This condition occurs in times when a shortage of the cash commodity is experienced. In times of shortage, very high demand is experienced in the spot month because buyers will be trying to lay their hands on every scrap of the commodity they can find.

The cash market is the market on which the physical commodity is traded. This is usually distinguished from the futures markets, where it is held that contracts are traded. The futures markets are derived from and dependent upon the cash market. It follows that the cash market and the futures markets are linked. Market conditions that prevail in the cash market must spill over and influence the derived market.

In order to demonstrate the linkage between the two markets, the two market conditions will be discussed under separate headings. Although the mechanism that links the two markets, namely the facility to deliver the cash commodity on a futures contract, remains constant, the effect of the linkage in a normal market differs from its effect in a market that is in backwardation.

The possibility of delivery on a futures contract also links one futures delivery month to the next. The result is that there is continuous price interaction between the cash market, the futures market and the different delivery months of the futures contract. Since the same mechanism allows all price interactions, price interaction between the different delivery months will be dealt with coincidentally to the price interaction between the cash and futures markets.

As was mentioned earlier on, carrying cost plays an important role in the market price mechanism. Thus, before the linkage and trading relationship between the spot market and the futures market can be properly dealt with, the concept of carrying cost must be understood.

CARRYING COST

Possessing or holding a commodity involves certain costs. The cost of holding a commodity includes the interest on the capital, the cost of storage, insurance and so on. The totality of these costs is referred to as the carrying cost. It is also variously known as carrying charges, the cost of carry, or simply the carry. The cost is expressed as a cost per quantity per period. For example, the carrying cost of copper is expressed in US cents per lb. per month.

The carrying cost of course depends on the commodity concerned. The carrying cost per period of 1000 tonnes of grain will be much less than the carrying cost of 1000 tonnes of gold for the same period. Although the rate of interest on the capital will be identical, consider the immense difference in the amount of capital invested and the difference in the sophistication of the storage facilities required, the cost of security, insurance premiums, etc. For these reasons, the carrying cost of grain will be expressed as a cost per tonne or per bushel per month, while the carrying cost for gold will be expressed as a cost per fine ounce per month.

Carrying cost is an important element in the trading relationship between spot and futures. It does not matter what particular commodity is being dealt with, there will always be cost involved in holding it. Keeping in mind the concept of carrying cost, the linkage and the interaction between the spot and the futures markets will now be discussed.

PRICE INTERACTION

The cash market consists of the spot market and the cash forward market. Cash forward transactions are contracts in terms of which cash commodity is bought and sold forward, i.e. for delivery in the future.

The spot price of a commodity is the ruling market price for the purchase of that cash commodity for immediate delivery. In the context of market terminology, the physical commodity is also referred to as 'cash', or 'the cash', or as the 'physical'. The spot price is the price of the commodity on the spot market. The spot market refers to the market where a commodity is purchased for delivery 'on the spot'. Reference is often made to the spot month. The spot month is the present month. 'Spot' in fact means 'now'.

'On the spot delivery' or 'immediate delivery' must nevertheless be understood in the context of the commodity being dealt with. If, for example, I wish to purchase an item of jewellery for my wife, delivery can be made by the jeweller 'on the spot', against payment being made. On the other hand, should I purchase 1000 barrels of crude oil, I would be appalled if the dealer were to ask me if I would like it wrapped or take it as it is. The term 'immediate delivery' therefore means that delivery will be made as soon as is practically possible.

As against spot delivery of course, a futures contract is a contract for the purchase of a commodity for delivery at an agreed date in the future. As is more fully discussed in another chapter, this is also the essence of cash forward agreements, with the exception that cash forward agreements are not exchange traded as futures contracts are. It must be mentioned however, that carrying charges as well as normal and inverse market conditions will shape cash forward prices as much as it does futures prices. The same considerations obviously apply in fixing forward prices as applies in fixing futures prices. Yet the prices are not exactly the same. The reasons for this need not detain this discussion. It is not necessary to go into all the differences between cash forward and futures contracts in the present context.

The spot market is by far the most important part of the cash market. The spot price of a commodity is its predominant price and it serves as the primary reference for all other derived and linked prices.

For reasons that will be explained presently, commodity futures prices will trade in a definite relationship to the spot prices of their underlying cash commodities. The cash and futures markets are linked to each other, through the facility of delivery on futures contracts that is provided by futures exchanges. Were it not for the possibility of delivery of the underlying cash commodity on a futures contract, there would be no link between the cash market and the futures market. The futures price would drift hither and thither in relation to the spot price of its underlying commodity. In fact, it is to be doubted whether the futures markets would have any role to play at all, were it not in principle at least, a purchase and sale of the underlying commodity for future delivery.

Notwithstanding the futures delivery facility, less than 2 percent of all futures contracts are settled by delivery of the cash commodity. It is estimated that the vast majority of contracts that are settled through delivery are so settled for arbitrage purposes. Arbitrageurs are traders who specialise in profiting from mispricings that occur in the market. This matter will be demonstrated below in an example of arbitrage trading in futures markets.

As previously mentioned the spot and futures markets interact differently under different market conditions. Their interaction under normal market conditions will be dealt with first.

price interaction in normal markets

A normal market exists when there is sufficient supply of the cash commodity to meet demand in the marketplace. This includes conditions of oversupply. Oversupply would still result in normal market conditions, since it would merely serve to drive general price levels down, without disturbing price relationships in the future. The question that is presently of interest is what the price relationship between the spot and the futures prices for a particular commodity is under normal market conditions.

As mentioned at the start, in a normal market the spot price will be lower than price of the first following futures delivery month. The first following futures delivery month is referred to as the near futures month. Futures delivery months that follow on the near futures month, are called deferred futures months. The price of the near futures month will be lower than the next deferred futures month and each following deferred futures month's price will be higher than the one before it.

The prevailing price structure in a normal market is as follows: prices ascend from spot (lowest) to the furthest futures deferred month (highest). The furthest deferred futures month can be trading as far as 2 years or more ahead, but it depends on the commodity and the exchange on which the contract is traded. Exchanges are guided by their experience and knowledge of the market for individual commodities, in determining how far ahead they will allow a particular contract to trade.

Futures contracts virtually never trade less than 18 months ahead. As near futures delivery months become current delivery months, deferred futures delivery month contracts start trading. Very often the nearer delivery months trade closer together (i.e. the next 3 consecutive delivery months all trade at the same time), but as the dates string out further into the future, the delivery months are spaced further apart (i.e. after the first 3 consecutive delivery months, only every third month trades out for the next 12 months, etc.).

The first rule in the price trading relationship between spot and futures markets is that, in a normal market, the premium of near futures to spot will tend not to be less than the carrying charge of the underlying commodity. This rule only applies under normal market conditions. The following example will illustrate the first rule. It will also serve to demonstrate how the facility of delivery on futures contracts influences and links the trading relationship between the prices in the two markets under normal market conditions. For the purpose of the example, assume that the carrying charge for corn is 3 cents per bushel per month and that at the end of March, spot corn is trading at $2.50 per bushel.

A miller decides to augment his inventory of corn. The first course of action open to him will be to visit a local farmer and to negotiate the purchase of the required quantity of corn, paying him $2.50 per bushel. The miller wishes to purchase the corn now to have it in stock when he requires it in the near future. He is reasonably certain however, that he will not use the corn in less than a month's time, which means the beginning of May. His total cost will thus amount to $2.53 per bushel ($2.50 purchase price + $0.03 for 1 month's carrying charge).

Before the miller embarks on this primary course of action however, he checks the price of the near month's (May) CBOT corn futures contract. He discovers that it is trading at $2.40 per bushel. In this case the miller will not wish to contract with the farmer. It will be to his advantage to purchase the required quantity of corn by buying May CBOT corn futures contracts at $2.40. He will then accept delivery of the corn through the exchange's delivery process. Since he will not possess the physical corn in the interim, he will avoid the 1 month's carrying cost. In effect he will save $0.13 per bushel ($2.53–2.40) by making his purchase through the futures exchange, rather than paying the spot price to the farmer.

In a free market system, where market information is freely available, all purchasers of corn can be expected to act in their own best interests, as the miller did in the above example. If all purchasers of corn acted in this way, there would be less demand in the spot market. The buying pressure will be transferred to the near futures month. The lessening of demand in the spot market will cause the spot market price to drop, while the buying pressure in the near futures month will cause the near futures price to rise. This dual effect will continue until the price difference equals the carrying cost, or the difference is so small that it is not worth the trouble.

The above example clearly illustrates the first rule of interaction between the markets, namely that the price difference between spot and futures must be equal or close to the carrying charge for the commodity in question. The important condition is of course, that normal market conditions prevail. Under inverse market conditions other, more powerful forces invert the price structure.

There is a second important rule that applies to the interaction between the markets. Its effect can only be seen under normal market conditions, but it holds true, with one exception, under all market conditions. The exception has nothing to do with the condition of the market, but with the nature of the commodity itself. This exception will be dealt with following the discussion of the rule. The second rule is dealt with under the heading of normal market conditions merely because it is only under these conditions that the rule can be clearly demonstrated.

The second rule is that the price increments between spot, near futures and deferred futures months cannot exceed the carrying cost of the commodity concerned for the periods involved. This is to be clearly distinguished from the first rule, namely that the price increments must be close to the cost of carry inasmuch as they cannot be markedly less. If the increments are markedly less, price corrections will take place, unless severe inverse market conditions prevail. This second rule is that, although the price increments can be equal to or slightly less than the cost of carry, they cannot be more. Examining a situation where the futures price exceeds the spot price by more than the cost of carry will test the validity of this rule.

Assume again that spot corn is trading at $2.50, but this time assume that the CBOT July futures contract is trading at $2.80. This constitutes a mispricing from which an arbitrageur can realise a neat risk-free profit.

Assume that an arbitrageur notices this mispricing. She immediately buys 500 000 bushels of corn in the spot market at $2.50 per bushel, simultaneously selling 100 CBOT July corn futures contracts at $2.80 per bushel. She would take delivery of the corn bought on the spot market and store it until the 1st of July. July 1 is the first delivery day of the CBOT July futures contract. Storage would involve a maximum of 4 month's carrying charges, amounting to 12 cents per bushel. She would then deliver the corn through the delivery process of the exchange, receiving payment through her broker.

Her total cost for the corn would amount to $2.62 per bushel ($2.50 spot market purchase price + $0.12 carrying charge), against which she has already sold the corn on the CBOT for $2.80 per bushel. From the very first day that she traded the corn, she would be 100 percent sure of an 18 cents ($2.80–2.62) per bushel profit. Since the size of each futures contract is 5000 bushels, this would net her a handy risk-free profit of $900 per contract, or a total profit of $90 000.

The arbitrageur in our example will not be the only person indulging in this sort of trade. Everybody's looking for a fast buck. One can imagine the activity on the markets the moment this mispricing becomes apparent. The spot market is suddenly flooded with purchasers buying up corn. The CBOT July contract is trading high volumes with aggressive selling.

The result of the activity on the market will be firstly to push up the spot price of corn. This will be due to the buying activity that is taking place on that market. Secondly, the July corn contract will experience a price decline as a result of the aggressive selling that is experienced. This market activity and its effect on prices will continue until the price difference between spot and the July futures contract is equal to, or slightly less than the 12 cents carrying charge.

Before the combined effect of the two rules is considered, the one previously mentioned exception to the second rule requires some explanation. The second rule applies only to non-perishables. It cannot apply to perishable commodities such as butter and eggs. The reason for this is that the price correcting mechanism invoked by the second rule depends upon the advantage to be gained by purchasing and storing the commodity against a future sale of that same commodity.

If the commodity is perishable, storage thereof involves the risk of spoilage. A spoilt commodity will not be deliverable against the short futures contract. All profit opportunity is lost. Consequently, in the case of perishables, the price premium of the distant month over the near month could exceed the cost of carry.

Thus, in summing up the first two rules, it can be stated that, given normal market conditions and aside from the exception of perishable goods, the difference between the spot market price of a commodity and the price of the near futures contract on that commodity must be close to and cannot exceed the carrying charges of the commodity. Similarly, the price premium of a deferred delivery month over an earlier delivery month must be close to and cannot exceed the carrying charge of the commodity for the period of deferment. The net result can thus be said to be that as far as non-perishable commodities under perfect normal market conditions are concerned, the price premium of any deferred delivery month over any the price of any nearer delivery month, will be equal to the carrying cost of the commodity concerned.

However, nothing is ever perfect. No market is ever so normal that it is perfectly normal. It may of course be completely normal under conditions of oversupply when the price premiums into the future will actually be equal to the carrying charges for the relevant periods. However, as will be shown when inverse markets are discussed, the price of spot can exceed the price of near futures with the inversion carried right through to the furthest futures delivery month. In addition, because the commodity markets are always chopping between degrees of shortage to degrees of oversupply, the market condition may vary in infinite gradations from extremely inverse to totally normal. In practice therefore, the premium of deferred months over near months will often be less than the carrying charges. This gives rise to spread trading, which is a subject that will be dealt with below.

Nevertheless, the second rule, namely that the price premium of non-perishables into the future cannot exceed the carry, is never breached except by short-lived mispricings in the market. It can thus safely be said that the maximum spread (price difference) between any non-perishable commodity's spot or near futures price and any price of that commodity for delivery at a date further into the future, will equal the carrying cost of that commodity. That is the bottom line as it were. It is the only fixed point to steer by as far as price relationships are concerned.

Next, the inverse market condition will be examined.

price interaction in inverted markets

Inverted markets are caused by shortages in the supply of the cash commodity. A shortage and a commodity will result in severe buying pressure in the spot market. Buyers will go to great lengths in order to secure supply. They will buy up as much of the commodity as is available in the spot market. Next they will focus their attention on the first or nearest futures delivery month.

Buying pressure will be slightly less severe in the near month than in the spot market. Because supply is uncertain, buyers will be anxious to lay their hands on whatever is available first. The result of this will be that the near futures month's price will be lower than spot. Some buying pressure will flow over into the next deferred futures month. The next deferred futures month's price will also rise, but the buying pressure will again, be less severe than in the near futures month. Therefore, the first deferred futures month's price will be less than the near futures month's price.

The picture that emerges from the description above, is a price structure that descends from the spot (highest price) to the furthest futures delivery month (lowest price). The descending order of prices is an inversion of the normal condition of the market, for which reason it is called an inverse market.

In the first example that was used when normal market conditions were discussed, it was detailed how the miller was able to take advantage of this type of price disparity. In an inverse market, the purchasers and hedgers who are prepared to buy their future requirements forward in the futures markets, will be able to avail themselves of this situation. Proper settlement of all the conditions of the contract is guaranteed by the clearing house. Even in times of severe shortage it is therefore not necessary to join the stampede. When the subject of hedging is discussed this matter will be investigated and discussed in greater depth.

As was pointed out in the first example however, the buying and selling actions of these forward-looking merchants will be inadequate to normalise the market's price structure. Depending on the severity of the backwardation, the correcting action will have a greater or lesser influence on the price structure as a whole. Since there is no other way of taking advantage of the price inversion, there is absolutely no limit to the premium that the spot price can trade over near futures and that near futures can trade over deferred months. The price structure will only be normalised once the physical supply of the commodity returns to normal.

The final rule of market interaction is that the spread (price difference) between the spot price and near futures will tend to zero in the near futures delivery month. The usual way of expressing this idea is to say that the spot and futures prices will converge during the futures delivery month. The latter rule applies to normal as a well as to inverse market conditions and will be the next subject of discussion.

price convergence in the futures delivery month

How the facility of delivery against a futures contract links the cash and futures markets under normal market conditions has been adequately demonstrated. From that discussion it is also apparent that market forces play off spot and deferred delivery months against each other to gain maximum price advantage: if futures delivery month's prices trade higher than spot by more than the carrying cost, traders will buy and take delivery in the spot market while selling and giving delivery in the futures markets. Conversely, if futures trade against spot by a margin that is lower than the carrying cost, traders will take advantage thereof by not purchasing in the spot market and making their purchases through the delivery mechanism of the futures markets.

Consider the situation in a carrying cost market first. Given these market forces, it is clear that the shorter the period between spot and the near futures delivery month, the less the carrying cost. The less the carrying cost becomes, the less the price difference between spot and futures must be. This process inevitably leads to the situation where the spot month and what used to be the near futures month become the same month. Then there should theoretically be no difference between the spot price and the futures price, because no carrying charges apply.

This is even true in the case of perishables. Because there is no storage period between the spot month and the futures delivery month, there is no chance of spoilage. Since the danger of spoilage is eliminated, its effect on prices is nullified. There can thus be no inherent economic reason for a difference in price.

It is worth repeating that things never work out perfectly. One would therefore very seldom find that the two prices are exactly equal. Nevertheless, in the futures delivery month the price difference between spot and futures will be insignificantly small.

Under inverse market conditions, carrying charges do not apply in any event. The question that arises is therefore whether there are forces at work in an inverse market that will neutralise the price inversion, as the spot and near futures months coincide.

Consider the situation where a shortage of a commodity exists. A frenetic scramble is taking place to buy up every scrap of the commodity that is available. When the spot month and the near futures month become the same month, buying pressure will be exactly the same in both markets. In other words, market conditions will be the same in the spot market as in the market for the futures delivery month because they are the same month.

As the period between the spot month and futures delivery months shorten, market forces that govern the spot market will become more and more evident and predominant in the approaching futures delivery months. The process will continue until the market forces in the spot and futures market are equal, which must happen at the time that the two months coincide.

As is demonstrated by this discussion, it is apparent that whether a normal market or an inverse market is encountered, the prices of spot and futures will converge and tend to zero when the near futures month coincides with the spot month.

the crop year in agricultural commodities

Agricultural commodities play such a vital role in so many industries that it is necessary to point out a significant exception to the price interaction discussed above. Although not all agricultural products have a crop year, there are many that do. Some examples of such commodities are corn, wheat, barley and potatoes.

In order to understand the price interaction of these particular agricultural commodities, the crop year must be taken into account. For this purpose the crop year is always considered to start with the harvest and run to the next harvest. The crop year for corn consequently runs from October 1 to September 30, while the crop year for wheat runs from July 1 to June 30.

In any agricultural commodity that is subject to a crop year, the price of the commodity will be the lowest for the year at harvest time. That is due to the fact that large amounts of new supplies of the commodity will be coming onto the market in the harvest month. There will consequently be a lot of selling pressure on the price of the commodity, since farmers will all be selling their harvest. Most farmers need to sell their crop as soon as it is harvested in order to repay production loans and to give them the necessary cash flow to prepare for the following crop year.

The result of all this selling pressure in the harvest month is that the price of that produce will be lower, or under the price of the preceding futures delivery month. Taking wheat as an example, July is the beginning of the wheat harvest in the Northern Hemisphere. The July futures price for wheat would be trading under the price of the preceding May contract. An inverse relationship results between 2 months in an otherwise normal market. The May futures price will still reflect the market conditions of the previous crop year, and supplies of that crop year will be at its lowest level, since it is the last futures delivery month of the previous crop year.

The above market situation represents the normal price expectation of crop year commodities, but it is subject to an exception. If the preceding crop year was especially large, a substantial amount of that crop may still be in storage and thus be available for supply. If, at the same time, the outlook for the new crop year is not good and a poor harvest is expected, it will be found that the May futures price will probably be under the July price. This situation may then signify the start of an inverse market after July.

It follows from the above discussion that, in a normal market, you will have a carrying cost price increase starting from the spot price to the near futures delivery month and then from one futures delivery month to the next. Deferred futures prices will therefore trade higher and higher until the month immediately before next year's harvest delivery month is reached. The latter (harvest) month's price will have an inverted relationship to the preceding futures delivery month's price.

Any company such as a supermarket, restaurant or bakery for example, that may wish to manage the risk of such agricultural commodities must therefore not be misled by this inverted price relationship. If it is merely the harvest month that is inverted in relation to its preceding futures delivery month, it is not an indication of an inverted market. If all the other months are trading at carrying cost differentials, the market is entirely normal.

It must thus always be kept in mind what the crop year of the product is. If a situation is encountered where the harvest month is trading at a higher price than the preceding futures delivery month, this will be a signal of an expected shortage of the commodity and even of an inverted market in the following crop year.

PRICE RELATIONSHIPS

Price interaction between the cash market and the futures market as well as between succeeding delivery months, gives rise to the existence of certain price relationships. The measure and monitoring of these price relationships form an extremely important part of the market information that is required to manage commodity risk.

Due to the multiplicity of factors that influence price relationships, it is not surprising to find that these relationships are virtually in a constant state of flux. When making use of commodity futures it is essential to understand how these relationships can be beneficial as well as how and when they can be detrimental. It is precisely because these relationships are in a state of flux that they can be either helpful or harmful. Were they to remain constant, they would not influence the results of our actions at all, since they would merely be neutral factors.

There are basically two important price relationships that concern the risk manager using commodity futures. At first glance they may appear to be one and the same thing, but they are not. The first price relationship is the relationship of the cash price to the price of futures. It is known as basis and it is the first subject that will be discussed.

The second price relationship is that which exists between one futures delivery month and another futures delivery month. This relationship was previously referred to as a spread. This type of spread is more precisely described as a calendar spread. The description is due to the fact that the two prices are only separated by calendar dates.

Indeed, other price relationships exist, just as other price interactions exist. There are interactions between the prices of different commodities. This interaction gives rise to the existence of a price relationship between the two commodities. If a relative futures position is taken in order to trade on the change in this type of price relationship, it is known as a commodity spread.

Spreads will be the second price relationship to be scrutinised.

the basis

The concept of basis is an extremely important one when dealing with futures markets. Through the discussions under the previous headings in this chapter, the mechanics of the price interaction between spot and near futures or deferred futures was explored. These price differences are known as the basis and when applied under specific circumstances, are also known as the hedge basis.

When the market situation of a particular commodity is referred to, the 'basis' of the commodity that is quoted will always be the relationship between the spot price of that commodity to the near futures price. In a different context it is expressed as the price of the cash to the price of the futures. It is never expressed the other way around. For example, if the spot price of a commodity is $250 per fine ounce and the near futures price is $265, the basis will be expressed as $15 under. This then means that the spot price is $15 under the futures price. Conversely, if the spot price were $250 dollars per fine ounce and the near futures price $242, the basis would be $8 over. This latter basis therefore indicates that the spot price is 'over' or greater than the futures price.

From the previous discussion it will immediately be apparent that if the basis is 'under', a normal market exists. Similarly, if the basis is stated to be 'over' the relevant market is in backwardation. Although basis is normally stated to be the price relationship between spot and near futures, this is not a rule of the Medes and the Persians.

When dealing with a particular situation, such as the market position of a gold mining company or of a manufacturer of electric cables, rather than a reference to the market in general, reference is made to the basis of that company, or manufacturer, if its market position includes futures. Consider the example of a mining company. The mining company produces gold at a gross cost of $220 per fine ounce. In the spot market, gold is trading at $250 per fine ounce. The mining company takes out a short futures position in order to protect its selling price. The short futures position is entered at a price of $265.

When referring to the market in general, it will be said that gold's basis is $15 under ($265 futures − $250 spot). The mining company's basis however, is $45 under ($265 futures price − $220 cash production price). Similarly, consider a cable-manufacturing firm that bought copper inventory some months ago at $75.40 per lb. The copper spot price is presently $74.70 per lb. In order to protect their inventory from further devaluation, the company sells futures contracts at $76.30. Again, in market terminology, copper's basis is $1.60 under ($76.30 futures − $74.70 spot). The cable manufacturing firm's basis however is $0.90 under ($76.30 futures price − $75.40 cash purchase price).

basis resulting from mismatches

There is a further dimension to the hedge basis in the futures markets. It still relates the cash price to the futures price, but the basis of a hedged position may be complicated as a result of certain disparities in the hedged position.

Consider the fact that futures contracts come in standard sizes, quantities or 'lots'. The cash position of a person or company may not equal any multiple of standard contract sizes. When the company takes in a futures position, it has to decide to either 'over-hedge' or 'under-hedge'. This implies that the futures position that is supposed to mirror the cash position will either be greater or smaller than the actual cash position. In an over-hedged position, the quantity of the futures position is greater than the quantity of the cash position. The excess in the futures position represents naked risk. The profit or loss on that portion of the futures position will not be offset by an opposite loss or profit in the cash market. Conversely, if the cash position is under-hedged, the cash position is greater than the futures position. There is thus a portion of the cash position that remains unhedged and which remains subject to the original market risk. This quantitative mismatch will thus influence the effectiveness of the hedge, because it will either leverage or dampen the effect of a move in the basis.

Apart from the quantitative mismatch, there is also the possibility of a mismatch in the commodity itself. This would be the result of hedging a secondary product that cannot be hedged directly with a futures contract. An example would be the electric cable manufacturer mentioned earlier. Copper-based electric cable cannot be hedged, since there is no futures contract offered on such cable. However, there will be a close price relationship between the price of copper and the price of copper cable.

Nevertheless, the two prices will not track one another completely. The effectiveness of the hedge will be affected by the fact that the price of cable will not move by the same amount, be it up or down, that the price of copper moves. This disparity in product therefore also causes either leveraging or dampening of any move in the basis, depending on the type of hedge and the move of the price.

basis movement

Having established that cash market prices and futures prices move in a definite, but variable relationship to each other, it is also clear that the actual basis changes all the time. Within certain limits, the spot and futures prices move independently from one another. These independent moves result in movement of the basis.

When the bases of the gold mining company and of the electric cable manufacturer were discussed in the previous section, they were calculated on the difference between the price at which each of them established their cash position (production costs, purchase price) and the price at which they entered their respective futures positions. The basis so calculated is referred to as the hedge basis since it is the prices at which the companies hedged their positions.

Having established their hedge bases, the companies will hold their respective cash and futures market positions until the time or event arrives that causes them to want to lift the hedge. During this time the price relationship between their respective cash positions and the price of the futures contracts they have hedged in will change continuously, widening and narrowing as market forces dictate the futures prices.

The hedge basis of course, does not change. It is the basis that was established when the hedge was entered and it is a fait accomplis. The basis that now concerns the companies is the basis that will exist at the time when the hedge is lifted.

At that time they will again transact in the spot market while simultaneously exiting their futures positions. Another, second basis will then be established, namely the basis between the then ruling spot price and the then ruling futures price. The difference between the original hedge basis and the second basis will determine the outcome of the hedge. This will be demonstrated presently. In the interim the companies will monitor their respective bases continuously to ensure that they exit their hedges at the most opportune time under all the circumstances.

They will obviously want to lift the hedge at the same time that they alter their cash position in the market. As previously stated, the effectiveness of the company's hedge will either be enhanced or diminished by the net movement of the basis. The effect will benefit by being illustrated with an example.

The instance of the previously mentioned cable manufacturer will serve sufficiently. After the company established its position in the futures market, its total market position is as illustrated in Table 4-1.

The company originally established its futures position in order to protect its inventory from a further fall in value. Some experimentation with the figures in Table 4-1 will demonstrate the effect of a move in the basis.

Table 4-1. A short futures hedge position

Cash Market		Futures Market		Basis
Buy Copper	$75.40	Sell Copper Futures	$76.30	$0.90 Under

Table 4-2. The outcome of a short hedge where no change occurs in the basis

Cash Market		Futures Market		Basis
Buy Copper	$75.40	Sell Copper Futures	$76.30	$0.90 Under
Sell Copper	$70.10	Buy Copper Futures	$71.00	$0.90 Under
Loss:	$5.30	Profit:	$5.30	

For the purposes of experimentation, ignore the fact that the company will not be selling the copper but will be selling the copper cable. The price of copper will always be a major factor in the price of copper cable. Whenever the company sells its cable therefore, it will be forced to take into account the then ruling price of copper. If the company ignores the ruling price of copper, they may well find themselves priced out of the market. For the purposes of the example, the figures will be treated as if the company is selling the copper at the ruling spot price.

Firstly, assume that when the company lifts its hedge, the copper price has plummeted. Assume further that there was no basis move. The company's situation could now look as illustrated in Table 4-2.

The company made a loss of $5.30 on the sale of the cash copper. Because the company took the opposite position in the futures market to its position in the cash market, i.e. selling futures against buying copper, the results were opposite. Against the loss on the cash market, the company thus made a profit in the futures market. The profit in the futures market exactly equalled the loss in the cash market. Consequently, it was a perfect hedge.

Now a real world situation will be illustrated. Assume the company lifts the hedge at the start of the futures delivery month. To make a fair comparison, assume that the spot price of copper dropped by $5.30 per lb., as it did in the previous example. However, spot prices and futures prices converge in the futures delivery month. The basis will therefore have narrowed when the hedge is lifted. The more likely outcome of the company's hedge would thus be as illustrated in Table 4-3.

As can be seen from the final column there was a narrowing of the basis from $0.90 under to $0.50 under. This means that the two prices moved closer together by 40 cents. This price narrowing was of course expected as a result of the working of those normal factors in the market that was discussed previously. The company's profit in the futures market is now greater than its loss in the cash market. The profit exceeds the loss by $0.40, the difference is exactly equalled by the basis move. The figures in both scenarios

Table 4-3. The outcome of a short hedge after a narrowing of the basis

Cash Market		Futures Market		Basis
Buy Copper	$75.40	Sell Copper Futures	$76.30	$0.90 Under
Sell Copper	$70.10	Buy Copper Futures	$70.60	$0.50 Under
Loss per lb.:	$5.30	Profit per lb.:	$5.70	Basis move: +$0.40

were kept the same, except that in the second scenario a basis move of 40 cents per lb. was allowed.

The example clearly demonstrates the principle that was expounded at the beginning, namely that the success of the hedge will depend on the move in the basis between the time the hedge is established and the time it is lifted. As can be seen, if there is no move in the basis, the hedge will be perfect. In other words, the profit in the futures will then neutralise the loss in the cash market exactly and completely.

The conclusion that a basis move will always result in a profit for the hedger, as illustrated in the example, is not warranted. There are a number of elements that need to be considered. Since there are at least some predictable elements in the move of the basis, the loss or the profit can be anticipated.

Suffice it to say at this stage, that in a futures hedge, the basis move can result in either a profit or a loss. Whether it will result in one or the other will firstly depend on the condition of the market, namely normal or inverse. Secondly, it will depend on whether the futures position of the hedger is long or short. This matter is fully dealt with in a later chapter.

spreads

Whereas basis is the term than denotes the price difference between a cash position and a futures position, the term 'spread' refers to the difference in the price between related commodity contracts. In order for a futures position to qualify as a spread position, it must be taken in related contracts that are recognised as such for the purposes of spreading, by the exchange or exchanges on which the contracts are traded.

Simultaneously purchasing a commodity futures contract against the sale of the same or a related futures contract establishes a 'spread' position on the futures markets. The term 'spread' is used synonymously with the term 'straddle'. These two terms should be distinguished from the same two terms when they are used in relation to commodity options. Although the meanings are similar, they are not the same.

spread types

As was suggested earlier, there are a number of different types of spreads.

- The first type of spread is known as a calendar or an intramarket or an interdelivery spread. The spread is entered into by simultaneously buying and selling the same number of futures contracts with the same underlying commodity on the same exchange in different contract delivery months. This is the most actively traded type of spread.
- The intermarket spread is the simultaneous purchase and sale of the same number of futures contracts with the same underlying commodity but on different exchanges. An example of such a position would be the selling of a December COMEX silver contract while buying a December CME silver contract.
- An intercommodity spread is the simultaneous purchase and sale of futures contracts

with different, but related commodities as their underlying, on the same or on different exchanges. Many commodities that have related uses track each other's prices. Especially commodities that can be used as substitutes for one another tend to react similarly to similar market stimuli. An example of this sort of spread would be to sell December oats and buy December corn on the CBOT. Corn and oats are both livestock feeds.

- The commodity product spread is used as a hedging technique. The spread consists of the purchase of a raw material and the simultaneous sale of the processed products and vice versa. The crack is the market term for one example of such a spread using crude oil as the raw material and heating oil and gasoline as the derived products.

using spreads

A spread transaction will enable the spreader to profit from either narrowing or widening of the price difference between the related contracts. Since a spread by definition refers to a transaction in which both a long and a short position in futures is taken, it is said that a spread consists of two 'legs'.

Keep in mind that in a spread situation, the trader is not concerned with the actual prices of the legs, but only with the price difference. The spread trader is not at risk of either a rise or a decline in the price. He is only at risk of a widening or narrowing of the spread.

If a trader buys the higher leg (futures contract with the higher price) and sells the lower leg (futures contract with the lower of the two prices), he expects that the spread (price difference between the contracts) will widen. In order to demonstrate this principle, assume that a trader enters an intramarket spread. Assume also that he buys a COMEX June gold contract at $250 per fine ounce and sells a COMEX October gold contract at $235 per fine ounce. The spread is $15, premium to June. The market position is shown in Table 4-4.

Now assume that the price of gold rises. The market is already in backwardation and it can be assumed that with a rise in price, the backwardation will increase. The price of the June contract rises to $265, while the October contract rises to $245. The trader closes out the spread and the profit and loss situation now is shown in Table 4-5.

From Table 4-5 it is apparent that the rise in price did not affect the fortunes of the trader. He made a profit on the deal of $5.00 per fine ounce, which is exactly the amount by which the spread widened.

As a control to this calculation, consider the situation if the spread had narrowed. Assume that when the trader closes out the spread, June gold has declined to $240.00,

Table 4-4. A long calendar spread position

June COMEX Gold		October COMEX Gold		Spread
Long at	$250.00	Short at	$235.00	$15.00 Premium to June

Table 4-5. The result of a long calendar spread after a widening of the spread

June COMEX Gold		October COMEX Gold		Spread
Long at	$250.00	Short at	$235.00	$15.00 Premium to June
Short at	$265.00	Long at	$245.00	$20.00 Premium to June
Profit:	$15.00	Loss:	$10.00	$5.00 Spread widening
Net Profit:	$5.00			

while October gold has declined to $230.00. Due to the decline in price, the market condition has become slightly less inverse and the trader's profit and loss position now is shown in Table 4-6.

Again, it is clear that the decline in price has not affected the profitability or otherwise of the spread. The trader made a net loss of $5.00 per fine ounce because the spread narrowed by $5.00.

In this example, where the higher leg is the 'bought' leg, the spreader's market position is said to be 'long the spread'. This spread is also known as a 'buy spread'. Were the higher leg of the spread the 'sold' leg, rather than the bought leg, the spread would be known as a 'sell spread'. The spreader's market position will then be referred to as 'short the spread'. In a sell spread the spreader will profit from a narrowing of the spread. The rules regarding both sell and buy spreads, apply to all spreads of whatever type.

From the example given above, it is also clear that generally speaking, a spread position carries less risk than an outright cash or futures position. For this reason also, the exchanges require less margin for a spread position than for an outright futures position.

Regarding the situation in an intramarket or calendar spread, the spreader's market expectations will determine in which leg a long position will be taken and in which leg a short position will be taken. If the price of a commodity is expected to rise, the near month's contract will be bought, while the deferred month's contract will be sold. This is known as a 'bull spread'. On the other hand, if the price of a commodity is expected to fall, then the near month's contract will be sold, while the deferred month's contract will be bought. The latter spread is known as a 'bear spread'.

The question arises why someone who expects a rise in price will buy the near leg and sell the deferred leg in a calendar spread. If there is a rise in the price of the commodity,

Table 4-6. The result of a long calendar spread after a narrowing of the spread

June COMEX Gold		October COMEX Gold		Spread
Long at	$250.00	Short at	$235.00	$15.00 Premium to June
Short at	$240.00	Long at	$230.00	$10.00 Premium to June
Loss:	$10.00	Profit:	$5.00	$5.00 Spread Narrowing
Net Loss:	$5.00			

the prices of both the near and the deferred futures contracts will rise. The spreader will profit on the long position and will lose on the short position. The spreader's expectation is thus that he will gain more on the long position than he loses on the short position. He therefore expects that if there is a rise in price, the rise in the near month will be greater than the rise in the deferred month. The question then really boils down to whether that expectation is a realistic one or not.

A rise in the price of a commodity will only occur if there is buying pressure. In the previous discussion on inverse market conditions it was concluded that buying pressure causes inverted markets, usually as a result of a shortage of the cash commodity. There are of course degrees of buying pressure, which in turn are dependent upon the degree of the shortage. Nevertheless, buying pressure in the commodity markets will always be greater in the near months and peter out into the future. Therefore, if there is an increase in buying pressure, its effect will be greater in the near month than in the deferred month. The spreader can therefore expect that if the price rises, the rise will be greater in the near month than in the deferred futures month. It is for this reason that a bull calendar spread is long in the near leg and short in the deferred leg.

As was also amply demonstrated in the previous discussion, the converse is also true. If supplies of a commodity are at normal levels and therefore reasonably balanced with demand, or if there is selling pressure due to an oversupply, a carrying charge market will prevail. If the spread between the near month and a deferred month is less than the carrying charge and an increasingly normal market is expected, it follows that the deferred month's price will increase over the price of the near month until it equals the carrying charge.

Therefore, if prices are expected to drop, it amounts to an expectation that a full-blown carrying charge market will eventuate. The near futures month will then experience a greater drop in price than the deferred futures month. The bear spread with its short futures position in the near month will thus show a profit over the loss incurred due to the smaller drop in price in the deferred month. The loss in the deferred month will be occasioned by reason of the long position held in that month.

From the discussion thus far, another generalisation about price action on the commodity markets can be made. Observe that when the price rises, the expectation is that the near month's price will rise more than the price rise in the deferred month. Again, when the price is expected to drop, it is expected that the near month's drop will be greater than the price drop in the far month. This leads to the inevitable conclusion that the general expectation in commodity markets is that there will be more price volatility in the near delivery months than in the deferred delivery months. The expectation is not affected by the market condition, i.e. normal or inverted.

This latter conclusion has implications for the risk manager, especially when use is made of commodity options on futures. Market volatility is directly linked to risk. In other words, as market volatility rises, so does risk. The prices of all options are higher as volatility rises and fall lower when volatility dies down. Volatility is of course influenced by many factors in the economy and the world markets. The foregoing is merely a general observation on volatility.

INTERPRETING MARKET INFORMATION

An important element in understanding the marketplace, is the ability to interpret the information that is received. So much information is constantly broadcast from the commodity markets that it is not always easy to know what is useful and what is not for one's own purposes. The aim of this section is to attempt to explain the meaning and value of some of the available market information for the risk manager. It will also be attempted to lay down some guidelines for understanding how market information may be interpreted to gain some insight into what is happening in the marketplace.

It is definitely not the purpose of this section to make the reader adept at either technical or fundamental market analysis. The risk manager does not require the ability to call the market. The ability of and the necessity for predicting market price movements are the domain of the speculator.

The risk manager hedges the markets precisely because he does not know where the market will go next. Even if a definite view is held, the risk manager must be unwilling to pay the price of being wrong. Nevertheless, the ability to read and understand the market is a prerequisite to managing risk. The knowledge and understanding to discern present market conditions must be acquired and developed. The purpose of this section is to serve as a basic guide to this enterprise.

price information

The first and most important information that is received from the markets is the prices of commodities. Prices are given in various forms. They are however, always available in plain, straightforward old figures, which is the first and major advantage. They are often arranged in columns, combined with different types of charts and generally dressed up in all sorts of ways. Nevertheless, our first concern must be to obtain the basic figures, before even looking at the rest.

The fresher the price information of course, the better the reaction to them can be. Prices are available on a daily basis or on 30-mine delay, 10-min delay or live quote basis. The source of daily prices will either be newspapers, data vendors, TV broadcasts, radio or even better, the commodity market's site on the Internet. Depending on the time of day, they will give you today's prices at the close, or the previous trading day's prices at the close. These prices, as well as the current delayed or live prices are available from many data vendors. The information can be had on a direct feed or over the Internet. One's broker may be a good starting point for finding the best source of information or data vendor for one's own purposes.

price quotations

It is important to understand how the price information from commodity markets is structured. Although the price information from commodity markets sometimes seems similar to the information received from the equity exchanges, there are also important differences.

Member firms of commodity futures exchanges receive the prices of commodity futures transacted on the floor of the exchange on a quotations board. The price information that is available in the daily press, is often merely a transcription of the quotations board of an exchange. The quotations board of a commodity futures exchange is of course similar to the board of a stock exchange.

The quotations board of a commodity futures exchange will show each commodity that is traded on an exchange. Under each commodity there will be columns representing the different delivery months that are trading at that time. Each column will show of the high and the low for the contract for the day, as well as the previous closing price. In each column the opening price, the high price and the low price for the day will be shown, as well as the closing price, which will either be the last price or the settlement price.

In order to understand the published price information correctly, the contract specifications of those commodities that are of interest, must be investigated. The price quote on the quotations board will only make sense in the light of the price quotation prescribed for a futures contract in the contract specifications of the exchange. For example, the price of a commodity might be given as '884'. Referring to the contract specifications of that commodity, it is made clear that the price quote for contract is given in cents per bushel. The 884 quoted as the price must therefore represent cents per bushel. Anyone who is familiar with the price of that particular commodity, whatever it may be, will then realise that a price of $8.84 per bushel could only be attained in a farmer's heaven.

The code of the price quote has thus not yet been cracked. Further inspection of the contract specifications reveals that the minimum 'tick', i.e. price movement, for the contract is 1/8 of a point. With this revelation comes the realisation that the last digit of the price quote must refer to this 1/8 point differential. The price quote of 884 thus translates as 88 and 4/8 cents per bushel. More correctly, the price for the commodity is $0.88 1/2 per bushel.

Price quotes can thus be confusing if the contract specifications are not well known. There are numerous contracts that have excise of 1/8, 1/32 and options that are quoted with differentials of 1/64. Thus, do not try to read and understand the published market information unless you are fully informed on the contract specifications for the commodity or commodities that you are watching.

commodity symbols

There is also a commodity price ticker that is similar to the stock ticker. A symbol is allocated to each commodity and it can be found in the contract specifications of a commodity. The reporting services all use the tickertape symbols of commodities. Thus, in order to obtain market information on a particular commodity from information vendors or from Internet sites, the symbol of the commodity is the key to finding the information. There are many commodity brokers who operate exclusively through orders placed over the Internet, using special software. The software incorporates the commod-

Table 4-7. The ticker symbols for some popular futures contracts

Propane Gas	PN	Swiss Franc	SF	Pork Bellies (Fresh)	FB
DJIA	DJ	Platinum	PL	Copper	HX
Oats	O	Wheat	W	Heating Oil	HO
S&P 500	SP	Silver	SI	US T-Bonds	US
Sugar	SU	Gold	GC	Cinergy Electricity	CN

ity symbols as the only recognised and accepted description of the contract. Table 4-7 lists the symbols of some of the more popular commodity contracts.

Options on futures contracts are also given symbols. They do not receive the same symbol as their underlying futures contracts. In order to obtain the market information on a particular option, it is first of all necessary to know the option's symbol. In addition to its symbol an option is identified as will or put by adding a 'c' or a 'p' at the end of the symbol. Table 4-8 sets out the option symbols of some popular commodity futures contracts.

Because of the unique element in commodity futures of delivery months trading into the future, price information on a commodity means nothing if it is not linked to a futures delivery month. It was thus necessary to develop a symbol for each delivery month that would be standard throughout the industry. Table 4-9 sets out the standard symbols for each futures delivery month.

Transactions on the tickertape are therefore indicated first of all by the symbol for the commodity, followed by the symbol for the delivery month, followed by the price. A transaction in May Swiss francs will thus be shown as 'SFK'. Orders that are placed over the Internet use all these symbols, thereby greatly simplifying the placing of orders.

analysing price information

For the purpose of gaining insight into the market, historic information is just as important as current market information. As this discussion will show, it is only when today's price action is compared with what has gone before, that an understanding of the markets starts to grow. The historic price information is available from the same sources that provide the current and up-to-the-minute price information.

Whether it is current or historic price information that is sought, the basic price information that is required remains the same. Firstly, the price at which the commodity traded at the opening of the market is required. That must be followed by the highest price of the day, which is followed in its turn by the lowest price of the day. Finally, the closing

Table 4-8. The ticker symbols of the options on some popular commodity contracts

Feeder Cattle	FC	British Pound	OB	Crude Oil	LO
Cheddar Cheese	CO	Japanese Yen	OJ	Entergy Electricity	OT
Oriented Strand Board	DO	Euro FX	EC	Palo Verde Electricity	VO
Dry Whey	DY	Nikkei 225 Index	ON	Gold	OG

Table 4-9. The standard symbols for futures delivery months

January	F	May	K	September	U
February	G	June	M	October	V
March	H	July	N	November	X
April	J	August	Q	December	Z

or settlement price for the day is required. This is the price information that appears on the quotations board mentioned previously. Usually the change in price will also be quoted, which is the difference between the previous trading day's settlement price and today's settlement price, or the previous day's settlement price will be given. In order to gain a full picture of the market for any one commodity, the foregoing price information must be obtained for every contract month that is traded.

Normally, the daily market information will include the spot price of the commodity in addition to the above daily price information. Other information, such as the volumes traded, open interest and visible supply will also be essential to gaining a proper understanding of the total market condition. In broad-brush strokes, a picture is thus painted of what took place in the markets on any day with respect to a wide spectrum of commodities. When the daily information over a period is linked together, a better appreciation of the totality of the market will be gained.

The price information also has a more immediate benefit for the user. If a position in either the cash or the futures market is held, the information will allow, inter alia, the calculation of profits or losses from day to day. However, as stated in the previous paragraph, the daily price information does not give the full picture of what is actually happening in the market place – not even as far as price movement is concerned. In order to be able to gain a better understanding of what the trends in the marketplace are, the daily price information is required for at least the past 20 consecutive trading days. Also, in order to facilitate the grasp and observation of price and other market trends, it is better to see the information graphically.

simple charts

Price information in its simplest graphic form is usually given using only daily settlement prices. The result is a simple line chart that usually connects the settlement prices for each day over a period of some 20 or more days. This may be sufficient to determine some of the trends that are prevalent in the marketplace.

As will become evident from the discussion that follows, bar charts are much more informative and useful than simple line charts. However, for the present purpose of introducing a discussion on charts, line charts will serve to explain the basic patterns and formations of price movement in the commodity markets.

Figure 4-1 represents a typical line price chart. A constant feature of a rising price is that it will, in the course of it rise, move downwards for short periods. These downward

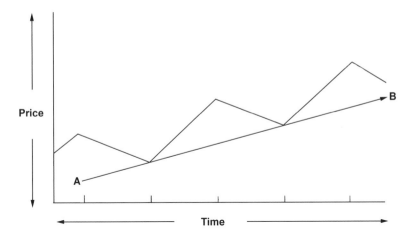

Figure 4-1   A basic line chart showing a rising price trend.

moves in an otherwise upward trending market are often referred to as 'corrections'. It is this tendency which gives rise to the jagged, saw toothed line of the graph.

It is only when this feature is graphically illustrated within the total context of the immediate price history, that it can readily be understood that the price of the commodity shows an upward trend. If one focused narrowly on the daily price reports, the picture may be somewhat confused because the price seems to go all over the place. You think it is rising, but the next day it is down again. That makes it hard to distinguish a pattern in the price movement.

The arrow AB in Figure 4-1 represents a trend-line. A trend-line is always achieved by drawing a line connecting the lowest prices achieved during the period. In Figure 4-1 the line clearly indicates an upward trend. In practice, a straight line may not always connect the lowest points. The trend-line will therefore be a straight line that comes closest to connecting the lowest points.

This feature of a rising market, which is incidentally mirrored by similar upward corrections in a declining market, is technically explained by profit taking. A profit-taker in a rising market will be someone who holds a long position. When the price rises he will be able to realise a profit by selling at a higher price than the price at which he entered the market.

Profit taking is an inevitable tendency that is observed in all markets. The markets are, after all, about making profits. It thus happens that when a market rises sufficiently, a number of market participants will start closing out their long positions by selling, thereby taking the profit that has accrued to them. The sudden selling pressure by profit-takers causes the price to decline, but as soon as they have eliminated themselves from the market, the price continues its upward movement.

A similar situation pertains when there is a decline in price. A declining price trend will be punctuated by short-lived rises in price. This situation is illustrated in Figure 4-2. Note again the saw toothed downward movement. Arrow CD is a trend-line connecting the lowest prices attained during the period. It clearly indicates that the price is in a downward trend.

The technical explanation for this phenomenon is again profit taking. A profit taker in a falling market will be someone who holds a short position and the falling market now presents that person with the opportunity of buying in at a lower price than the commodity was sold for in the first instance. The buying pressure exerted on the market by these profit takers causes the price to a rise. When the profit takers have bought themselves out of the market, the price continues its downward trend.

The next question that arises is whether one can tell when the price trend in a market has turned around. Actually, is it possible to tell when a market trend has turned around soon after it has done so, and if so, how soon? There is really only one generally accepted test, although there are as many techniques as there are traders.

What follows is not an exercise in attempting to predict whether or when a market will turn around. This is an attempt to identify at the soonest possible moment that an existing trend has been reversed.

In fact, the test is quite straightforward. When the two trends illustrated in Figures 4-1 and 4-2 are simply combined, the distinguishing feature is immediately apparent. This is illustrated in Figure 4-3.

Figure 4-3 illustrates a chart feature that is known as a top head and shoulders. As one can readily discern, it is simply a combination of a graphic line portraying an upward tending price and another graphic line portraying a downward trending price. The line connecting points 1 and 2 forms the left shoulder, while the line connecting points 4 and 5 forms the right shoulder. The open triangle formed by the two lines connecting points 2, 3 and 4 is known as the 'head'.

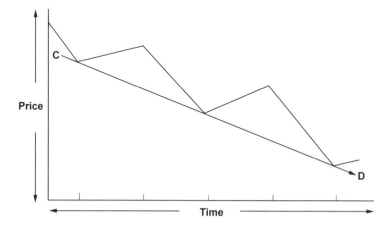

Figure 4-2   A simple line chart showing a declining price trend.

The top head and shoulders chart formation will always appear when an up-trending market turns into a downtrending one. The formation is a natural result of the saw-toothed formation of price charts.

Upon an examination of the formation, it is apparent that point 3 on the chart is the turning point in the upward trend. There is however nothing in the chart formation to indicate that it is so when point 3 is reached and the rest of the chart has not happened yet. Even when the price starts to rise after point 4 is reached, it still seems that the price is in an upward trend and that the downward move from point 3 to 4 is just another correction. Point 4 is, after all, still at a higher level than point 2. If a trend line were to be drawn immediately after the price started rising beyond point 4, it would still show a strong upward trend.

The first time that it can be said with any measure of certainty that the market has turned, is when the price starts declining after point 5 has been established. It is only after point 5 has been established that both shoulders and the head are in place. It is in place because point five has broken the saw-toothed upward movement. The price beyond point 5 is heading down, whilst point 5 is lower than point 3. If the price drop from point 3 to point 4 was merely a price correction, point 5 would be higher than point 3.

Some commentators are of the opinion that one should be very conservative in deciding that a market has turned. On the basis of Figure 4-1, they will not judge that the market has turned before the price has moved down to under point 4. Then it is certain that the market has turned.

Even though the downward trend is now evident after point 5, it cannot be said how far it will continue down or for how long. The only thing that can be said with certainty is that the same type of chart formation will be in evidence when it turns up again. When the price turns up again it will form a 'bottom head and shoulders'. A bottom head and

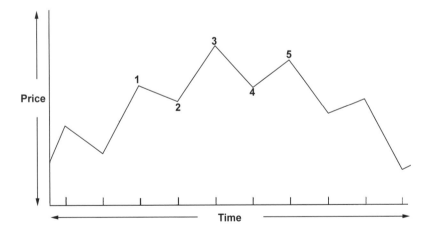

Figure 4-3 **A simple line chart combining an up and a downtrend and showing a 'top head and shoulders' formation.**

shoulders is merely a mirror image of the formation in Figure 4-3. There will again be a left shoulder and then the right shoulder, but the sharp point of the head will point down. The formation is upside-down compared with the one in Figure 4-3. Where the left shoulder in Figure 4-3 is formed by a downward correction in an upward trending market, the left shoulder in a 'bottom head and shoulders' formation will be formed by an upward correction in a downward trending market.

The right shoulder in Figure 4-3 is formed by what is in fact an upward correction of a down trending market, although this will not be evident at the time it happens. In a 'bottom head and shoulders' formation, the right shoulder will in fact be formed by a downward correction in an already up trending market.

In summary, it can thus be said that a top head and shoulders formation is a bearish indicator, because it indicates that the price trend of the market has turned down or has turned bearish. In contrast, a bottom head and shoulders is a bullish indicator since it indicates that a previously down trending market has reversed itself upwards and has turned bullish.

reading bar charts

As was mentioned previously, drawing a line chart from the price information received from the markets is not really a totally satisfactory way of visually illustrating the market. It means that a lot of the value of the available information is lost. A bar chart gives a more useful graphic image.

Figure 4-4 illustrates a single price bar, which incorporates the opening price, the highest price reached, the lowest price reached and closing price for the period indicated by the bar. If the bar indicates the price information for one day, it includes all the price information that is obtained from the markets for the day that it indicates. One bar as illustrated in Figure 4-4 can incorporate the price information for 1 day, 1 week or 1 month. In fact, there is no limit to the time period that can be represented by one bar. The usual application however, is to have daily and weekly price bars in charts.

Upon investigation of a price bar some further observations can be made. The length of the bar between the high and the low indicates the volatility of the market for the period represented by the bar. The longer the line, the higher the price volatility of the market during that period. When a number of consecutive bars are graphically illustrated in a chart, it becomes relatively easy to compare the different daily and weekly volatilities. Apart from market volatility, one can also judge what is happening to price resistance and price support for that commodity.

The high of the bar represents the level at which real price resistance occurred in the market on that day or week. The low of the bar indicates the level of price support for the same period. By looking at a bar chart therefore, it can be judged whether the level of support for the price of a commodity is rising or falling. A judgement will also be possible as to whether the level of price resistance is rising or falling. These are both indicators of market sentiment and are often not directly related to whether the price is in an upward or a downward trend. Some technical trading systems combine all these trends into market 'models' that attempt to predict future market moves and prices.

Another significant feature that can be observed in a price bar is the relationship of the opening price to the closing price. In Figure 4-4 an 'up' day is represented. That is to say, it represents a day when the price closed higher than it opened. This phenomenon is usually associated with an up trend in the price. The inverse situation, when the closing price is lower than the opening price, is associated with a downtrend.

However, care must be taken not to read too much into any single feature of a chart. As will be demonstrated presently, many features are normal to uptrends and many others to downtrends, but there are reversals of the phenomena in both trends. There are no absolute truths.

Figure 4-5 is a bar chart comprised of daily price bars, reflecting the price of CBOT corn. Upon closer inspection, a number of the features that have been discussed will become evident. Firstly, note from the dates at the bottom of the chart, that prices are only shown for trading days. No blanks are left for weekends and other non-trading days. This improves the observable price flow.

The first noticeable feature is the price volatility. Notice the high volatility on July 28, the low of which is the lowest point that can be seen on the present chart. Other high volatility days are September 19 and October 7. Notice the extremely low volatility from September 19 through October 2.

Inspecting the chart from left to right, it is immediately evident that the price was clearly trending up from July 28 to August 4. The high on August 4 represents the high point of that particular trend. August 4 was thus the pivotal day for this trend. For the whole period of the up-trend, the price resistance level rose daily, as did the level of support. Notice that both the high and the low of each successive day after July 28 was

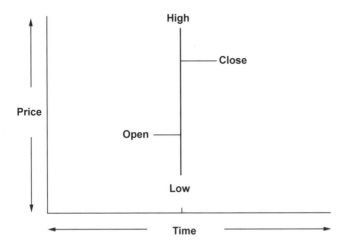

Figure 4-4   A single price bar.

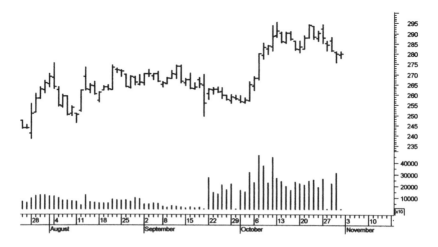

Figure 4-5   A composite chart with daily price bars and contract volumes.

higher than that of the previous day. Comparing the opens and closes of the days reveals that every day, from and including July 28 were 'up' days.

The only exception to all the mentioned features is presented by the data of August 4, the pivotal day. Although the price resistance level rose on that day by as much as it did on any of the other days, the price support level was actually lower than that of the previous trading day. In addition, it was a 'down' day. The price opened higher than it closed.

It would be very convenient if one could generalise 'rules' from the above observations. That would however be extremely dangerous. At best one could say that the contrary indications of August 4 were danger signals, indicating a possible change in the price trend. However, there is no way of telling from those indications, how seriously the price trend will be altered.

Nevertheless, it is interesting to observe how the price trend actually did alter after August 4. At first it appears to trend down for a few days, but in fact it trades sideways until October 6. That is how one would describe the price movement, since the price fluctuates up and down, but it never goes as low or lower than the low of July 28 and it never challenges the high of August 4. It actually keeps on trading within, or inside the range set by that one rally which started on July 28 and ended on August 4. Then on October 7 the price shoots past the high of August 4 and continues to rally until October 12.

There is clearly no strong price trend in this market. The reason or reasons for this will have to be sought in the fundamentals that underlie the market. To an observer on October 31, the market would still seem rather directionless. Unless a price driving change takes place in the underlying fundamentals of the market, prices will remain choppy with a lower support level of around 250 and a resistance level of around 300.

volume and price

Apart from the basic price information that was used above, there are a number of additional statistics that provide further insight into the market. The two most important concepts in commodity futures are those of volume and open interest.

The figures for both volume and open interest are published daily. These figures constitute a very important base on which both market sentiment and market conditions are gauged. One of the best ways to examine these statistics is by means of visual aids, such as graphs and charts. Very often, the data vendors will supply the figures together with a price chart. Otherwise, it is essential to have the necessary software to be able to display the data as a chart.

Open interest is a statistic that is peculiar to the futures markets and will be dealt with under the next heading. Volume is a statistic that can be misleading if regard is not given specifically to what units it is given in. On some futures contracts, volume indicates the number of contracts traded, while in respect of other contracts, volume may indicate the number of units of the underlying that was traded. Then the size of each contract must be taken into account in order to appreciate the number of trades. First, the inter-relationship of price and volume will be investigated.

At the bottom of Figure 4-5 the number of contracts traded are indicated in bars. You will notice that there is a different scale running up to 50 000 on the right-hand side of the chart. It is indicated before the start of the commodity price scale on the same axis. Volume refers to the total number either of purchases or of sales of futures contracts that were made during that day's trading session. It does not indicate the total number of purchases and sales, because for every contract purchased, one must obviously be sold as well. The total number of purchases and sales are therefore not added together to obtain the trading volume. They equal each other. Either the one or the other is thus used to indicate the volume of trades.

A market works like a democracy. If only a few people bother to vote, they can elect a representative, but that representative might not enjoy the support of the majority of the voters. If everybody had taken the trouble to vote, a different candidate might have been elected. So it is with price. Only one contract needs to trade on the market for a price to be established. The question that arises is, how meaningful can a price or even a trend be that is established by only a small number of trades?

The answer is that such a price or such a trend may not be very strong. When prices are fixed or trends established with relatively low volumes, market commentators will always refer to trading in a 'thin market'. This is an indication that things are very likely to change when all 'voters' come to the 'polls'.

Consider the relatively low volumes reflected in Figure 4-5 during the period that it traded sideways. It seems that many buyers were waiting on the sidelines, watching to see if the price would drop. When the price did not drop by October 7, the buyers came to market in droves, immediately buying the price higher and increasing market volatility in so doing. Higher volumes of trading thus supported the higher price level that was achieved and maintained through to the end of October.

However, there is no indication from the information on the chart, what the fundamental reasons were why buyers were sitting on the sidelines in the first place. If these fundamental reasons were known at the time, a somewhat better understanding and perhaps even a slight anticipation of their actions might have been possible.

open interest

The second important concept that was mentioned previously, is open interest. Open interest refers to all the futures contracts that are 'open' and in force at any particular time. Open interest is thus a figure that is given out by an exchange for every trading month of every futures contract. It reflects the total number of open futures contracts that exist at the time the figure is given. In order to understand the importance of knowing the figure for open interest, an understanding is required of how open interest comes about and how it changes. Then changes in open interest can be related to changes in the price of the contract.

The best way of explaining the concept is by examining some examples. Assume a new futures contract starts trading on the London exchange today. Its underlying asset is immaterial. A hedger in London wishes to take a long position in the contract and puts in a bid. A speculator in Paris, through his broker, notices the bid and accepts it by making an equal offer. In effect the hedger in London has now bought a contract from the speculator in Paris. Incidentally, this transaction is recorded as a volume of one. Thus, the transaction resulted in an open interest of one and also a volume of one. The situation on the market now is shown in Table 4-10.

What has in effect happened, is that two new market participants, i.e. participants without any existing positions in the present contract, have come to the market and have taken up positions in it. It is thus apparent that a new buyer and a new seller who enter a new long and a new short position, together create one new open position. In addition, any existing long position holder who increases the number of long positions held, plus either an existing short position holder increasing the number of short positions held, or a newcomer who enters a new short position, together create new open positions for the number of contracts traded. Keep in mind that open positions refer to open contracts. The numbers of traders in the market who hold open positions are never known.

The same increase in open interest occurs when an existing short increases his number of short positions by selling to an existing long who is increasing his number of long positions. In all these instances, new open positions are created which are added to the other existing open positions and the open interest grows. Open interest is thus a cumulative total over the life of the contract, while volume is a daily statistic.

Table 4-10. A transaction resulting in open interest of one

Long	Short	Open Interest
The London Hedger	The Paris Speculator	One Open Contract Exists

Table 4-11. A transaction that creates a new open position

Long	Short	Open Interest
The London Hedger	The Paris Speculator	One Open Contract Exists
The New York Trader	The Brussels Hedger	One Open Contract Exists
		Total Open Interest: 2

Taking the example further, consider that a trader in New York purchases a contract from a hedger in Brussels. The market situation is shown in Table 4-11.

Again, this is a single transaction giving a volume of one. If two contracts were traded of course, the volume would be two and the number of open contracts to be added to the existing open interest, would also be two. For the purposes of this explanation it will be assumed that in each instance to be discussed only one contract is traded.

In both the previous examples, two new longs contracted with two new shorts. As was previously explained, each instance would consequently result in one additional open contract. A further transaction can now be introduced. The Paris speculator decides to liquidate his position through the process of offsetting. This requires him to buy one contract. He succeeds in this, through his broker, by buying a contract from a speculator in Los Angeles. As this is a transaction, the volume is one. The situation with open positions now is shown in Table 4-12.

Although a transaction was done, open interest remains the same. When the process of offsetting was explained, it was stated that a person who holds long and short positions simultaneously in the same futures contract in the same delivery month is out of the market. The two opposite positions cancel one another out. This situation is again clearly demonstrated by the example in Table 4-12.

The speculator from Los Angeles has in fact taken the place of the Paris speculator as the short counterparty to the London hedger's long position. Because the LCH (London Clearing House) acts as seller to all buyers and buyer to all sellers, the London hedger is not concerned at all. He is not even aware of the fact that a new 'counterparty' has been allocated to him. As far as the situation of the Paris speculator is concerned, it is also clear that he cannot contract with himself, acting as both buyer and seller to himself. It follows that he must be out of the market.

In this instance a volume of one was thus achieved, but no new open position was

Table 4-12. A transaction with no change in open interest

Long	Short	Open Interest
The London Hedger	The Los Angeles Speculator	One Open Contract Exists
The Paris Speculator	The Paris Speculator	No Contract Exists
The New York Trader	The Brussels Hedger	One Open Contract Exists
		Total Open Interest: 2

Table 4-13. A transaction with no effect on open interest

Long	Short	Open Interest
The London Hedger	The Los Angeles Speculator	One Open Contract Exists
The London Trader	The Brussels Hedger	One Open Contract Exists
The New York Trader	The New York Trader	No Contract Exists
		Total Open Interest: 2

created. Had this been the only transaction for the day, the market report would have shown a volume of one and open interest of two. One should therefore never attempt to 'balance' the volume in the market report with the change in open interest. The figures will not make sense in that way.

The example can be taken even further. The New York trader offsets his position by going short one contract, which is bought by another trader in London. The open interest is now shown in Table 4-13.

Once again, no change takes place in the open interest. There was a volume of one. The London trader has now taken the place of the New York trader as the long against the short position of the hedger from Brussels. The situation is thus that an existing holder of a position on the market has 'changed places' with a newcomer to the market. As was the case in the previous instance, the result is that the total number of open contracts does not change, although volume is traded.

In the final iteration a transaction will be demonstrated that gives a volume of one, but which actually diminishes open interest. Consider what the situation will be should the London hedger decide to offset his position, whilst at the same time, the Brussels hedger also decides to do the same.

Assume, for the purpose of this transaction, that no other parties join in the market. The long hedger in London now sells his contract to the short hedger in Brussels. The open interest situation now is shown in Table 4-14.

Although there has been a transaction, the open interest has declined to only one. Only the London trader and the Los Angeles speculator are left in the market.

From this extended example it becomes apparent that transactions in the market can have the effect of increasing open interest, not affecting open interest at all, or of actually decreasing open interest. The importance of open interest is that it tells us how many

Table 4-14. A transaction which diminishes open interest

Long	Short	Open Interest
The London Hedger	The London Hedger	No Contract Exists
The Brussels Hedger	The Brussels Hedger	No Contract Exists
The London Trader	The Los Angeles Speculator	One Open Contract Exists
		Total Open Interest: 1

people have an interest in the market. It also tells us how many contracts there are in existence against which delivery of the underlying commodity may have to be made and given.

The open interest will differ from one delivery month to the next delivery month. Therefore, from the open interest an estimate can be made of what the possible needs of the market in a particular month might be. This is not an exact science, but it is an indication, giving a feel for the market.

Even more important than the figure for open interest, is the way it changes. A lot can be learnt about the market by watching how open interest moves against how the price of the commodity moves. In order to explain this more clearly, the combinations that change open interest can be summarised as follows:

- Open interest increases – whenever a new short position and a new long position are established
- Open interest is unchanged – whenever a person with an existing long position sells his contract to a new long position holder or when an existing short position holder buys a contract from a new short position holder
- Open interest decreases – whenever a person who holds an existing long position sells that contract to a person with an existing short position.

Consideration can now be given to what can be learnt from the marketplace by comparing changes in open interest to price movement. This assessment will assist in determining the condition of the market and will help in the making of risk management decisions.

open interest increases and the price rises

It has been clearly demonstrated that open interest increases because new positions are being taken in. New positions will probably result from a mixture of new entrants coming into the market as well as from existing position holders increasing their positions. Buyers are taking in positions more aggressively than sellers, which is why the price is rising.

It is technically incorrect to ascribe the rise in price to the supposed fact that there are more buyers than sellers in the market. It may be factually correct that there are more buyers trying to find sellers, but the price is made when a transaction is done. A transaction is only done when there is both a seller and a buyer. Thus, the price that is established is 'made' by an equal number of buyers and sellers. What can safely be said is that buyers are being more aggressive in their dealings. They are more anxious to enter into transactions than sellers are. They are more easily persuaded to bid up the price. That is why the price is rising.

Technically, this type of market is considered strong. If prices continue rising however, the market can easily become overbought. Once the market is overbought, a correction is on the cards. It does not mean of course, that there will necessarily be a reversal of the uptrend. Rather, the probability of a longer and somewhat deeper correction than one that

is merely the result of profit taking is indicated. One is thus well advised to take cognisance of these factors when deciding what the state of the market is.

open interest increases while the price goes down

Due to the fact open interest is increasing, it is certain that new buyers and new sellers are
entering the market. It is also just as certain that existing long position and short position
holders are increasing their positions. The sellers are however being more aggressive in
their dealings than the buyers. It is for this reason that the price is going down.

Technically this market is considered weak. If these two factors continue influencing
the market in tandem, it may become oversold. Like an overbought market, an oversold
market is subject to imminent correction. An over sold market will of course, experience
a correction in an upward direction.

open interest decreases while the price rises

A decrease in open interest signals the fact that people are leaving the market. Both
existing long positions and existing short positions are being liquidated. Whatever new
entrants there may be in the market, they are being far outnumbered by those people who
are in the market and are closing out or covering their existing positions.

Existing short positions are being liquidated more aggressively than existing long
positions. This means that it is mostly the existing short position holders will are
doing the buying that is taking place, resulting in the price rise. These short position
holders are being aggressive in their buying.

Although the price is rising, it is technically considered to be a weak market. Existing
short position holders in a futures market are often producers of the underlying commodity who will offset their short positions during the delivery month. They will normally
provide price support through their buying activity towards the end of the contract in the
delivery month. Since the shorts are now aggressively leaving the market, that buying
potential is being eliminated. Once the holders of short positions have covered their
positions, they cannot be relied upon to provide buying strength in the market at a future
time.

open interest decreases while the price declines

The fact that open interest is decreasing again indicates that market participants are
leaving the market. In other words, more existing positions are being covered while
their new positions are being taken up. In this instance however, existing long position
holders are covering their positions more aggressively than the short position holders are.

These existing long position holders are selling the market down. Keep in mind that
they have to sell in order to cover their existing long positions. It is clear that they are
offering the contracts at progressively lower prices in order to leave the market. This type
of market is technically regarded as a strong market. The declining price trend in

conjunction with the decrease in the open interest is also referred to as a liquidating market.

open interest and the crop year

The previously discussed agricultural commodities that are subject to crop years have their own pattern of growth and decline in open interest. The tendency is for open interest to be at its highest for the crop year at harvest time. This is because farmers, elevator operators and other users of the commodity generally establish their hedges in the harvest month. As the crop year progresses, the hedges are systematically lifted. As the hedges are lifted, the open interest tends to diminish.

The above is the normal tendency for these commodities. That does not mean that the tendency will be followed every crop year or even throughout the year in any single crop year. Aberrations from the expected norm should however be noticed immediately and considered seriously. There should be fundamental factors at work in the market that cause the aberration. The potential user of the market should determine the nature of these factors, before any position is taken on the market.

certificated stock

It is trite that the market price of any commodity is determined by supply and demand. It is therefore quite surprising to see how often these two basic factors of price determination are ignored when market conditions are discussed. In the commodity markets, the relevant information is not hard to come by. Volume and open interest are clear indicators of the demand situation in the market.

The quantity of a commodity that is available for delivery against short futures positions is called certificated stock. The number of short futures positions against which the stock can be delivered is obviously equal to the open interest in the near futures month. Each futures exchange supplies a daily report on certificated stock for each commodity on which futures contracts are offered on the exchange. Certificated stock is the supply of a commodity that has been inspected and approved for delivery on futures contracts.

In the grain markets certificated stock is referred to as visible supply. In the United States, the CFTC publishes a weekly report on grain that is deliverable against short futures positions. The CBOT also issues a report on visible supply every Monday morning. In the case of grains, visible supply refers to stocks of the grain that are presently held in public elevators, afloat on barges and such stocks as are in store at certain loading centres. It excludes stocks of grain that are held on farms and in country elevators.

CHECKLIST FOR THE REVIEW OF CHAPTER 4

General overview: the overall control objectives of the material dealt with in this chapter are to identify the major market forces, key price relationships and their importance for a business in managing commodity risk

	Key Issues	Illustrative Scope or Approach
4.1	Does the company review the condition of the commodity markets on an ongoing basis?	Risk management criteria are influenced by the condition of the market. It is therefore necessary for a business to know and be aware of the market condition of all relevant commodities on a continuous basis
4.2	Does the business take account of the known price interactions of spot and futures when it makes hedging decisions?	• In an inverse market there is a premium of spot over the near futures delivery month and of near futures over deferred futures months. The possible premium is unlimited • In a normal market there is a premium of deferred months over near futures months and of the near futures month over spot. The premium cannot exceed the cost of carry • The prices of spot and near futures will converge and the difference tend to zero in the near futures delivery month
4.3	Does the business consider the hedge basis when establishing hedges with futures?	The hedge basis results from the difference between the cash market price of the business and the price at which the futures hedge is entered The effect that the movement of the hedge basis will have on the hedge will be amplified by over-hedging or under-hedging In a spread position, only the movement of the spread will result in a profit or a loss on the hedge
4.4	Does the business have any program of collecting commodity market data and of interpreting it?	Market data are available from a number of data vendors as well as from exchanges themselves. From the latter, it is available on a more limited scale It is important for a company to keep itself abreast of market data in order to be in control of its commodity risk management function. Before risk management can be initiated and executed properly, the business will have to equip itself with the necessary services, hardware and software to collect and collate market information usefully
4.5	What are the minimum data required by a business to execute a proper risk management function?	The minimum data required would be to obtain the following daily information: • The spot price of the commodity • The open, high, low and settlement prices of the near futures and deferred futures months' contracts

continued

	Key Issues	Illustrative Scope or Approach
		• The volume traded for each contract
		• The open interest on each contract
		• The certificated stock
4.6	What are the key factors that a business should use in assessing the market?	The business should observe and interpret the following:
		• Particular price formations such as a top or a bottom head and shoulders, ascending and descending hooks as well as sideways trading
		• By comparing spot and futures prices to determine the market condition
		• By comparing the volume traded with the price to determine whether the price was set in a strong or a thin market
		• By comparing changes in open interest to changes in the price
		• Monitor changes in certificated stock against open interest to anticipate floods and famines

five

hedging with commodity futures and options – the user's hedge

INTRODUCTION

A hedger is always a company, a firm or person involved in a business that, in one way or another, uses the underlying cash commodity. Hedging is a technique of neutralising financial risk that involves the taking of a risk that is negatively correlated with the risk being hedged. It is not necessary to discuss risk correlation as such in the context of this book. It is merely necessary to point out at this stage that hedging with commodity futures involves the taking of a position in futures contracts that is opposite to the cash position held. This is a matter that will presently be dealt with in greater detail.

As is clearly implied from the foregoing, this book is concerned with the technique of hedging in so far as it is used to hedge commodity risk through the use of commodity futures and options. The options that will be dealt with are limited to options on commodity futures. During the course of the discussion, reference will only be made to options, which must therefore be understood as a reference to options on commodity futures.

Since the purpose here is to discuss the hedging of commodity risk, it will be necessary to investigate and attempt to define what exactly is meant by the term 'commodity risk'.

COMMODITY RISK

Commodity risk forms part of market risk. It can be readily defined as being the risk faced by a business due to the possibility of adverse changes in the prices of commodities.

Although essentially correct, the definition requires some fleshing out. A fuller definition will be suggested later in the discussion.

However, before a satisfactory definition of commodity risk can be arrived at, it will be necessary to investigate what the term 'commodity' means. What exactly the nature of a commodity is, is a slightly more involved question than would be supposed at first. This question will thus be dealt with first.

what is a commodity?

Like many other financial terms, the term 'commodity' is not a static one. The definition has undergone substantial changes and development over the last 100 or more years. It started off as meaning any primary agricultural product. This definition was later expanded by force of circumstance to include minerals and metals. Today however, the tendency among many commentators and academics is to have an open-ended definition whereby a commodity is defined as anything that can form the underlying asset of a futures contract.

The problem presented by this definition is that the term would include everything from interest rates and foreign currency to pork bellies and frozen orange juice. Although it does make a valid point for certain purposes, it does not reflect normal market terminology. It is also insufficiently focused to be really helpful for the purpose of this book. As will become apparent though, the definition does contain an important element that will lead to a narrower definition of commodities. It can therefore not summarily be dismissed.

In normal business parlance, the term 'commodity' is applied to physical goods of commercial value. Nevertheless, not all physical goods are regarded as commodities. Motor cars, furniture and jewellery for example are physical goods, but they are not understood to be commodities. These are examples of compound manufactured goods. They are constructed by putting together numbers of other physical goods, some of which are commodities.

The essence of what is termed a commodity is still missing. It does not lie in whether or not the physical goods concerned are primary or secondary products. The mere fact that physical goods have been processed in some way does not deprive them of commodity status. Mention only has to be made of metals to demonstrate this. The primary product from which metals are produced is the mineral ore. The ore has to pass through a good deal of processing before the extracted metal is ready to be cast into a basic form such as ingots. Metals in ingot or bar form are definitely and universally regarded as commodities. Similarly, soybean meal, gasoline and heating oil are all secondary products that are classified as commodities.

The quality that distinguishes a commodity from other physical goods is to be found elsewhere. It is for good reason thus, that the open-ended definition requires physical goods to be of such a nature that they could form the underlying asset of a futures contract in order to qualify as commodities. This is not a facile element at all. In order for physical goods to be suitable for the purpose of forming the underlying asset of a futures contract, two basic qualities are required.

Firstly, the commodity needs to be something that can be bought and sold in standard quantities. The quantitative measurement may be weight, volume, or some other suitable measurement, such as British thermal units (Btu's). Secondly, the commodity must be easily graded and standardised. The requirements are also dealt with in the chapter on futures contracts.

These qualities are essential in underlying assets of futures contracts. Since futures contracts are standardised contracts for future delivery of the underlying commodity, only the price of the underlying needs to be agreed between the parties. The type of goods purchased, the quantity and the grade are all prescribed terms of a futures contract. If the goods do not lend themselves to this type of quantification and standardisation, they cannot form the underlying asset of a futures contract.

A more restricted definition of a commodity consequently suggests itself as being 'any physical good that have the qualities to form the underlying asset of a commodity futures contract'. The accent on 'physical' does not preclude intangible commodities. Energy commodities such as petroleum products, coal and electricity are measured in intangible quantities such as Btu and Mwhs. It is thus not necessarily the physical properties of the products that are regarded as commodities, but rather, it is the intangible quantities of energy that are delivered.

Not all goods that thus qualify as commodities are actually traded on the commodity futures markets. However, the numbers of those that do not trade are shrinking daily. New futures contracts are continuously being added to those already on offer in order to meet the growing demands of commerce and of the trading public.

categories of commodities

Commodities, as defined above, are divided into three broad categories. The first category is agricultural products, the second category is metals and the third category is energy. Each category has a number of sub-divisions.

Agricultural products are the oldest recognised category. They include products such as corn, wheat, soybeans, barley, cocoa, coffee and sugar among many others. They are not limited to foodstuffs. Non-foodstuff agricultural products, such as cotton, lumber and other timber board products have also been traded for many years. Livestock contracts include cattle and hogs. Butter, eggs, cheese and milk make up livestock produce while a wide variety of meats, including boneless beef and fresh and frozen pork bellies are available. The potato is the only vegetable traded on futures markets.

The LIFFE (London Interest and Financial Futures Exchange) offers UK agricultural contracts, while the CBOT, CME and KCBT are the major agricultural products futures exchanges in the US. All these exchanges offer a wide variety of non-agricultural contracts as well.

The metals category is sub-divided into precious metals, base and non-ferrous metals. Precious metals consist of gold, silver and platinum. Base metal is limited to pig iron, while a wide variety of non-ferrous metals such as copper, aluminium and nickel are traded on the LME (London Metals Exchange). Both precious and non-precious metals are traded in the US, mainly on the NYMEX, COMEX and the CBOT exchanges.

Energy commodities are a recent and extremely fast-growing category. Crude oils and certain refined oils such as heating oil, fuel oil and gas oil are traded. In addition, natural gas is also traded on London's IPE (International Petroleum Exchange). In the United States, a coal contract will shortly be offered by the NYMEX (New York Mercantile Exchange), with four contracts on electricity already trading on the same exchange.

hedging physical goods

As argued above, not all physical goods of commercial value are commodities. Nevertheless, companies are exposed to the risk of adverse price movements of all goods that they buy, sell, use or produce. Why then the emphasis on commodity risk?

The definition of a commodity makes it clear that the concept is linked to futures trading. Futures contracts form part of the gallery of financial derivative instruments that are available to control and manage financial risk. What was said of the qualities that are required of goods for futures trading is equally valid for such goods to form the underlying asset of any other derivative instrument. In the premises, only commodities underlie derivative instruments.

On the basis of what was said at the beginning of this chapter, namely that hedging is accomplished by the taking a position in a derivative that is opposite to the cash position, it follows that the risk of adverse price movement of commodities can be hedged by means of derivative instruments. The prices of physical goods that do not enjoy the qualities required of commodities can therefore not be hedged directly. This does not mean that price moves of such goods cannot be managed.

Physical goods that do not qualify as commodities are usually comprised of commodities. A motor car for example, is mostly comprised of various types steel and other metals. The price movements of these metals will greatly influence the cost of a car. A wedding cake does not qualify as a commodity, but it is made by combining a number of commodities such as wheat flour, butter, eggs, sugar, some cocoa or coffee perhaps, and some energy for baking.

In order to guard against adverse price movements of goods that are not commodities in themselves, it is necessary to hedge the prices of commodities that have the greatest influence on the cost of such goods. Although principally correct, this statement is subject to a serious caveat: secondary product hedging involves basis risk. The subject of basis risk is dealt with in another chapter, but its effects will become more apparent when the subject of hedging with commodity futures is discussed.

Thus, when the risks of adverse price movement are identified and assessed, a company must reduce the physical goods that it produces or uses in the course of its business, to their constituent commodities. Since only the adverse price movement of commodities can be hedged, it will then be necessary to calculate the impact that the possible price moves of each of the component commodities has on the financial well being of the company. The result of that calculation will reflect the totality of the commodity risk faced by the firm.

the financial risk in commodities

Having determined and discussed the nature of commodities, the risk incurred by their production, use and trading can be identified. The definition of commodity risk as expounded at the start of this section is thus in need of some revision.

The risk that this book is particularly concerned with, is the financial risk to business that follows from trading in commodities. Financial risk in this context refers to the risk of the financial condition of a business. Furthermore, it bears repeating that the risk that forms the subject matter and focus of this book is the risk faced by businesses from adverse moves in the prices of commodities.

The risk of loss and damage to goods due to other causes, are not risks that can be addressed by the use of commodity futures. The risk of adverse price moves is exacerbated by price volatility in the commodity markets. It would thus be wrong to limit the definition of commodity risk solely to adverse price moves. Adverse price moves may be the actual cause of financial loss, but the risk is directly proportional to volatility.

Given the considerations discussed above, a definition of commodity risk, for the purpose of this book, can be suggested as follows:

Commodity risk is the risk to a firm's financial condition resulting from adverse price moves and increases in the price volatility of such tangible or intangible commodities as are produced, held, traded and/or used by it in the course of its business.

This definition will serve adequately to guide the discussion on hedging that follows.

THE BUYING HEDGE USING FUTURES

The buying hedge is so called because it is the technique used by the buyer of the commodity as opposed to the producer or manufacturer thereof. In other words, it is the technique that will be used by a business that is short the cash. The technique is consequently also known as a long hedge. The latter appellation is due to the fact that the buyer or user of a commodity will hedge the cash position of the business by taking in a long position in the futures markets.

The opposite hedge is known as a short hedge or as the producer's hedge. The latter hedge is fully dealt with in the next chapter. Since the two types of hedges mirror each other, it is suggested that the reader reads either what follows in this chapter or alternatively, the whole of the next chapter, depending upon which one of the hedges is appropriate to the business of the reader's concern. This will save the reader the tedium of slogging through what is essentially a repeat of the same material, albeit the converse.

At the end of the next chapter, a checklist of the differences between the two hedges will be found in a comparative table. If either the long hedge or the short hedge is thoroughly understood, it will be quite simple for the reader to gain an equally thorough understanding of the other hedge by reading through the summary of the differences.

Thus, returning to the subject under discussion, it can be said that the purpose of the buying hedge is to protect a short cash position from an adverse move in price. A short cash position is at risk of a rise in price. A rise in the price of the underlying commodity will increase the cost of purchasing the cash commodity at a date in the future. The working and dynamics of the hedge will be best illustrated by means of an example. The effect and efficacy of a buying hedge will differ depending on the market condition, namely whether the market is normal or inverse. It will therefore be appropriate also to demonstrate and discuss the long hedge by using an example and then iterating the example by assuming different market conditions. However, in order first to demonstrate the basic concept of using a long hedge, the condition of the market will be ignored.

the perfect long hedge

Consider the situation of a gas station owner situated in Buffalo, New York. The major retail product of this particular station is unleaded gasoline, delivered from the New York harbour area. During January, the prices of crude and refined oil are constantly rising. The owner's concern is that the pressures of rising prices on the one hand and a resultant price-cutting by his competitors will squeeze his profit margins. The owner wishes to maintain at least the present profit margins through to the end of March. In order to protect his purchase price, he decides to hedge using the futures contract on New York Harbour unleaded gasoline.

Ignoring transport costs to Buffalo, NY, the spot price of unleaded gasoline at the end of January is $0.8425 per US gallon. At the same time, the March futures contract on the NYMEX is trading at $0.7461. The oil market is thus in a state of inversion; a condition to which it is often prone.

The last trading day of this contract will be the last business day of the February. The gas station owner intends to purchase his unleaded gasoline requirements for March on that day. The estimated requirements of the station for March will be 126 000 US gallons. Since one futures contract equals 42 000 US gallons, the station will require three contracts to cover its March purchases.

The owner thus telephones his broker and instructs him to buy three NYMEX March New York Harbour unleaded gasoline contracts. Later in the day, the broker reports back with a fill of $0.755. His hedged position now appears in Table 5-1.

Notice that this example illustrates the position where a business uses the technique of hedging without actually holding any cash position. The gas station owner is technically not short the 126 000 US gallons of unleaded fuel since he has not sold it without owning or possessing it. In this case, the business is making use of the facility of hedging in order to protect its competitiveness in the market and not its actual cash holding. It is a frequent and very effective use of hedging.

Table 5-1. A long hedge at its initiation

Cash Market		Futures Market		Basis
Jan. 'Short' 126000 Galls.	$0.8425	Jan. Long Three Contracts	$0.7550	0.0875 Over

As is fully discussed elsewhere, a market can move in any one of three ways: it can trade up, down or sideways. A market that trades sideways does not have a stationary price. A sideways market merely means that the price of fluctuates up and down in a reasonably narrow range. Thus, prices will change up or down, even in a sideways trading market.

In order to demonstrate the basic mechanics of a hedge, the result of an upward and of a downward move in price will be discussed. Since the example demonstrates a long hedge, which is intended to protect the hedger against a rise in price, this contingency will be investigated first.

the price rises

Assume that on February 28, when the gas station owner orders his March inventory of unleaded gas, the spot price has increased to $0.8750. Assume further that on the same date, the March futures contract is trading at $0.7860 and rising. Obviously, if the spot price of a commodity rises, the futures price of that commodity will also rise. When the gas station owner places his inventory order at the ruling spot price, he simultaneously telephones his broker and instructs him to close out the futures position. Assume that the broker sells the three long futures contracts at a price of $0.7875. The result of the hedge is shown in Table 5-2.

The spot price of unleaded gasoline rose by $0.0325 per US gallon and the futures price reacted by rising by the same amount. From Table 5-2 it is clear that the 'loss' on the cash purchase of the gasoline is totally offset by the profit realised on the futures trade. This is due to the fact that there was no basis move. There was no basis move precisely because the spot price and the futures prices moved by the same amount. This therefore illustrates a perfect hedge.

Of course, the business did not suffer a loss on the cash market. The 'loss' merely indicates the amount that the station is paying more in March than it was in January. Nevertheless, this was the reason for the hedge – to avoid paying more and putting profit margins under pressure. The result of the hedge is that the net purchase price of the

Table 5-2. The result of a perfect long hedge in an inverse market with a rise in price

Cash Market		Futures Market		Basis
Jan. 'Short' 126000 Galls.	$0.8425	Jan. Long Three Contracts@	$0.7550	0.0875 Over
Feb. Long 126000 Galls.	$0.8750	Feb. Short Three Contracts@	$0.7875	0.0875 Over
'Loss':	$0.0325	Profit:	$0.0325	Change: 0

Table 5-3. The result of a perfect long hedge in an inverse market with a decline in price

Cash Market		Futures Market		Basis
Jan. 'Short' 126000 Galls.	$0.8425	Jan. Long Three Contracts@	$0.7550	0.0875 Over
Feb. Long 126000 Galls.	$0.8050	Feb. Short Three Contracts@	$0.7175	0.0875 Over
'Profit':	$0.0375	Loss:	$0.0375	Change: 0

unleaded gasoline amounts to $0.8425 per gallon ($0.8750 paid; $0.0325 profit on the futures market). The gas owner therefore managed to purchase his March inventory at the same price that it was in January.

The situation of a decline in price can now be investigated.

the price declines

For the purpose of this iteration, assume that the spot price for unleaded gasoline on February 28 is $0.8050. The price that the broker realises on the sale of the futures is $0.7175. Again, the futures price would be expected to fall in sympathy with the fall in the spot price. The result of the hedge is now shown in Table 5-3.

Again, the was no basis move and the profit in the cash market therefore neutralises the loss in the futures markets exactly. The net result of the hedge is thus that the purchase price for the March inventory equals $0.8425 per gallon – exactly the same as in the previous iteration where the price of gasoline rose. The hedge has not come up to the expectations of the gas station owner, as the cost for his March inventory is now higher than the cost to his competitors.

discussion: the result of the hedge

From the above two iterations of the example, it is clear that the purpose of a hedge is to ensure price stability. Ignoring for a moment any move in the basis, it is evident that once a hedge has been established, it does not matter whether the price rises or falls, the result will be the same. The greatest benefit of a hedge is therefore that it allows a business to budget, to have price certainty and to dampen price volatility in the market.

The downside of a hedge is that it does not allow the advantage of a favourable price move. In a perfect hedge all risk is hedged away, even the risk of a profit. This is not intended as a criticism of a perfect hedge – it is merely an accurate observation. It means though, that a perfect hedge will not be desirable under all circumstances. The general thesis of this book is thus supported by illustrating that hedging is a multi-faceted facility. It should not be indulged in without proper consideration of all aspects and requirements of the situation. This question will be discussed in greater detail in the next chapter.

THE LONG FUTURES HEDGE IN AN INVERSE MARKET

As it happens, a perfect hedge is highly improbable when using futures and options. Basis move is a constant factor that has to be taken into consideration at all times. It is one of the aspects that make hedging with futures and options such a fascinating subject. It seems that there are so many aspects and perspectives that one is continually being confronted with something new – an old Roman might have been tempted to exclaim 'ex futurae semper alliquid novo'. In order to demonstrate a more realistic approach to the example, two more iterations are discussed below. This time however, basis moves, predicated on proper market considerations, will be employed.

MOVES IN THE BASIS RESULT IN AN IMPERFECT HEDGE

An imperfect hedge is by definition, one in which the profit in the one market does not perfectly neutralise the loss in the other market. Basis movement can therefore result in either a profit or a loss on the hedge. It is the purpose of the discussion that follows to examine and indicate profit and loss situations resulting from a long hedge.

the imperfect long hedge: the price rises

For the purposes of the next iteration, the facts in the previous example in which a price rise was discussed will be used unaltered, except for allowing for an appropriate basis move. This will also allow for a better comparison between iterations in order to focus attention on only one important aspect, namely the changes in the hedge basis.

Assume therefore that the gas station's hedge, using March New York Harbour unleaded gasoline futures contracts, is lifted on February 28. The long positions are covered at a price of $0.7725. The result of the hedge is now as illustrated in Table 5-4.

It is well known that the spot price of a commodity and the its near futures contract price will converge and tend to zero in the futures delivery month. Since the last trading day of February is the last trading day of the March futures contract and March is the delivery month, it is reasonable to suggest a basis of no greater than $0.0325. In fact, the basis could even be much smaller, and had the market reverted to normal, there could even have been a slightly negative basis.

The exact figure of the eventual basis is not of such great importance. What is of extreme importance though, is that the basis would have narrowed. In order to narrow

Table 5-4. An imperfect long hedge in an inverse market with a rise in price

Cash Market		Futures Market		Basis
Jan. 'Short' 126000 Galls.	$0.8425	Jan. Long Three Contracts@	$0.7550	0.0875 Over
Feb. Long 126000 Galls.	$0.8750	Feb. Short Three Contracts@	$0.8425	0.0325 Over
'Loss':	$0.0325	Profit:	$0.0875	Change: −0.055

from an inverse position the basis must technically weaken. It does not matter whether it weakens from very positive to mildly positive or right through to downright negative. The extent of the weakening will influence the quantitative outcome of the hedge, but it will not influence the outcome in principle – the long hedge will show a profit when the basis weakens. A closer inspection of the last iteration of the example will reveal this more clearly.

The only change that was made to the figures used in the first iteration of the example was that the price the March futures contracts fetched upon their sale was considerably higher. This change made the example more realistic, as explained above. Any increase in the price of the futures contracts would result in a greater profit on the futures trade. Since a narrowing of the basis absolutely requires a greater futures price, it is inevitable that the futures price must increase from its January level by more than the spot price increases from that same date. This demonstrates the inevitability of a profit on a hedge under these conditions.

Calculating the actual purchase price of the March inventory, it comes to $0.7875 per US gallon ($0.8750 actual price paid − $0.0875 profit on the futures). The gas station is now in an enviable position. Its March inventory has cost it less than its February inventory had done at the end of January. While the competitors will be raising prices, this station will actually be in a position to cut prices if it so wished. Keep in mind that this is not the result of blind luck. Having found itself in a market that was in backwardation, the result of the hedge is only what the gas station owner would have expected.

Next, the result will be put to the test to see whether the profit remains inevitable if there is a drop in price rather than a rise.

the imperfect long hedge: the price declines

The assumption now is that the spot price has declined. With a decline in price, it is likely that the market would will go into contango, i.e. become a normal market. However, it is not necessary to drive the example that far in order to illustrate the principle. Only the futures price needs to be adjusted from the first price decline iteration in order to reflect the expected narrowing of the basis. Assume therefore, that the futures position of the gas station was covered at a price of $0.7725. The result of the hedge is now shown in Table 5-5.

In fact, the price of the futures rose even though the spot price declined. This is due to the fact that the market would be less inverse when a drop in buying pressure results in

Table 5-5. The result of an imperfect long hedge in an inverse market after a decline in price

Cash Market		Futures Market		Basis
Jan. 'Short' 126000 Galls.	$0.8425	Jan. Long Three Contracts@	$0.7550	0.0875 Over
Feb. Long 126000 Galls.	$0.8050	Feb. Short Three Contracts@	$0.7725	0.0325 Over
'Profit':	$0.0375	Profit:	$0.0175	Change: −5.5

lower prices. It is apparent again that a narrowing of the basis can only happen if it (the basis) weakens, that is to say, when the basis becomes anything from less positive through to downright negative. The only way that the basis can weaken is for the futures price to improve relative to the spot price. This change, depending on its size, will result in anything from a smaller loss on the futures right through to a massive profit.

If the actual purchase price of the inventory is recalculated in the light of the information in Table 5-1, a result of $0.7875 is obtained. This is incidentally the same actual price that was obtained when the price rose in the previous iteration. The reason that the net purchase prices are identical is that in addition to the fact that identical basic price information was used, the change in the basis was the same in both instances. If the futures prices were to be adjusted to give different basis changes, the actual price paid for the inventory would be different. This again demonstrates how absolute the influence of basis is in hedging with commodity futures.

Again, because of the basic rule that the spot price and the near futures price will converge and tend to zero in the futures delivery month, it can be stated with confidence that a buying hedge in an inverse market will result in a profit on the hedge. There is a condition however. The condition is that the hedge must be held until or at least very close to, the futures delivery month. The basis will tend to narrow and widen continuously during the currency of a futures contract and nothing can be said with any certainty concerning the state of the basis before the close approach of the futures delivery month. Monitoring the basis is therefore an important part of successful hedging. It is a subject that will be returned to in more detail later.

THE LONG FUTURES HEDGE IN A NORMAL MARKET

The investigation and discussion must now turn to the effect of a buying hedge in a normal market. A buying hedge remains the same in principle, whatever the market condition. The purpose of this discussion is thus to demonstrate how the hedge behaves under normal market conditions.

The only relevant difference between a market in backwardation and one in contango for the purposes of this discussion, is the way the basis moves. In an earlier chapter, this whole phenomenon was fully discussed and it was pointed out then that under both markets conditions, the spot price and the futures price will converge and tend to zero in the futures delivery month. Therein lies the difference.

Under inverse market conditions, the spot price is trading higher than the near futures price. The higher the spot price is over the futures price, the more positive or stronger the basis. A convergence of the two prices therefore inevitably means a weakening of the basis. The basis must become less positive. Under normal market conditions, the converse is true. The spot price will be under the futures price. The basis will therefore be negative or weak. When these two prices converge, they are moving closer together, the basis is thus becoming less negative. It is, in other words, strengthening.

The rule on price convergence can thus be phrased differently in order to differentiate the situation in a normal market from that in a market in backwardation. It can be said that in a normal market, the basis between the spot price of a commodity and its near futures contract price will strengthen and tend to zero in the near futures delivery month. Conversely, it can be said that in an inverse market, the basis between the spot price and the near futures price of a commodity will weaken and tend to zero in the near futures delivery month.

The effect of these factors on a long hedge in a normal market may best be illustrated by means of an example, iterated as in the previous section. Consider a manufacturing jeweller that among other things manufactures gold rings for high school graduates. The rings are normally presented to the graduating students by the High School juniors at a ceremony in May, before the year-end of the schools. The manufacturing jeweller has to quote a firm price for the rings in February, when the orders are placed by the schools. The jeweller does not intend to start manufacturing the rings before the beginning of May, since they need only be shipped after the 15th of that month.

They know they find themselves in a highly competitive market and therefore do not wish to pad their prices unduly in order to protect themselves against price rises. That is in any event a very risky strategy. On the other hand, they want to make sure that they do not supply the rings at a loss. They therefore quote for the rings based on the ruling spot price of gold in February, which is $283.00 per fine troy ounce. The May gold futures contract on the Chicago Board of Trade is simultaneously trading at $292.00 per fine troy ounce.

The jewellery firm calculates that it will require no more than 2000 ounces of gold to fill their orders. The CBOT contract trades in multiples of 1000 ounces. The firm therefore places an order with their broker to buy two CBOT May Kilo Gold futures contracts at the market. Assume that they receive a fill at $292.50. Their hedged position is now shown in Table 5-6.

From the prices illustrated in Table 5-6, it is clear that the gold market is in contango. For the purposes of this, and all other iterations based on this example, it will be assumed that the initial basis as illustrated in this table represents a full 2-month carrying charge for gold.

Once the firm had accepted the orders for the rings at their fixed price, they were obviously short the gold. They had sold it, or at least a product containing it, without owning or possessing it. They must therefore employ a long hedge to protect their position. Keep in mind that their alternative strategy was actually to purchase the gold and hold it until required, thereby incurring a 2-month carrying charge. The carrying charge would probably not be the worst consideration either. The worst part of this alternative would be to tie up $536 000 of capital for 2 months. Such a substantial

Table 5-6. A long hedge in a normal market

Cash Market		Futures Market		Basis
Feb. Short 2000 oz. Gold	$283.00	Jan. Long Two Kilo Gold	$292.50	9.50 Under

Table 5-7. The result of a long hedge in a normal market after a price rise

Cash Market		Futures Market		Basis
Feb. Short 2000 oz. Gold	$283.00	Jan. Long 2 × kg Gold	$292.50	9.50 Under
April Long 2000 oz. Gold	$289.50	April: Short 2 × kg Gold	$293.75	4.25 Under
Loss:	$6.50	Profit:	$1.25	Change: +4.25

sum would undoubtedly have a negative effect on the size and scope of the firm's other activities during this time.

the imperfect long hedge; the price rises

In the first iteration of the example, a rise in the price of gold will be assumed. At the end of April, when the manufacturing jeweller firm wishes to purchase the gold, the spot market price it pays is $289.50. At the same time, the firm instructs the broker to lift the hedge. The broker reports back that the long futures positions were closed out at $293.75. The result of the hedge is illustrated in Table 5-7.

The firm clearly made a loss on the hedge. The profit on the futures trade fell short of the loss on the spot market by $5.25 per troy ounce or, to put it differently, the firm's net loss after taking account of the hedge is $10 500. The actual purchase price of the gold was thus $288.25 per fine troy ounce ($289.50 paid on the spot market − $1.25 profit on the futures) giving a total price of $576 500.00 for 2000 ounces.

Two main questions arise from the result of the hedge. Firstly, was the firm better off by hedging, and secondly, what was the maximum loss, if any, that they could suffer on the hedge? These two questions will be discussed after the second iteration has been dealt with.

the imperfect long hedge: the price declines

For the purposes of this iteration, it will be assumed that gold suffered a decline in price between February and the end of April. When the jeweller firm makes its purchase at the end of April, they pay a price of $275.50. This is $7.50 per fine ounce better than they had based their quote on. However, when the firm receives the fill on the lifting of the hedge, the discover that the long futures positions were covered at $279.75, resulting in a loss on the futures market of $12.75. See Table 5-8 for the full result.

Table 5-8. The result of an imperfect long hedge in a normal market after a decline in price

Cash Market		Futures Market		Basis
Feb. Short 2000 oz. Gold	$283.00	Jan. Long 2 × kg Gold	$279.75	9.50 Under
April Long 2000 oz. Gold	$275.50	April: Short 2 × kg Gold	$292.50	4.25 Under
Profit:	$7.50	Loss:	$12.75	Change: +4.25

As in the previous iteration, the basis strengthened by 4.25 from 9.5 under to only 4.25 under. It is therefore not surprising that the net loss suffered on the hedge amounts are the same as in the previous iteration, namely $5.25 per fine troy ounce. The net price paid for the gold is thus $288.25 per fine troy ounce or a total of $576 500, exactly as in the previous iteration. Of course, if the basis strengthened more, the loss on the hedge would have been greater. Had it strengthened less, the loss would likewise have been smaller.

Notice the central role played by the move in the basis. The difference between the profit made on the cash market and the loss made on the futures market equals $4.25, which in its turn is equal to the amount by which the basis strengthened. Monitoring the basis is thus central to managing risk with commodity futures.

discussion: the result of the hedge

As is apparent from the above two iterations of the example, once the position has been hedged, the result of the hedge is totally independent of the price move. It does not matter whether the price moves up or down, the result of the hedge is determined solely by the move in the basis and by nothing else.

The iterations also demonstrate the fact that a long hedge with commodity futures in a normal market will inevitably result in a loss on the hedge. As previously mentioned, two main questions arise from this:

- what, if any, are the limits of the possible basis move; and
- is a long hedge with commodity futures in a normal market a viable risk management option for a business?

Dealing first of all with the limits of the risk, the rule of price convergence must be kept in mind, because it is the key to answering the question. The risk of loss is, as has been demonstrated, limited to the extent that the basis narrows. Since we are dealing exclusively with a basis move in a normal or carrying charge market, the question can thus be put differently. The question is really, by how much can the basis strengthen during the term of the hedge?

The realistic answer to the question put in this way is that the amount by which the basis can strengthen is unlimited. This means that the risk of loss on a basis move is unlimited. That is however not the end of the matter. The answer as postulated requires some further examination. Consider the fact that in a normal market, the maximum basis that can exist between the spot price and the price of the futures in any futures delivery month is limited to the carrying charge. Should a long hedge be established with a basis equal to the carrying charge for the period, the risk is that the basis move may wipe out the whole of the carrying charge. If the basis strengthens to zero, then the loss on a long hedge will amount to the total of the initial basis. If the basis was the carrying charge, then the loss on the long hedge will be the carrying charge.

Unfortunately, the carrying charge is not the limit of the loss. A market in contango can, during the currency of a hedge, turn into an inverse market. That means that the basis could start of as a negative one, equal to the carrying charge and then strengthen, wiping out the carrying charge, and continuing to strengthen as the market becomes increasingly inverse. As there is no limit to the amount that the price of the spot month can trade over the price of the near futures month, there is no limit to how far the basis can strengthen. Since it is a strengthening of the basis that causes a loss on a long hedge, it follows that there is no limit to the amount of the loss.

The above argument is however subject to one very important condition. That condition is that no matter what the condition of the market may be the spot price and the price of the near futures will converge and tend to zero during the futures delivery month. Thus, although there is no limit to how far the basis can strengthen during the currency of a hedge, the ultimate situation in the futures delivery month will be that the spot price will be just over or just under the price of that futures contract.

The first question can thus be answered. The maximum risk that a long hedge in a normal market entails, on condition that it is held until or close to the futures delivery month, will approximate the carrying charges of the commodity for the period of the hedge. As can be expected, the foregoing statement is not intended to be a mathematical law. It is however, a practical guide and a rule that will serve the user well if it is applied with circumspection. It will never be leagues off the mark.

The second question can now be investigated. It must be stressed at the outset, that the discussion that follows is relevant only to the use of futures contracts to establish a long hedge in a normal market. It certainly does not apply to the use of futures in any other hedge in any other market condition, much less to the use of futures generally.

As to whether or not a long hedge using commodity futures is a viable option for a business in general terms, the answer must be an unqualified yes. Whether it is a viable option for a particular company at a particular point in time is a matter that must be properly considered. A number of the main considerations that should be taken account of are discussed below, without any pretension that these considerations are in any way exhaustive of all considerations.

It is suggested that the primary and most important question is to determine the alternatives. If the risk that it is intended to hedge has minimal impact on the financial wellbeing of the business, then obviously the question of hedging it should not have arisen in the first place. However, in all other instances the evil of not hedging should be weighed against the evil of the loss of the possible basis move. Not hedging always involves unlimited risk, against which a long hedge in a normal market involves limited risk as discussed.

Another alternative is to purchase the inventory now and hold it until it is required for use. A long futures hedge may be adjudged superior to this course of action. If the inventory is purchased in anticipation of its later use, the carrying charges will be incurred in full and a substantial amount of capital will be tied up in inventory. This will doubtless have a deleterious effect on the firm's ability to carry on with the normal course of its business successfully. It may also curb the firm's ability to avail themselves of profitable opportunities that come its way during this time. Any business would be ill advised to embark upon such a course of action.

Therefore, regard should first be given to the alternative financial hedging instruments that may be available. Swaps, cash forward agreements and over the counter (OTC) options, as well as exchange-traded options that do not have futures contracts as their underliers, do not involve basis moves. A properly constructed swap or other OTC instrument will result in a perfect hedge every time.

The problem in the commodity markets however, is that these OTC instruments are often not available at all and even if they are, they might be available only in larger quantities that could far exceed the requirements of the firm. Nevertheless, depending on the requirements of the situation, it may be the best alternative to select another derivative instrument for a long hedge in a normal market. This is a question that only a business faced with the problem will be able to resolve at the appropriate time. Some factors that will weigh when other derivatives are considered will be discussed presently.

However, first keep in mind that when dealing with the question of the limits of the risk, the conclusion was reached that the maximum possible loss on a long hedge in a normal market will approximate the carrying charge for the period of the hedge. The maximum loss will be a rarity in practice. The prudent action to take would be to start of by inspecting the price of the futures delivery month that it is intended to use for the hedge. Then determine the basis by using the actual price that the business would have to pay now for the cash commodity. This might of course be the spot price or the business might normally enjoy the facility of a discount on the spot price. It is the actual price that the business has to pay for the physical commodity that determines the cash leg of the hedge basis. It is not basis in general that determines the business's hedge performance, but its own particular hedge basis. Therefore, if the business enjoys a discounted price, it is the discounted price that must be used to determine the hedge basis. It follows that it is also the discounted price that must be used to calculate the result of the hedge when it is lifted.

As previously stated, swaps result in a perfect hedge every time. If a perfect hedge is what the business requires and swaps are liquid and available in the required lot sizes, they may be the best choice under all the circumstances. The other alternatives of non-futures based options and cash forward agreements require some further consideration and evaluation.

Cash forward agreements and other options again, may be available or they may not. If cash forward agreements are available, the price will be at a premium to the spot price. The price premium will, inter alia, have the carrying charges of the commodity for the period factored in. There are no free lunches. One way or another, somebody has to pay for the carrying charges. The only time that carrying charges are not applicable is when the commodity in question must still be produced, such as agricultural products that will only be harvested at the start of the new crop year. The price premium on a cash forward purchase will have to be compared with the possible loss on a futures hedge.

Any option product that is available for consideration will carry a premium. The premium is not linked to carrying charges of course, but many other elements go into the pricing of options. The question of option pricing is dealt with elsewhere in this book. It is always a question of investigation therefore, as to whether the premium on an option is greater or smaller than the carrying charge. Although this is certainly not the only element to consider when deciding upon the question of using options, it is an important element that needs to be given due consideration.

Thus, the hedge basis, determined using the actual cash price to the business as previously explained, must then be compared with the price premium of a cash forward purchase and to the premium to be paid on an option. If the basis is anything less than the price premium to be paid on a cash forward purchase or the premium on an option, the long hedge with futures has the advantage. Even if the price test results in a tie, there are other matters to consider.

Focussing on the cash forward agreement for the moment, if the difference between the price premium on the cash forward and the hedge basis of the futures is insignificant, there are other factors to consider. A cash forward agreement involves counter party credit risk, while a futures contract does not. In addition, a futures hedge allows a business freedom to seek out the best price deal in the cash market when the day of reckoning arrives. In a cash forward agreement the business is legally bound to purchase the goods from the vendor with whom the cash forward transaction was concluded.

Considering the alternative of using options, some further factors require consideration. It may well be that the business is in a similar position to that of the manufacturing jeweller in the previous example. It has given a quote to which it is contractually bound. Its main concern therefore is to ensure that the purchase of the gold will be at a price that was catered for in the quote. Incidentally, being both prudent and knowledgeable about hedging, the jeweller would have factored the expected loss on the basis move of the hedge into the price quotation. Similarly, the premium on the option would also have been factored in, had they decided to follow that course. Picking up windfall profits along the way, which is the other much vaunted advantage of options, may not be especially important to the firm, since that is only a possibility and will not to be indulged in, especially if greater cost is involved.

In the premises therefore, a buying hedge even in a normal market where a loss on the hedge due to a strengthening of the basis will be incurred, is nevertheless a viable option for a business. More consideration of the total situation may be required before a final decision is reached, but hedge with futures can certainly not be dismissed out of hand.

THE BUYING HEDGE USING OPTIONS

The concern is of course, with commodity options. The term 'long' hedge would be somewhat of a misnomer in this case since this hedge is not particularly distinguished by the hedger taking a long position in options. At the start of the section on the buying hedge, it was stated that the purpose of the buying option is to protect the hedger against a rise in the price of the underlying commodity. This remains the purpose when using options.

The foregoing statement requires some further elucidation. Keep in mind that, as is fully discussed elsewhere, a commodity option has a commodity futures contract as its underlying and as such is the only known derivative of a derivative. The commodity option is thus related to the physical commodity twice removed, one might say. Nevertheless, the concern here is to deal with hedging the price of the physical commodity that underlies the futures contract, rather than with hedging the price of the underlying of the option.

It is quite correct of course, to assume that a position in futures contracts can be hedged by means of a commodity option. It is a combination often described as a fution and is greatly favoured by many speculative traders. Technically, such a combination of a futures contract with a hedging option would be styled a synthetic option. It can also be used to very good effect by hedgers. Synthetic futures and options will thus be dealt with during the course of this chapter. However, the first question that arises is how options might best be employed for the purpose of establishing a buying hedge.

Since the purpose of a buying hedge is to protect the hedger against a rise in the price of the commodity, the hedging position must be such as to allow a profit to the hedger in the futures market on a rise in the price, to offset the loss in the cash market. This would normally be achieved by taking a long futures position, as was discussed under the previous section. It thus follows that if a long futures position is eschewed in favour of an option, it must be an option to gain a long futures position. A call option is precisely such an option. A call option will upon its exercise result in a long futures position.

The whole purpose of using options rather than futures is to avoid any possibility of loss. With an option, the greatest possible loss is the loss of the premium paid on the option. Against this advantage, there is the cost of the premium that the hedger will have to factor into the cost structure of the business. An example will serve to illustrate the situation.

Consider the case of a heavy haulage contractor with its main base of operations situated in Antwerp. The volatility of the price of crude oil is of concern to the company. It serves a number of very big customers. The company needs to quote ahead to their clients on a per kilometre per contract basis. Because the market is very competitive, the company is well aware of the fact that their prices have to be keen in order to maintain its custom. After a quote has been accepted therefore, the company must ensure that the cost basis of the quote is not upset by adverse price moves. They therefore have to hedge their major costs, such as fuel. On the other hand, because their profit margins are constantly under pressure, it would be a welcome relief if they could gain more margin in a quote by any drop in the price of oil.

Based on the foregoing considerations, the treasurer of the haulage company decides in November to use Brent Crude options on the IPE to hedge the price of the fuel involved in a contract the company has just been awarded. The contract is to convey copon wrapped and lined pipes from a factory in Milan to a pipeline site in the Balkans. Conveyance will start at the end of February. The fuel requirements to complete the contract have been carefully calculated.

The treasurer has previously used Brent crude contracts for hedging and knows that its price tracks the price of their fuel costs more closely than any other contract. She also knows the differential required to convert Brent Crude quantities into the quantities of fuel oil they require. Based on her calculations, the company requires 126 000 US gallons, or 3000 barrels of Brent crude to hedge the fuel required to execute the pipeline contract.

The Brent Crude futures contract trades in quantities of 42 000 US gallons, or 1000 barrels of oil per contract. One Brent crude option has one Brent Crude futures contract as its underlier. When the treasurer supplied the cost figures to be used in preparation of the quote, she gave the then ruling spot price of their fuel, which equals a spot price for Brent Crude of $25.97 per barrel. When the treasurer draws the current prices from the Internet after having received confirmation of the acceptance of their quote, she finds that the Brent Crude spot price is $26.30 per barrel. The futures contracts closed on the previous trading day as follows:

January: $25.78 per barrel
February: $24.71 per barrel
March: $23.75 per barrel

The market is clearly in backwardation. The treasurer telephones the company's broker and instructs him to purchase three IPE March Brent Crude 2400 Calls at $1.53 stop. The 2400 strike is the call strike closest to the money. The broker later reports that the order was filled at a price of $1.53 per barrel. The total premium for the three options thus amounts to $4590.00 ($1.53 per barrel × 1000 barrels per contract × three contracts). The hedged position of the company now is shown in Table 5-9.

Because of the 'twice removed' nature of an option, there are in fact two relevant bases. The first basis is that between the cash position of the hedger and the strike price of the option. Since the strike of the option is fixed, this basis will only move as a result of the movement of the cash price. The often-discussed trading relationship between spot and near futures does not apply to this particular basis. This basis, being dependent only on the movement of one of the prices involved, can move in any direction at any time. It is as unpredictable as the price itself. The second basis shown in Table 5-9 is that well-traversed basis, about the movement of which a lot is known at this stage.

Because commodity options have a commodity futures contract as its underlier, the profit to be realised at expiration or earlier exercise is determined by the price of the futures contract relative to the strike of the option. It is not determined by the spot price of the commodity. The spot price of the commodity of course influences and governs the price of the futures contract due to the specific trading relationship, as has been thoroughly discussed up to now. Nevertheless, the option will be in the money or out of the money depending on the state of the price of the underlying futures contract.

The effectiveness of a hedge with a commodity option is therefore still determined by

Table 5-9. A buying hedge using a call option

Cash Market		Futures Market		Basis
Nov. Short 3000 Barrels@	$25.97	Nov. Long Three March calls	$24.00	
		Nov. Premium on calls	$1.53	1.97 Over
		Nov. Underlying March Futures	$23.75	2.22 Over

the movement of the cash/futures basis. Consequently, the condition of the market plays a similar role tot the one demonstrated in the previous examples. Given these considerations, the example will be further iterated in terms of the two possible market conditions.

THE BUYING HEDGE USING LONG OPTIONS IN AN INVERSE MARKET

As was demonstrated in the case of the long hedge using futures contracts, the result is not influenced by the up or down movements of the price. The result of the hedge stays the same. The major factor that influences the effectiveness of the hedge was demonstrated as being the condition of the market. With an options hedge there is the promise of a different result when the price rises or declines. This is due to inherent feature of long options, namely that one cannot lose more than the premium on the option. This matter will now be further investigated.

the price rises

Assume firstly that the price rises. When the haulage company orders its fuel requirements during the first half of February, the spot price of Brent Crude has risen to $27.45 per barrel. The March futures contracts are trading at $27.23 and the call options are thus in the money.

The treasurer immediately instructs the company's broker to lift their hedge by exercising the calls and simultaneously selling three March Brent Crude futures contracts. The results of the futures trades are that the calls are exercised and the company is consequently assigned three long futures positions at $24.00. The order to short three March futures is filled at a price of $27.25. The result of the hedge is set out in Table 5-10.

As Table 5-10 clearly demonstrates, the result is a gross profit on the hedge. The gross profit on the hedge is equal to $1.77 ($3.25 profit on the futures $-$1.48 loss on the cash market) which is identical to the weakening of the cash/option strike basis. The weakening of this basis in an inverse market has, as was the case with a futures hedge, resulted

Table 5-10. Result of a buying hedge in an inverse market using long call options, after a price rise

Cash Market		Futures Market		Basis
		Nov. Long Three March Calls	$24.00	1.97 Over
		Nov. Premium on Calls:	$1.53	
Nov. Short 3000 Barrels@	$25.97	Feb. Long Three March Futures	$24.00	1.97 Over
Feb. Long 3000 Barrels@	$27.45	Feb. Short Three March Futures	$27.25	0.20 Over
Loss:	$1.48	Profit:	$3.25	
		Net Profit After Premiums:	$1.72	Change: -1.77
		Nov. Underlying March Futures	$23.75	2.22 Over
		Feb. Underlying March Futures	$27.25	0.20 Over
		Potential Profit:	$3.50	Change: -2.02

in a profit on the buying hedge. Unfortunately for the company, this is not the net result of the hedge. The premium of the option must still be accounted for from the profit on the hedge. After that calculation, the net result for the company is a net profit on the hedge of $0.24 per barrel ($1.77 hedge profit−$1.53 option premium). The effect of the hedge on the cost of the fuel to the haulage company is thus to bring it down from the $27.45 level paid to $25.73 ($27.45 payment−$3.25 profit on the hedge+$1.53 option premium). This is naturally a $0.24 improvement for the company on the $25.97 per barrel that they based their quote on.

On the basis that the purpose of a buying hedge is to give protection against an adverse upward movement in price, the result in the example was totally adequate. For comparative purposes however, Table 5-10 illustrates that a straight futures hedge would have given a far more favourable result. As is indicated by the basis change, there would have been a substantial profit of $2.02 on a futures hedge, without a premium cost to factor in. This would have resulted in a net cost to the company of $23.95 on the oil.

The cost of the premium on an option always presents a dilemma. It can be factored into other costs of the operation, but yet it remains. The main considerations in using options are always two-fold: less risk and opportunity to gain from a favourable price move. It is easy to see in retrospect that a futures hedge should have been used, but at the time the hedge was established nobody could say with any certainty where the price would be when the hedge was lifted. Nevertheless, the problem remains that the effectiveness of exchange traded options as a protective measure is inhibited by two factors.

The first factor is that the strike prices are pre-set at certain intervals. If the first strike out of the money is used for the hedge, the hedger enjoys no protection for the difference between the price of the underlying and the strike price of the option. Buying the first option in the money does not solve the problem either. That in the money option will entail paying that much higher premium.

The second factor is the premium itself. The price of the underlying must move adversely by more than the premium of the option before any protection is given by the option. These two factors operate against the effectiveness of the protection afforded by an option against an adverse price move. Whether that is compensated for by the incurring of less risk is a matter that risk managers must decide for themselves. The risks presented by a straight futures hedge is clearly illustrated in the examples and their iterations that were dealt with in the previous sections of this chapter.

The next iteration will serve to examine whether the vaunted opportunity to gain from a favourable move makes up for the option's shortcomings as a protective hedge against an adverse price move.

the price declines

For the purposes of this iteration, the same basic information that was used in the first iteration will be kept intact. Only now, it will be assumed that there was a decline in the price of Brent Crude.

When the company placed its order for fuel in the first week of February, the spot price

Table 5-11. The result of a buying hedge in an inverse market using long call options, after a price decline

Cash Market		Futures Market		Basis
Nov. Short 3000 Barrels@	$25.97	Nov. Long Three March Calls	$24.00	1.97 Over
Feb. Long 3000 Barrels@	$21.45	Nov. Premium Paid	$1.53	
Profit:	$4.52	Loss:	$1.53	
		Nov. Underlying March Futures	$23.75	2.22 Over
		Feb. Underlying March Futures	$21.25	0.20 Over
				Change: −2.02

of Brent Crude had dropped to $21.45 per barrel. The market was still in backwardation and March futures were trading at $21.25. The options were out of the money and the treasurer merely allowed them to expire. The result of the hedge is now illustrated in Table 5-11.

The profit in the cash market, which is due to the decline in price under the budgeted figure, must now be offset only against the premium paid. The options expired out of the money and consequently no futures positions were taken in. The loss in the futures market is thus limited to the premium paid on the options. The net result is thus a profit of $2.99 per barrel of crude ($4.52 − $1.53) on the favourable price move. The net cost of the oil to the company is consequently $22.98 ($21.45 actually paid + $1.53 premium on the options).

discussion: the result of the hedge

The example with its two iterations suggests that an option hedging strategy can be very successful. However, in the final analysis the success of the strategy depends on the size of the adverse or favourable move.

In both iterations of the example, the price moves were sufficient to overcome the cost structure of the option. Even in the favourable downward move, the price must move by more than the premium of the option before any advantage is gained. Fortunately, in the favourable move, there is no additional difference between the strike price and the initial futures price to be made up.

The restrictions on the protection afforded against an adverse move have already been discussed. Given the examples thus far, it is clear that a buying hedge using options will have a greater chance of giving a desirable result when there is a volatile underlying market. Then the odds are better that whatever price moves there are will be substantial moves.

Nevertheless, the discussion has again demonstrated that the buying hedge will tend to show a profit, whichever way the price of the underlying moves. This is not as true in a hedge with options as it is with futures, but it will be the case with options on condition that the price move is large enough to neutralise the option cost. It now remains to discover what the result of the buying hedge with options will be under normal market conditions.

THE BUYING HEDGE USING LONG OPTIONS IN A NORMAL MARKET

The purpose is again to protect the hedger against a rise in price of the underlying commodity, but to make use of call options. Consider the situation of International Foods Inc., whose US head-office is situated in Chicago, Illinois. At the start of February, its baby foods division was granted a large contract to supply a national supermarket chain with a consignment of their products. The chain required delivery during the first half of May.

The treasurer had been given the production schedule for the baby foods division. It was apparent that the inventory for the contract had to be purchased at the start of April in order to complete production and delivery on schedule. One of the major price factors that could influence the profitability of the contract, was the price of milk. The treasurer had intended from the outset to make use of options on the BFP milk futures contract in order to hedge the price of milk. The board of the company had previously directed that preference should be given to long options when hedges were constructed to manage the company's commodity risks.

Consequently, the treasurer accessed the website of the CME to determine the previous day's settlement prices of the BFP Milk futures contract and options. They would require the equivalent of 400 000 lbs. of BFP milk to complete the contract. The futures contract trades in quantities of 200 000 lbs. and the company would therefore use two option contracts to hedge their position. He had participated in the preparation of the original quote and his records showed that he had based the quote on an average milk price that would be equivalent to a price of $9.25 per 100 lbs. on the BFP contract standard.

His enquiry on the website indicated that the prices of the futures contracts had settled as follows:

February: $9.65 per 100 lbs.
March: $10.01 per 100 lbs.
April: $10.26 per 100 lbs.

This clearly shows that the market was in contango, but not very strongly so. Depending on the exact price of milk and the current interest rate, which taken together establishes the total interest portion of the carrying cost, the carrying charges for BFP milk was around $0.85 per month per 100 lbs. at the time that the quotation was prepared. This is the figure that the treasurer had used to base his calculations on. As against that, the deferred futures were trading at a premium of $0.36 (March/February) and $0.25 (April/March), respectively.

Having also accessed that part of the website that showed the previous day's settlement prices of the options, the treasurer telephoned the company's commodity futures broker.

Table 5-12. A buying hedge in a normal market using call options

Cash Market		Futures Market		Basis
Feb. Short 400000 lbs.@	$9.25	Feb. Long Two April 1050 Calls	$10.50	1.25 Under
		Feb. Underlying April Futures	$10.27	1.02 Under

They contacted each other before the market opened and put in an order to buy two CME April BFP Milk 1050 calls at $0.34stop. Later in the morning the broker called back with a fill at $0.34. The company's hedged situation was now as shown in Table 5-12.

The hedge basis, calculated on the spot price used in the quote and the strike price of the calls, is 1.25 under as indicated in Table 5-12. The market goes into backwardation from time to time, a fact of which the treasurer is well aware. Nevertheless, because he intends to hold the hedge to a time as close as possible to the delivery of the futures contract, he knows that the greatest probable loss on this hedge is $1.25 give or take a few cents. This is a contingency for which he had already made some provision in the quote.

The two possibilities, namely that of a rise in price and that of a decline in price can now be discussed.

the price rises

Assume that when the company places their order for milk at the end of March, spot BFP milk is $10.34. At the same time the April BFP milk futures contract is trading at $10.86. The treasurer goes through to the broker and instructs her to lift the hedge. The broker thereupon exercises the two options on behalf of the company and simultaneously shorts the futures with two BFP Milk contracts. She manages to sell the two contracts at a price of $10.83 per 100 lbs. When the fills are reported back to the treasurer, he calculates the result of the hedge shown in Table 5-13.

The actual price of the milk to the company, ignoring the option premium for the moment, was $10.54 ($10.87 actual price paid − $0.33 profit on the futures). This is $1.29 more than the price that the quote was based on and falls within the contingency provided by the treasurer. The premium on the call options was $0.34. If it is factored into the cost of the milk, the total cost paid reaches $10.88, which represents an adverse price

Table 5-13. Result of a buying hedge in a normal market using call options after a price rise

Cash Market		Futures Market		Basis
Feb. Short 400000 lbs.@	$9.25	Feb. Long Two April 1050 Calls	$10.50	1.25 Under
March Long 400000 lbs.@	$10.87	March Long Two April Futures	$10.50	1.25 Under
Loss:	$1.62	March Short Two April Futures	$10.83	0.04 Over
		Profit:	$0.33	Change; +1.29
		Feb. Underlying April Futures	$10.27	1.02 Under
		March Underlying April Futures	$10.83	0.04 Over
				Change: +1.06

situation of $1.63 per 100 lbs. ($10.88 total cost − $9.25 budgeted cost; also $1.29 basis change + $0.34 option premium). This is incidentally $0.01 worse than not having been hedged at all, since the total adverse price move was $1.62 (loss on the cash market). However this is happenstance and is not an inevitable corollary of this type of hedge. Only hindsight makes this conclusion possible.

However, note that if straight futures contracts had been used, the adverse strengthening of the basis would have been only $1.06, resulting in a total cost of $10.31 ($9.25 budgeted cost + $1.06 basis change, or $10.87 actual price − $0.56 profit on futures). The hedge with options thus resulted in an additional cost to the company of $0.57 per 100 lbs., which comes to a total of $2280 on the total contract. If a futures hedge had been used, the total cost of the milk would have been $41 240 and the $2280 additional expense caused by the use of options consequently represents a 5.5% cost increase on that hedge.

the price declines

In the next discussion, the buying hedge will be examined, using options under conditions where the price of the underlying commodity has declined. For this purpose, it will be assumed that when International Foods lifts the hedge, the spot price of BFP Milk has declined to $8.94 per 100 lbs. and the April futures contract is trading at $8.50 per 100 lbs. on the CME.

The hedge consequently requires no action in order to be lifted, because the futures price is then trading at below the $10.50 strike price of the call options. Consequently the options are out of the money and cannot be exercised. Because of the expiry date for the options, they are also not sold back into the market to recoup some of the premium paid, but are allowed to expire. The resulting cost implication is merely that the total premium of $1360 ($0.34 per 100 lbs. per option for two options) is forfeited. The result of the hedge is shown in Table 5-14.

Taking into account the premium of $0.34 paid on the call options, the actual cost of the milk amounts to $8.88 ($8.54 actual price + $0.34 option premium). The only inhibiting factor in this hedge is the premium of the option itself. If a straight hedge with futures had been used, the net cost of the milk would have been $10.31 per 100 lbs. ($9.25 budgeted cost + $1.06 basis change, or $8.54 actual cost + $1.77 loss on the

Table 5-14. Result of a buying hedge in a normal market using long call options, after a price decline

Cash Market		Futures Market		Basis
Feb. Short 400000 lbs.@	$9.25	Feb. Long Two April 1050 Calls	$10.50	1.25 Under
March Long 400000 lbs.@	$8.54	Feb. Premium on Call Options	$0.34	
Profit:	$0.71	Loss:	$0.34	
		Feb. Underlying April Futures	$10.27	1.02 Under
		March Underlying April Futures	$8.50	0.04 Over
		Loss:	$1.77	Change: +1.06

futures). In this case therefore, the use of options resulted in a $1.43 per 100 lbs. ($10.31 cost using futures − $8.88 cost using options) cost advantage using options to hedge rather than using futures contracts.

In this particular iteration, the hedge with long call options at least allowed a portion of the $0.71 profit to be realised notwithstanding the inherent adverse basis move.

discussion: the result of the hedge

It is apparent that the discussion of the relative advantages of using options to hedge over using straight futures is an unending one. There are too many variables to which the respective instruments are subject to to ever give a final answer. The advantage of one over the other will always only be manifest after the event. In the result, it is up to management in every business to determine how they favour one above the other. Some clear guidelines could be laid down for using either one or the other.

What is perfectly clear however, is that hedging is always better than not hedging. There was one example, using options, where the result was actually worse by $0.01 by hedging than by not hedging. This only serves to illustrate that such an outcome is possible. It will happen rarely in practice and results from the small move in the price of the underlying. This stresses again that options are really more appropriate where the market of the underlying commodity is reasonably volatile and that any move, be it up or down, will be a big move. On the buying hedge, market volatility will improve the odds that the protection afforded by the option against an adverse upward price move will bear fruit. It will also increase the likelihood that the opportunity afforded by options to take advantage of a favourable move will be meaningful.

THE BUYING HEDGE USING SYNTHETIC LONG FUTURES IN AN INVERTED MARKET

The synthetic futures and synthetic options that will be dealt with below achieve variations in results that should be carefully considered, since they might provide certain benefits that could be specifically sought by management. They are known as synthetics because they are positions created by using combinations of options or options and futures that give the same profit/loss profile as a straight futures position or that of a different option. The advantages and disadvantages of using each of the synthetic instruments can only be demonstrated by comparing the results of their use with the results obtained when the direct instrument is used.

A synthetic long futures is created by buying a call option and simultaneously selling a put option at the same strike price. The advantage is that, depending on the strikes that are selected, the premium gained by the sell of the put will partly or completely offset the premium paid for the call. The net cost position could thus be a small profit on the premiums, a zero cost situation or a relatively small cost to take in the position. The net combined profit/loss profile of this position is the same as that of a long futures

Table 5-15. A buying hedge using synthetic futures in an inverse market

Cash Market	Futures Market		Basis
Nov. Short 3000 Barrels@ $25.97	Nov. Long Three March Calls	$24.00	1.97 Over
	Nov. Short Three March Puts	$24.00	
	Profit on Premium:	$0.25	
	Nov. Underlying March Futures	$23.75	2.22 Over

position. If the price rises, the call will gain value while, if the price drops, the put will lose value. The comparative advantage or disadvantage of this strategy will now be investigated.

The example of the heavy haulage contractor will be revisited to enable some comparisons to be made. The basic facts of the example remain the same. Assume that instead of using call options to hedge the position, as was done in previous iterations of the example, the treasurer decides to make use of synthetic futures.

She has the choice of buying the 2400 OTM calls while selling the slightly ITM 2400 puts, or buying the ITM 2350 call while selling the OTM 2350 puts. She decides to use the first combination as it allows her to start her position at a profit, since the premium she will receive for the puts is greater than the price she will have to pay for the calls.

She therefore contacts the company's broker and instructs him to buy three IPE March Brent Crude 2400 calls at $1.53 stop and to sell three IPE March Brent Crude 2400 puts at $1.78 stop. Later he reports back that both orders were filled at the stop prices. The hedged position is now as illustrated in Table 5-15.

The synthetic long futures thus established has a profit/loss profile as if the futures were bought at a price of $24.00. As was the case with the previous hedge using call options, the position leaves a difference between the actual price of the futures and the price of the synthetic futures of $0.25. In the case of the hedge using options this was one of the two factors that inhibited the effectiveness of the hedge, because the option only afforded protection from the time the futures price reached the strike price. The company is 'self-insured' for the difference.

In the present case, the synthetic futures seem to suffer from the same disadvantage, but the disadvantage is more apparent than real. The reason is that the net result of taking in the position has already realised a profit of $0.25 per barrel. The cash in the kitty thus already bridges the gap between the synthetic futures price and the actual futures price, placing them on a par, at least as far as a rise in price is concerned. A price rise is therefor the first iteration to be discussed.

the price rises

The same price assumptions will be made as were made in the first round of iterations when discussing the hedge with options. Therefore, it will be assumed that when the Heavy Haulage contractor ordered its inventory of fuel in February for the purpose of

Table 5-16. Result of a buying hedge in an inverted market, using synthetic long futures, after a price rise

Cash Market		Futures Market		Basis
Nov. Short 3000 Barrels@	$25.97	Nov. Long Three March Calls	$24.00 ⎫	1.97 Over
Feb. Long 3000 Barrels@	$27.45	Nov. Short Three March Puts	$24.00 ⎬	
Loss:	$1.48	Profit on Premium:	$0.25	
		Feb. Long Three March Futures	$24.00	1.97 Over
		Feb. Short Three March Futures	$27.25	0.20 Over
		Profit on Futures:	$3.25	Change: −1.77
		Total Profit:	$3.50	
		Nov. Underlying March Futures	$23.75	2.22 Over
		Feb. Underlying March Futures	$27.25	0.20 Over
		Profit on Futures Hedge:	$3.50	Change: −2.02

executing the pipeline contract in March, the spot price of Brent Crude was $27.45. It will further be assumed that the March futures contract was trading at around $27.00.

Thus, in the present iteration, the call option is in the money and the put option is out of the money. The call option is consequently exercised by the futures broker on behalf of the company on its expiration date while the put option is allowed to expire. It is also assumed that the treasurer's order to short three IPE March Brent Crude futures contracts is filled at $27.25, which is identical to the assumption that was made in the first iteration. When the put option expires out of the money, it has no value and consequently the premium that was received on the sale of the options is kept by the company. The profit that was realised by selling the more expensive ITM put while buying the less expensive OTM call is therefore calculated as part of the result of the hedge. The result of the hedge is as shown in Table 5-16.

As the illustration in Table 5-16 clearly demonstrates, the result of the hedge is identical to the result of a hedge using a long futures, as if it was entered at the price of the futures at the time the options were traded. The total profit in the futures market is calculated by taking the profit realised on the calls and adding it to the profit made on the sale and purchase of the options (£3.25 profit on the futures resulting from the call options + $0.25 profit on the option premiums). The net cost of the 3000 barrels, taking into account the result of the hedge is $23.95 ($27.45 price actually paid − $3.50 total profit in the futures markets). The same result would have been obtained if a straight futures hedge had been used ($25.97 budgeted cost − $2.02 favourable basis change).

the price declines

All the assumptions will again remain as they were in the second iteration of the example. It is thus assumed that when the cash market purchase of the fuel is made, the spot price of Brent Crude has declined $21.45. The March futures contract was trading around $21.30. The call is thus out of the money, but the put option is in the money.

Table 5-17. Result of a long hedge in an inverted market using synthetic long futures, after a price decline

Cash Market		Futures Market		Basis
Nov. Short 3000 Barrels@	$25.97	Nov. Long Three March Calls	$24.00	1.97 Over
Feb. Long 3000 Barrels@	$21.45	Nov. Short Three March Puts	$24.00	
Profit:	$4.52	Profit on Premium:	$0.25	
		Feb. Short Futures@	$24.00	1.97 Over
		Feb. Long Futures@	$21.25	0.20 Over
		Loss:	$2.75	
		Total Loss:	$2.50	
				Change: -1.77
		Nov. Underlying March Futures	$23.75	2.22 Over
		Feb. Underlying March Futures	$21.25	0.20 Over
		Loss on Futures Hedge:	$2.50	Change: -2.02

When the hedge is lifted on the date of expiration of the put option, it expires in the money and is consequently exercised against the company. Before expiration, the treasurer instructed the company's broker to buy three March Brent Crude futures contracts. These three long futures would offset the short futures positions that would be assigned to the company. The broker fills the order at $21.25. The result of the hedge is as set out in Table 5-17.

This iteration again demonstrates that a long or buying hedge consistently results in a hedge profit in an inverted market. The result is that the net cost of the oil, after taking the hedge into account is $23.95 ($21.45 actual price paid $-$ $2.50 net loss on the futures). The net loss on the futures is calculated by deducting the $0.25 profit on the original purchase and sale of the respective options, from the $2.75 loss suffered on the short and long positions of the futures contracts. The result is exactly the same as the one that would have been attained if straight futures had been used: $25.97 budgeted cost $-$ $2.02 basis change = $23.95.

discussion: the result of the hedge

The reason that the net result of this iteration is exactly identical to the previous result is that the basis changes were the same: a weakening of the basis from $2.22 over to $0.20 over. The interposition of the options thus makes no difference to the overall outcome. If the results are identical, the question then arises what reason is, if any, would induce one to use synthetic futures rather than futures or vice versa. The answer concerns the company's overall strategy, because there is in fact a potential difference between using one rather than the other.

Using the synthetic futures involves spending more time and energy on the hedge than is required when using a straight futures hedge. The synthetic option allows a dynamic strategy to be followed because it is made up of two options. If, in a long hedge with long futures contracts, the price of the underlying starts declining (i.e. moving adversely) there is very little adjustment that can profitably be made.

It is true that one could offset the futures position in order to stop the loss, but then the protection against an upward move will be lost. There is therefore considerable danger in trying to hedge by 'jumping' in and out of futures contracts. Indeed, it is strongly suggested that experience shows that this is a course of action that should be avoided altogether.

On the other hand, in a synthetic long futures, the short put can be bought back if the price of the underlying is seen to make a substantial downward move. If the put is bought back the profit on the original purchase and sale will be lost, but this must be balanced against the gain on the hedge because of the favourable basis move. Furthermore, if the call option is left intact, the protection against an adverse move is maintained. When the price moves favourably again, a put can be sold at a strike below the futures price. The original call and the new short put need not be at the same strike.

This latter strategy will result in a very effective and extremely profitable hedge on occasions where the price is volatile. However, as will be apparent from this discussion, to take advantage of the possibilities afforded by a hedge with synthetic long futures, the company will have to be prepared to spend some time and effort on monitoring the hedge. This may or may not be acceptable. It is a matter that each business must decide for itself based on its own circumstances.

THE LONG HEDGE USING SYNTHETIC LONG FUTURES IN A NORMAL MARKET

The same example as the one previously employed in illustrating the buying hedge with long calls in a normal market will be used. In this iteration, it will be assumed that the company's treasurer decides to hedge with synthetic futures rather than with long calls. In the previous example it was noted that the most advantageous way, and in fact the only correct way of establishing a long synthetic futures position, is by buying the call at the first strike out of the money and by selling the put at the same strike. It follows that the short put will be at the first strike in the money.

In the example to be used in this iteration, it was assumed that the price of April futures at the time that the hedge is established is $10.27. The strike to be used is therefore the 1050, since that is the strike of the first call out of the money and the first put strike in the money. Consequently, the treasurer instructs the company's broker in February to buy two CME BFP Milk 1050 calls at $0.34 stop and simultaneously to sell two CME BFP Milk 1050 puts at $0.57 stop. The orders are filled at the stop prices. The hedged situation now appears as set out in Table 5-18.

Note that although the prices and the contracts are entirely different to the previous ones where the synthetic futures in an inverted market was discussed, the synthetic futures hedge is at its establishment equal to the hedge using straight futures. If the profit on the premium is subtracted from the basis, the result is a basis of 1.02 under. This is

Table 5-18. A buying hedge in a normal market, using synthetic long futures

Cash Market	Futures Market		Basis
Feb. Short 400000 lbs.@ $9.25	Feb. Long Two April 1050 Calls	$10.50	1.25 Under
	Feb. Short Two April 1050 Puts	$10.50	
	Profit on the Premium:	$0.23	
	Feb. Underlying April Futures	$10.27	1.02 Under

identical to what the basis on a straight futures hedge would have been, as is indicated in Table 5-18.

the price rises

As was the case in the first iteration, it will be assumed that when the milk inventory is purchased, the spot price has risen to $10.87 and April futures are trading at around $10.80.

The call is in the money and the treasurer gives instructions for it to be exercised. At the same time two April BFP Milk futures contracts are sold at a price of $10.83. The short put is allowed to expire out of the money. The result of the hedge is set out in Table 5-19.

The net cost of the milk after taking the result of the hedge into account is $10.31 ($10.87 actual cost − $0.56 net profit on the futures market). Predictably, the result is again identical to the result that would have been obtained if the hedge had been established with straight futures contracts: $9.25 budgeted cost + $1.06 basis change = $10.31. Another constant that is as much expected, as it is apparent is that there has been a loss on the hedge. The loss of course equals the basis move, which in its turn is slightly greater than the original basis.

the price declines

As was the case in the previous iteration, the basic price information of the first iteration will be maintained. The assumption is therefore that at the end of March, when the milk is purchased by the company, the spot price has declined to $8.54 per 100 lbs. while April futures are trading at around $8.50 per 100 lbs. The call option is consequently out of the money and is allowed to expire.

The put option is however in the money and it is exercised against the company. The company, being short the option, cannot exercise the option. The counter party, has the right to exercise the option, but it will be exercised automatically upon its expiry in the money. Anticipatory to the exercise of the option, the company's broker had been instructed to buy two BFP Milk futures, which she managed to do at a price of $8.50. The result of the hedge is set out in Table 5-20.

The net loss on the futures markets amounted $1.77 per 100 lbs. ($2.00 loss on the futures − $0.23 profit on the option premium). Taking into account this loss, the net cost

Table 5-19. The result of a buying hedge in a normal market using synthetic long futures, after a rise in price

Cash Market		Futures Market		Basis
Feb. Short 400000 lbs.@	$9.25	Feb. Long Two April 1050 Calls	$10.50	1.25 Under
March Long 400000 lbs.@	$10.87	Feb. Short Two April 1050 Puts	$10.50	
Loss:	$1.62	Profit on the Premium:	$0.23	
		March Long Two April Futures	$10.50	1.25 Under
		March Short Two April Futures	$10.83	0.04 Over
		Profit on Futures:	$0.33	
		Total Profit:	$0.56	Change: +1.29
		Feb. Underlying April Futures	$10.27	1.02 Under
		March Underlying April Futures	$10.83	0.04 Over
		Profit on Futures	$0.56	Change: +1.06

of the milk to the company was $10.31. This is again identical to the result that would have been obtained had the hedge been done with futures contracts instead of option combinations: $9.25 budgeted cost + $1.06 basis change = $10.31.

discussion: the result of the hedge

All the iterations again demonstrate that once a hedge is in place, the direction of the price move is irrelevant. The result remains the same whether the price of the underlying rises or declines. In the case of a synthetic futures hedge, it is clear that it is just as effective as a hedge with straight futures. In all calculations, the brokerage and exchange fees have been ignored, since they are small in relation to hedging the numbers that are usually encountered in business. Nevertheless, they are an expense that will have to be taken into account. The only disadvantage that a synthetic futures would therefore have would be trading costs. That is because, in order to establish the hedge, two positions

Table 5-20. The result of a buying hedge in a normal market using synthetic futures, after a price decline

Cash Market		Futures Market		Basis
Feb. Short 400000 lbs.@	$9.25	Feb. Long Two April 1050 Calls	$10.50	
March Long 400000 lbs.@	$8.54	Feb. Short Two April 1050 Puts	$10.50	1.25 Under
Profit:	$0.71	Profit on the Premium:	$0.23	
		Feb. Short April Futures@	$10.50	
		Feb. Long April Futures@	$8.50	
		Loss on the Futures:	$2.00	
		Total Loss:	$1.77	
		Feb. Underlying April Futures	$10.27	1.02 Under
		March Underlying April Futures	$8.50	0.04 Over
		Loss on Futures	$1.77	Change: +1.06

have to be taken in options against every one taken in futures. Furthermore, additional futures trades are required to offset the futures positions that are assigned. The multiplicity of trades that increase trading costs are therefore the only real difference between the two strategies.

However, the flexibility and real expectation of a much better outcome of the hedge, especially in a normal market where a loss on the hedge is otherwise unavoidable, makes the synthetic futures a better choice. Nevertheless, there is no reason to make use of this more complex instrument if the business does not have the real intention and capacity to take advantage of the flexibility offered by the features of the instrument. Then the additional trading costs, small as they may be, are indeed merely a waste of good money.

THE BUYING HEDGE USING SYNTHETIC LONG CALL OPTIONS

This is the final hedging instrument that will be the subject of the discussion in this book. There are other possible combinations of instruments, but the main ones that should primarily be mastered and used are the ones discussed herein. These are the major futures instruments and between them, they should satisfy the hedging needs and preferences of most businesses.

The synthetic call, like the synthetic long futures, adds a certain flexibility that is lacking in a straight options position. This will become clear as the discussion progresses. Nevertheless, all such advantages come at a price. There will be additional trading costs, but more importantly, it will require more time and resources from the person or persons who are entrusted with the carrying out of hedging strategies in a firm.

A synthetic long call is created by buying a futures contract and a long put at the first strike out of the money. The long futures position will profit from a rise in price, while a rise in price will not affect the value of the long put at expiration. The long put will profit from a decline in the price of futures, but this gain in value will be neutralised by the loss in value of the long futures position. The cost of establishing the position equals the premium paid for the long put. Assessing the profit/loss profile of the position at option expiry, it appears that the potential for profit on a rise in price is unlimited while the maximum loss that can be incurred will be the loss of the premium on the put. This corresponds exactly to the profit/loss profile of a long call.

It is also interesting to note that the profit/loss profile of the synthetic long call corresponds to that of a long call option with the same strike as the strike of the put option. In order to replicate the ordinary long call option, the long puts that are used to construct the synthetic position, must be at the same strike as the straight call option would have been. It will therefore be advantageous to compare the outcome of the following iterations with the outcome of the previous hedges using long calls. Therefore, the same examples will be used to demonstrate the former as were used to demonstrate the latter.

For the purposes of this example, it will be assumed that the treasurer telephones the company's broker and instructs her to purchase three IPE March Brent Crude futures contracts at $23.75 stop. The 2400 strike is the first strike at which calls are out of the money, although the puts are in the money at that strike. Nevertheless, the broker is instructed to buy three IPE March Brent Crude 2400 puts at $1.78 stop. The broker later reports that all the orders were filled at the stop prices. The total premium for the three put options amounts to $4500 ($1.50 per barrel × 1000 barrels per contract × three contracts).

The synthetic long call, so constructed, thus has a nominal strike of 2400, which is identical to the strike of the long calls in the first iteration of this example. The premium of the synthetic option's premium is greater than the premium of the long call in the previous iteration and the net effect of that will be demonstrated in the results. The hedged position of the company now appears in Table 5-21.

The oil market is in backwardation at that stage. The result of this hedge will thus be investigated under inverse market conditions.

THE BUYING HEDGE USING SYNTHETIC LONG CALLS IN AN INVERSE MARKET

the price rises

Assume firstly that the price rises. When the haulage company orders its fuel requirements during the first half of February, the spot price of Brent Crude has risen to $27.45 per barrel. The March futures contracts are trading at $27.23 and the put options are thus out of the money.

The treasurer immediately instructs the company's broker to lift the company's hedge by selling three March Brent Crude futures contracts. The order to short three March futures contracts is filled at a price of $27.25. The result of the hedge is set out in Table 5-22.

As Table 5-22 clearly demonstrates, the result is a profit on the hedge. The gross profit on the hedge is equal to $2.02 ($3.50 profit on the futures − $1.48 loss on the cash market) which is identical to the weakening of the hedge basis. The weakening of the basis in an inverse market has, as was the case with a futures hedge, resulted in a profit on the buying hedge.

Table 5-21. A buying hedge using a call option

Cash Market	Futures Market		Basis
Nov. Short 3000 Barrels@ $25.97	Nov. Long Three March Puts	$24.00	1.97 Over
	Nov. Premium on Puts	$1.78	
	Nov. Long Three March		
	Futures@	$23.75	2.22 Over

Unfortunately for the company, this is not the net result of the hedge. The premium of the option must still be accounted for from the profit on the hedge. After that calculation, the result for the company is a net profit on the hedge of $0.24 per barrel ($2.02 hedge profit − $1.78 option premium). This is identical to the $0.24 net profit shown by the hedge where straight long calls were used.

The effect of the hedge on the net cost of the fuel to the haulage company is thus to bring it down from the $27.45 price level actually paid to $25.73 ($27.45 payment − $3.50 profit on the hedge + $1.78 option premium). This is naturally a $0.52 improvement for the company on the $25.97 per barrel that they initially based their quote on ($25.97 budgeted cost − $25.45 actual net cost; or $2.02 basis change − $1.50 option premium).

Table 5-22 still indicates that a straight futures hedge would have given a more favourable result. As is indicated by the basis change, there would have been a substantial profit of $2.02 on a futures hedge, without a premium cost to factor in. This would have resulted in a net cost to the company of $23.95 on the oil.

Nevertheless, it has been demonstrated that the result of a hedge with synthetic options will be equal to the result obtained with normal options of the same type at the same strike price.

The next iteration will serve to examine whether the hedge using synthetic options grants as much opportunity to profit from a favourable price move, as the hedge with straight call options does.

the price declines

For the purposes of this iteration, the same basic information that was used in the first iteration will be kept intact. Only now, it will be assumed that there was a decline in the price of Brent Crude.

When the company placed its order for fuel in the first week of February, the spot price of Brent Crude had dropped to $21.45 per barrel. The market was still in backwardation

Table 5-22. The result of a buying hedge in an inverse market using synthetic calls, after a price rise

Cash Market		Futures Market		Basis
Nov. Short 3000 Barrels@	$25.97	Nov. Long Three March 2350 Puts	$24.00	2.47 Over
Feb. Long 3000 Barrels@	$27.45	Nov. Premium on the Puts	$1.78	
Loss:	$1.48	Feb. Long Three March Futures	$23.75	2.22 Over
		Feb. Short Three March Futures	$27.25	0.20 Over
		Profit:	$3.50	
		Net profit after Premiums:	$1.72	Change: −2.02
		Nov. Underlying March Futures	$23.75	2.22 Over
		Feb. Underlying March Futures	$27.25	0.20 Over
		Potential Profit:	$3.50	Change: −2.02

and March futures were trading at $21.25. The put options were in the money and they were exercised by the broker on instructions from the treasurer. As a result of the short futures positions assigned to the company upon the exercise of the put options, the original long futures positions were automatically offset at a price equal to the strike price of the put options. The result of the hedge is illustrated in Table 5-23.

The decline of the futures price against the fixed strike price of the put option has resulted in a profit in the futures markets, albeit a small one of $0.25. That profit is offset again, by the $1.78 premium paid for the option, resulting in a net loss of $1.53 in the futures market.

The profit in the cash market, which is due to the decline in price under the budgeted figure, will be diminished by the net loss in the futures market. The net result is thus a profit of $2.99 per barrel of crude ($4.52 profit on the cash − $1.53 loss on the futures) on the favourable price move. As is to be expected by now, the result is identical to the $2.99 profit allowed by the hedge when straight call options were used.

The net cost of the oil to the company is consequently $22.98 ($21.45 actually paid + $1.53 net loss on the futures).

discussion: the result of the hedge

As was the case with a hedge using straight call options, the success of the strategy depends on the size of the adverse or favourable move.

The discussion has again demonstrated that the buying hedge will tend to show a profit, whichever direction the price of the underlying moves in. This is not as true in a hedge with options as it is with futures, but it will be the case with options on condition that the price move is large enough to neutralise the option cost.

It now remains to be seen what the result of the buying hedge with synthetic options will be under normal market conditions.

Table 5-23. The result of a buying hedge in an inverse market using synthetic calls, after a price decline

Cash Market		Futures Market		Basis
Nov. Short 3000 Barrels@	$25.97	Nov. Long Three March Puts	$24.00	2.47 Over
Feb. Long 3000 Barrels@	$21.45	Nov. Premium on Puts	$1.78	2.22 Over
Profit:	$4.52	Nov. Long Three March Futures@	$23.75	0.20 Over
		Feb. Short Three March Futures@	$24.00	
		Profit:	$0.25	
		Net Loss After Premiums:	$1.53	
		Nov. Underlying March Futures	$23.75	2.22 Over
		Feb. Underlying March Futures	$21.25	0.20 Over
		Potential Loss:	$2.50	Change: −2.02

THE BUYING HEDGE USING SYNTHETIC LONG CALLS IN A NORMAL MARKET

The purpose of the hedge is still to protect the hedger against a rise in price of the underlying commodity, but also to make use of synthetic long call options. In the present iteration it will be assumed that when the treasurer got hold of the company's broker, he put in an order to buy two CME April BFP Milk futures at $10.27 stop. He also put in an order to buy two CME April Milk 1050 puts at $0.43 stop. This was the first strike where calls were out of the money, although at that strike the puts are actually in the money. Later in the morning the broker called back and reported that all the orders had been filled at the stops. The company's hedged situation is shown in Table 5-24.

The treasurer could have chosen the out of the money 1025 puts to construct the synthetic position. That choice will however not give a desirable result, as will be demonstrated.

The two possibilities, namely that of a rise in price and that of a decline in price can now be discussed.

the price rises

For the purpose of this iteration, it will again be assumed that when the company places their order for the required milk inventory at the end of March, spot BFP milk is $10.34. At the same time the April BFP Milk futures contract is trading at $10.86. The treasurer telephones through to the broker and instructs her to lift the hedge.

The broker thus proceeds to sell two March BFP Milk futures contracts in order to offset the two long futures contracts that had been entered at the start of the hedge. She manages to sell the two contracts at a price of $10.83 per 100 lbs. The broker allows the two put options to expire since they are completely out of the money. The premium paid on them is therefore forfeited.

When the fills are reported back to the treasurer, he calculates the result of the hedge as shown in Table 5-25.

The actual price of the milk to the company, ignoring the option premium for the moment, was $10.31 ($10.87 actual price paid − $0.56 profit on the futures). This is $1.06 more than the price that the original quote was based on and it corresponds to the basis move of the futures ($10.31 net cost before premium − $9.25 budgeted cost). The premium on the put options was $0.57. If that is factored into the price of the milk, the total cost reaches $10.88 ($10.87 actual price paid − $0.56 profit on the futures + $0.57 premium on the puts).

This outcome is identical to the total cost of $10.88 that resulted from the hedge with long calls. This, despite the fact that the premium of the puts was higher than the premium on the calls. The example demonstrates that when a synthetic option is constructed with a strike identical to the strike of a straight option, it will give an identical result if used as a hedge. There may be infrequent mispricing of options that will cause a

Table 5-24. A buying hedge in a normal market using synthetic call options

Cash Market		Futures Market		Basis
Feb. Short 400000 lbs.@	$9.25	Feb. Long Two April 1050 Puts	$10.50	1.00 Under
		Feb. Premium on Puts:	$0.57	1.02 Under
		Feb. Long Two Milk Futures@	$10.27	
		Feb. Underlying April Futures	$10.27	1.02 Under

deviation from this rule. A synthetic option is therefore identical to its ordinary counterpart in every way, except in flexibility.

Had the treasurer selected the puts at the lower strike of 1025 where the premiums were at $0.43 at the same time, a better result would have been obtained in this case. Whereas the hedge with long calls and synthetic long calls at a strike of 1050 resulted in a hedge that was $0.01 per 100 lbs. worse than an unhedged position, the hedge with synthetic long calls at a strike of 1025 would have limited the net increase in cost to $1.49 ($10.74 net cost after the hedge − $9.25 budgeted cost). The hedge at a lower strike would thus have resulted in a $0.13 improvement on the unhedged position, but it would have given a worse result under conditions of a rise in price.

the price declines

In the following iteration, the result of a hedge using synthetic long calls will be examined under normal market conditions where the price of the underlying commodity has declined. As in the initial iteration of the example, it will be assumed that when International Foods lifts the hedge, the spot price of BFP Milk has declined to $8.54 per 100 lbs. and the April futures contract is trading at $8.50 per 100 lbs. on the CME.

The put options are in the money and the treasurer gives instructions for them to be exercised. The short futures positions that are assigned as a result of the exercise of the

Table 5-25. Result of a buying hedge in a normal market using synthetic long calls, after a price rise

Cash Market		Futures Market		Basis
Feb. Short 400000 lbs.@	$9.25	Feb. Long Two April. 1025 Puts	$10.25	1.00 Under
March Long 400000 lbs.@	$10.87	Feb. Premium on Puts:	$0.57	
Loss:	$1.62	Feb. Long Two Milk Futures@	$10.27	1.02 Under
		March Short Two April Futures	$10.83	0.04 Over
		Profit:	$0.56	
		Net Loss After Premiums:	$0.01	Change: +1.06
		Feb. Underlying April Futures	$10.27	1.02 Under
		March Underlying April Futures	$10.83	0.04 Over
				Change: +1.06

options will automatically offset the long futures positions that were taken up at the outset of the hedge. No further action is therefore required of the broker. As the short futures positions are assigned at the strike price of the puts, there is no fill at a price to be reported. The broker merely reports that the puts were exercised.

The result of the hedge is shown in Table 5-26.

Taking into account the premium of $0.57 paid on the put options, the actual cost of the milk amounts to $8.87 ($8.54 actual price + $0.34 loss on the futures). This compares favourably with the $8.88 cost of the milk when straight calls were used for the hedge. The $0.01 disparity is the result of a slight discrepancy in the pricing of the options. If it is considered that options are priced by the market under auction conditions, it is remarkable that the disparities are so rare and so small. The results are therefore identical for all practical purposes.

However, if a straight hedge with futures had been used, the net cost of the milk would have been $10.31 per 100 lbs. ($9.25 budgeted cost + $1.06 basis change, or $8.54 actual cost + $1.77 loss on the futures). In this case therefore, the use of either straight call options or synthetic options would have given a better result than a straight futures hedge.

discussion: the result of the hedge

From the examples discussed, it is clear that using synthetic options in a selling hedge will usually give the same result as a hedge using straight options, although there are exceptions. If used to their full potential, synthetic options have definite advantages over using straight put options in a hedge. The potential for using different strategies with synthetic options is discussed in a later chapter.

The same comment however applies as was made with reference to the use of synthetic futures. Because a synthetic put involves two positions against the one position required for a straight options hedge, it involves greater trading costs. As has been pointed out, these costs are minimal in relation to the numbers at issue in a hedge and they are further dwarfed by the advantages to be gained.

Table 5-26. Result of a buying hedge in a normal market using synthetic long call options, after a price decline

Cash Market			Futures Market		Basis
Feb. Short 400000 lbs.@	$9.25		Feb. Long Two April 1025 Puts	$10.50	1.25 Under
March Long 400000 lbs.@	$8.54		Feb. Premium on Puts:	$0.57	
Profit:	$0.71		Feb. Long Two Milk Futures@	$10.27	1.02 Under
			March Short Two April Futures	$10.50	
			Profit:	$0.23	
			Net Loss After Premiums:	$0.34	
			Feb. Underlying April Futures	$10.27	1.02 Under
			March Underlying April Futures	$8.50	0.04 Over
			Loss:	$1.77	Change: +1.06

The advantages to be gained are fully discussed earlier in this chapter. However, all of these advantages follow from strategies that the make-up of synthetic options allows. Their use will require more time and resources to be spent on monitoring and managing the hedge. If the business is willing to devote the necessary time and resources to this enterprise, the rewards will be forthcoming and they can add substantial value. However, if there is no intention, capacity or need in the business to make use of these strategies, then using synthetic options will serve no purpose.

CHECKLIST FOR THE REVIEW OF CHAPTER 5

General overview. The overall control objectives of the material dealt with in this chapter are to employ the long hedge with futures instruments to the best advantage of a business

	Key Issues	Illustrative Scope or Approach
5.1	How can the business protect its financial well being from adverse price moves of commodities that it purchases?	The company can protect its commodities purchasing prices by means of a user or long hedge in the futures. It is done by: • Buying a futures contract for an appropriate delivery month • Buying a call option • Buying a synthetic futures contract. This is constructed by buying a call option and selling a put option at the same strike price • Buying a synthetic call option. This is constructed by buying a put option and selling a call option at the same strike price
5.2	What effect will a rise or a decline in the price of the underlying commodity have on the result of a hedge?	• If the cash position of the business is fully hedged, the price move of the underlying commodity will not affect the outcome of the hedge in any way • If the futures position is quantitatively smaller than the cash position, a drop in price will result in a profit in the cash market on the unhedged portion, while a rise in price will result in a loss on the unhedged portion • If the futures position is quantitatively greater than the cash position, a drop in price will result in a loss in the futures on the excess, while a rise in price will result in a profit on the excess

continued

	Key Issues	Illustrative Scope or Approach
5.3	What effect will it have on the hedge if the underlying market is in backwardation?	A buying hedge in an inverse market will result in a profit on the hedge, if it is held to the futures delivery month. The profit will be equal to the amount by which the basis weakens
5.4	What effect will it have on the hedge if the underlying market is in contango?	A buying hedge in a normal market will result in a loss on the hedge, if it is held to the futures delivery month. The loss is caused by a strengthening of the basis. The maximum loss might exceed the cost of carry only marginally
5.5	What advantage, if any, will the business gain by using options on futures instead of straight futures contracts in a hedge?	• Conventional wisdom has it that options carry less risk than futures. This is certainly true if the profit/loss profiles of the two instruments are compared, but it is not so when they are properly used in a hedge • Its main advantage lies in the facility it creates of allowing a profit to be realised on a favourable price move, which is not possible in a true hedge. The condition is that the price of the underlying must move sufficiently to neutralise the cost of acquiring the option • Options allow a variety of hedging strategies to be followed that can enhance the hedge result
5.6	What advantage, if any, will the business gain by using synthetic futures instead of straight futures contracts in a hedge?	A hedge with synthetic futures will give the same result as a hedge with simple futures taken at the same time. The trading costs for the synthetic futures will be two to two-and-a-half times as much as the trading costs for a simple future hedge The flexibility of synthetic futures will allow certain hedging strategies to be used that are not available with a simple futures hedge
5.7	What advantage, if any, will the business gain by using synthetic options instead of straight options on futures in a hedge?	A hedge using synthetic options will give exactly same result as a hedge using the straight option at the same strike price taken at the same time The trading costs for a synthetic options hedge will be two to two-and-a-half times as much as a hedge using straight options

continued

Key Issues	Illustrative Scope or Approach
	The flexibility of a synthetic option will allow additional hedging strategies to be used to enhance the result of a hedge

SIX

hedging with commodity futures and options – the producer's hedge

THE SELLING HEDGE USING FUTURES CONTRACTS

The producer's hedge is also known as the selling hedge. The selling hedge is so called because it is the technique used by the seller of the commodity as opposed to the buyer or user thereof. In other words, it is the technique that will be used by a business that is long the cash. The technique is consequently also known as a short hedge. The latter appellation is because the buyer or user of a commodity will hedge the cash position of the business by taking in a short position in the futures markets.

The opposite hedge is known as a long hedge or as the producer's hedge. The latter hedge is fully dealt with in the previous chapter. Since the two types of hedges mirror each other, it is suggested that the reader reads either the whole of this chapter or alternatively, the previous chapter. The choice depends upon which one of the hedges is appropriate to the business of the reader's concern. This will save the reader the tedium of slogging through what is essentially a repeat of the same material, albeit the converse. At the end of this chapter, a checklist of the differences between the two hedges will be found in a comparative table. If either the short hedge or the long hedge is thoroughly understood, it will be quite simple for the reader to gain an equally thorough understanding of the other hedge by reading through the summary of the differences.

Returning to the subject under discussion, it can thus be said that the purpose of the selling hedge is to protect a long cash position from an adverse move in price. A long cash position is at risk of a drop in price. A drop in the price of the underlying commodity will decrease the cost of purchasing the cash commodity at a date in the future, thus causing a lessening of income and a loss to the seller. The working and dynamics of the hedge will be best illustrated by means of an example.

The effect and efficacy of a selling hedge will differ depending on the market condition, namely whether the market is normal or inverse. It will therefore be appropriate also to demonstrate and discuss the short hedge by using an example and then iterating the example by assuming different market conditions. However, in order to first demonstrate the basic concept of using a short hedge, the condition of the market will be ignored.

the perfect short hedge

Consider the situation of an oil refinery situated in New York. The major retail product of this refinery is unleaded gasoline, delivered from the New York harbour area. During January, the prices of crude and refined oil are constantly rising. The refinery's concern is that the rising prices cannot continue indefinitely and the fear that a drop in prices may be imminent. They wish to maintain at least the present profit margins through to the end of March. In order to protect their selling price at current levels, they decide to hedge the price of a portion of their production that will be sold and delivered in March, with futures contracts. They decide to use the New York Harbour Unleaded Gasoline futures contract that trades on the NYMEX for this purpose.

The spot price of unleaded gasoline at the end of January is $0.8425 per US gallon. At the same time, the March futures contract on the NYMEX is trading at $0.7461. The oil market is thus in a state of inversion; a condition to which it is often prone.

The last trading day of the March futures contract will be the last business day of February. The refinery intends to start shipping their unleaded gasoline production for delivery in the month of March on that day. The portion of production that the refinery decides to hedge with futures is 210 000 US gallons. Since one futures contract equals 42 000 US gallons, the refinery will require five contracts to cover its March sales.

The refinery's treasurer thus telephones their broker and instructs him to sell five NYMEX March New York Harbour Unleaded Gasoline futures contracts. Later in the day, the broker reports back with a fill at $0.7550. Their hedged position now appears in Table 6-1.

The movement of prices in the market can now be considered. As is fully discussed elsewhere, a market can move in any one of three ways: it can trade up, down or sideways. A market that trades sideways does not have a stationary price. A sideways market merely means that the price fluctuates up and down in a reasonably narrow range. Thus, prices will change up or down, even in a sideways trading market.

In order to demonstrate the basic mechanics of a hedge, the result of an upward and of a downward move in price will be discussed separately. Since the example demonstrates a

Table 6-1. A short futures hedge in an inverted market

Cash Market		Futures Market		Basis
Jan. 'Long' 210000 Galls.	$0.8425	Jan. Short Five Contracts	$0.7550	0.0875 Over

Table 6-2. The result of a perfect short hedge in an inverse market with a decline in price

Cash Market		Futures Market		Basis
Jan. Long 126000 Galls.	$0.8425	Jan. Short Three Contracts@	$0.7550	0.0875 Over
Feb. Short 126000 Galls.	$0.8050	Feb. Long Three contracts@	$0.7175	0.0875 Over
Loss:	$0.0375	Profit:	$0.0375	Change: 0

short hedge, which is intended to protect the hedger against a drop in price, this contingency will be the first to be investigated.

the price declines

For the purpose of this iteration, assume that on February 28 the spot price for unleaded gasoline is $0.8050. In order for the refinery to lift this hedge, they will have to purchase five futures contracts. Keep in mind that the hedge was originally established by taking up five short positions in futures contracts, an offsetting trade would therefore be constituted by buying five identical contracts in the same delivery month.

The treasurer of the oil refinery therefore instructs their broker to lift the hedge by covering the five short futures positions. Assume that the price the broker realises on the purchase of the futures is $0.7175. Again, the futures price would be expected to fall in sympathy with the fall in the spot price. The result of the hedge is now shown in Table 6-2.

There was no change in the basis between the time the hedge was entered and the time it was exited. The profit in the futures market therefore neutralises the loss in the cash markets exactly. The net result of the hedge is thus that the selling price for the March inventory equals $0.8425 per gallon, exactly what it was at the outset. The example clearly illustrates that if there in no basis move, the result of the hedge will be to maintain the price status at the start of the hedge. Such a hedge is described as a perfect hedge.

The hedge has done exactly what was expected of it by the oil refinery, since the net income from their March production is now higher than the net income realised by their competitors.

the price rises

The result of the previous hedge will now be compared with the result when a rise in price occurs. Therefore, it will be assumed that the spot price for unleaded gasoline rises to trade at $0.8750 at the end of February. Assume also that the broker buys the three offsetting futures contracts at a price of $0.7875. The result of the hedge is shown in Table 6-3.

Again, there was no change in the basis. The spot price of unleaded gasoline rose by $0.0325 per US gallon and the futures price reacted by rising by the same amount. From Table 6-3, it is clear that the profit realised on the cash purchase of the gasoline is totally offset by the loss on the futures trade. This is due to fact that there was no basis move.

Table 6-3. The result of a perfect short hedge in an inverse market with a rise in price

Cash Market		Futures Market		Basis
Jan. Long 126000 Galls.	$0.8425	Jan. Short Three Contracts@	$0.7550	0.0875 Over
Feb. Short 126000 Galls.	$0.8750	Feb. Long Three Contracts@	$0.7875	0.0875 Over
Profit:	$0.0325	Loss:	$0.0325	Change: 0

There was no basis move precisely because the spot price and the futures price moved by the same amount. The hedge therefore remains perfect.

The result of the hedge is that the net income produced by the hedged quantity of unleaded gasoline amounts to $0.8425 per gallon ($0.8750 actually received − $0.0325 loss on the futures market). The refinery is not ecstatically happy, because they missed out on an increased profit opportunity. Nevertheless, they reached their hedging goal, which was to maintain at least the January profit level through to March.

discussion: the result of the hedge

From the above two iterations of the example, it is clear that the purpose of a hedge is to ensure price stability. Ignoring for a moment any move in the basis, it is evident that once a hedge has been established, it does not matter whether the price rises or falls, the result will be the same. The greatest benefit of a hedge is therefore that it allows a business to budget, to have price certainty and to dampen price volatility in the market.

The downside of a hedge is that it does not allow the advantage of a favourable price move. In a perfect hedge all risk is hedged away, even the risk of a profit. This is not intended as a criticism of a perfect hedge – it is merely an accurate observation. It means though, that a perfect hedge will not be desirable under all circumstances. The general thesis of this book is thus supported by illustrating that hedging is a multi-faceted facility. It should not be indulged in without proper consideration of all aspects and requirements of the situation.

THE SHORT FUTURES HEDGE IN AN INVERSE MARKET

As it happens, a perfect hedge is highly improbable when using futures and options. Basis move is a constant factor that has to be taken into consideration at all times. It is one of the aspects that make hedging with futures and options such a fascinating subject. It seems that there are so many aspects and perspectives that one is continually being confronted with something new – an old Roman might have been tempted to exclaim 'ex futurae semper alliquid novo'. In order to demonstrate a more realistic approach to the example, two more iterations are discussed below. This time however, basis moves, predicated on proper market considerations, will be employed.

Basis moves result in an imperfect hedge. An imperfect hedge is by definition, one in which the profit in the one market does not perfectly neutralise the loss in the other market. Basis movement can therefore result in either a profit or a loss on the hedge. It is the purpose of the discussion that follows to examine and indicate profit and loss situations resulting from a short hedge.

the imperfect short hedge: the price declines

The assumption now is that the spot price in the example will have declined. With a decline in price, it is likely that the market would go into contango, i.e. – become a normal market. However, it is not necessary to drive the example that far in order to illustrate the principle. Only the futures price needs to be adjusted in order to reflect the expected narrowing of the basis. Assume now therefore, that the futures position of the refinery was covered at a price of $0.7725 when the hedge was lifted. The result of the hedge is now shown in Table 6-4.

In fact, the price of the futures rose even though the spot price declined. This is because the market would be less inverse when a drop in buying pressure results in lower prices. It is apparent that in an inverse market, a narrowing of the basis implies its weakening, that is to say, when the basis becomes anything from less positive through to downright negative.

In the example illustrated in Table 6-4, the net income to the refinery on sales of unleaded fuel for March would have been based on a net price of $0.7875 ($0.8050 actual selling price − $0.0175 loss on the futures). This is $0.055 worse than the selling price during January ($0.8425 January selling price − $0.7875 net selling price after the hedge). The worsening of the selling price is exactly equal to the change in the basis. This demonstrates that the determining factor in the effectiveness of a hedge is the change in the basis and not the change in the price of the underlying.

discussion: the short hedge results in a loss in an inverse market

It is well known that the spot price of a commodity and its near futures contract price will converge and tend to zero in the futures delivery month. Since the last trading day of February is the last trading day of the March futures contract, it is reasonable to suggest a basis of no greater than $0.0325, as was done in the previous example. In fact, the basis could even be much smaller than indicated in the above iteration of the example. Had the market reverted to normal, there could even have been a slightly negative basis – slightly

Table 6-4. The result of an imperfect short hedge in an inverse market after a decline in price

Cash Market		Futures Market		Basis
Jan. Long 126000 Galls.	$0.8425	Jan. Short Three Contracts@ $0.7550		0.0875 Over
Feb. Short 126000 Galls.	$0.8050	Feb. Long Three Contracts@ $0.7725		0.0325 Over
Loss:	$0.0375	Loss:	$0.0175	Change: −0.055

negative because the basis cannot be too great, positive or negative, in the futures delivery month.

The exact figure of the eventual basis is not of such great importance for the purpose of this example. What is of extreme importance though, is that the basis would have narrowed or weakened as was previously observed. The extent of the weakening will influence the quantitative outcome of the hedge, but it will not influence the outcome in principle – the short hedge will show a loss when the basis weakens.

In the example, the only change that was made to the figures used in the first iteration was that the price the March futures contracts fetched upon their sale was considerably higher. This change made the example more realistic, as explained above. Any increase in the price of the futures contracts would obviously result in a loss on the futures trade since the initial position in a short hedge is short futures.

In an inverse market, a narrowing of the basis requires that the futures price must either rise to meet the spot price, or the spot price must drop to meet the futures price. In either case, it is inevitable that the futures price must either increase from its previous level by more than the spot price increases from that same date, or it must drop ever so slightly against a massive drop in the spot price. The circumstances thus demand a loss in both markets, as was the case in the example. Alternatively, a great loss will be suffered in the futures market as the price rises to meet the spot price, or a substantial loss in the spot market as its price drops to meet the futures price. Whatever the specifics may be, the inevitability of a loss on a short hedge under inverse market conditions is demonstrated. This thesis will be revisited after the following iteration.

the imperfect short hedge: the price rises

Assume that the hedge of the refinery is lifted on February 28. The spot price has risen to $0.8750 per gallon. The March futures price has also risen and is trading around $0.84 per gallon. The short positions are covered at a price of $0.7725. The result of the hedge is illustrated in Table 6-5.

Calculating the actual selling price of the March sales, the result comes to $0.7875 per US gallon ($0.8750 actual price paid − $0.0875 profit on the futures). This is the same net price as was realised in the previous iteration. The results are identical because the change in the basis was identical.

There was a loss on the hedge again. The net selling price is worse than the selling price in January by $0.055 per gallon ($0.8425 January selling price − $0.7875 net

Table 6-5. An imperfect short hedge in an inverse market with a rise in price

Cash Market		Futures Market		Basis
Jan. Long 126000 Galls.	$0.8425	Jan. Short Three Contracts@ $0.7550		0.0875 Over
Feb. Short 126000 Galls.	$0.8750	Feb. Long Three Contracts@ $0.8425		0.0325 Over
Profit:	$0.0325	Loss:	$0.0875	Change: −0.055

March selling price), which is equal to the change in the basis indicated in Table 6-5. In this iteration, the company would have been better off had it not hedged.

Two main questions therefore arise from the outcome of these two hedge results. Firstly, was the firm better off by hedging, and secondly, what was the maximum loss, if any, that they could suffer on the hedge?

discussion: the result of the hedge

Dealing with the first question, it is clear that in both of the above iterations the company would have been better off had it not hedged. In the first iteration, the loss in the cash market was $0.0375, which was exacerbated by a further loss on the futures markets. In the second instance, the large loss in the futures market wiped out the profit in the cash market to give a $0.055 loss on the hedge. The net result is inevitable in both instances.

The basis move will always result in the final net price being worse than the hedged price by the amount that the basis weakens. That means that the benefit of any favourable move will always be wiped out into a deficit as great as the weakening of the basis. Thus, on a favourable price move of the underlying, the short hedger in an inverse market will always be worse off by hedging than by not hedging.

This is however not true in the case of an adverse price move. Keep in mind that it has been demonstrated that a hedge always gives the same result, whether the price goes up or down. An adverse price move for a short hedger occurs when the price drops, as was the case in the first iteration above. Had the price in that instance dropped by more than $0.055 with the same move in the basis, the move would have been neutralised for the amount by which it unfavourably dropped by more than $0.055. The $0.055 basis move is not capricious. As will be fully explained, the size of the basis move is reasonably predictable from the start. The result of a short hedge in an inverted market is also predictable. The company must decide at the outset whether it can accommodate the result of the situation. The choice is further elaborated below.

Two main questions arise from the discussion thus far:

- what, if any, are the limits of the possible basis move; and
- is a short hedge with commodity futures in a normal market a viable risk management option for a business?

Dealing first of all with the limits of the risk, the rule of price convergence must be kept in mind, because it is the key to the answer to the question. The risk of loss is, as has been demonstrated, limited to the extent that the basis narrows. Since we are dealing exclusively with a basis move in an inverse market, the question can be put differently. The question is really, by how much can the basis weaken during the term of the hedge?

There is indeed a limit to the amount by which the basis can weaken. Consider the fact that in an inverse market, there is no maximum basis that can exist between the spot price and the price of the futures in any futures delivery month. However, in a market in contango the maximum negative basis is equal to the carrying charge for the period between the spot month and the futures delivery month.

The question should therefore be approached in a practical way. In every case, it should be observed what the actual basis is. The amount constituting the basis at the time that the short hedge is entered, is the primary amount that can be lost. If the basis weakens to zero, then the loss on a short hedge can amount to the total of the initial basis. However, during the currency of a hedge, a market that was originally in backwardation can turn into a normal market. That means that the basis could start off as a positive one and then weaken and continue to do so until it is completely in contango. The limit of the weakening of the basis is thus the amount by which it starts off as being positive, up to a negative basis of no greater than the carrying charge for the period left to the futures delivery month. That is the theoretical maximum.

The theoretical maximum will never eventuate because, on condition that the hedge is held to the futures delivery month, the basis will be either positive or negative by only a small amount. That is because the prices will converge and the basis will tend to zero during the futures delivery month.

The first question can thus be answered. The maximum risk that a short hedge in an inverse market entails, on condition that it is held until or close to the futures delivery month, will approximate the basis that exists at the start of the hedge.

The second question can now be investigated. It must be stressed at the outset, that the discussion that follows is relevant only to the use of futures contracts to establish a short hedge in a normal market. It certainly does not apply to the use of futures in any other hedge in any other market condition, much less to the use of futures generally.

As to whether or not a short hedge using commodity futures is a viable option for a business in general terms, the answer must be an unqualified yes. Whether it is a viable option for a particular company at a particular point in time is a matter that must be properly considered. A number of the main considerations that should be taken account of are discussed below, without any pretension that these considerations are in any way exhaustive.

It is suggested that the primary and most important question is to determine the alternatives. If the risk that it is intended to hedge has minimal impact on the financial wellbeing of the business, then obviously the question of hedging it should not have arisen in the first place. However, in all other instances the evil of not hedging should be weighed against the evil of the loss of the possible basis move. Not hedging always involves unlimited risk, against which a short hedge in a normal market involves limited risk as discussed.

Regard should first be made to the alternative financial hedging instruments that may be available. Swaps, cash forward agreements and over the counter (OTC) options, as well as exchange-traded options that do not have futures contracts as their underliers, do not involve basis moves. A properly constructed swap or other OTC instrument will result in a perfect hedge every time.

The problem in the commodity markets however, is that these OTC instruments are often not available at all and even if they are, they might be available only in larger quantities that could far exceed the requirements of the firm. Nevertheless, depending on the requirements of the situation, it may be the best alternative to select another derivative instrument for a short hedge in an inverse market. This is a question that only a business faced with the problem will be able to resolve at the appropriate time. Some factors that will weigh when other derivatives are considered will be discussed presently.

The prudent action to take would be to start of by inspecting the price of the futures contracts for the delivery month that it is intended to use for the hedge. Then determine the basis by using the actual price that the business would receive now for the cash commodity. This might of course be the spot price or the some derived price that the business normally sells at. It is the actual price that the business receives for the physical commodity that determines the cash leg of the hedge basis. It is not 'basis' in general that determines the business's hedge performance, but its own particular hedge basis. It follows that it is also the actual price received by the firm that must be used to calculate the result of the hedge when it is lifted.

As previously stated, swaps result in a perfect hedge every time. If a perfect hedge is what the business requires, and swaps are liquid and available in the required lot sizes, they may be the best choice under all the circumstances. The other alternatives of non-futures based options and cash forward agreements require some further consideration and evaluation.

Cash forward agreements and other options again, may be available or they may not. If cash forward agreements are available, the price received by the company would normally be negotiated at a premium to the spot price. The price premium would normally, have the carrying charges of the commodity for the period factored in. The only time that carrying charges are not applicable is when the commodity in question must still be produced, such as agricultural products that will only be harvested at the start of the new crop year. A cash forward agreement involves credit risk. The firm will be exposed to the creditworthiness of the purchaser. If this is acceptable and cash forwards are available, they may be a better choice than futures under these particular circumstances.

Options present other considerations to be taken into account. Any option product that is available for consideration will carry a premium. It is always a question of investigation therefore, as to whether the premium on an option is greater or smaller than the possible loss on a futures position. Although this is certainly not the only element to consider when deciding upon the question of using options, it is an important element that needs to be given attention to.

Thus, the hedge basis that can be lost, determined by using the actual cash price to the business as previously explained, must then be compared with the premium to be paid on an option. If the basis is anything less than the price premium to be paid on an option, the short hedge with futures obviously has the advantage.

Focussing on the cash forward agreement for the moment, apart from the already mentioned counter party credit risk, there are other factors to take account of when these instruments are considered. A futures hedge allows a business freedom to seek out the best price deal in the cash market when the day of reckoning arrives. In a cash forward agreement the business is legally bound sell the goods to the vendor with whom the cash forward transaction was concluded, on the agreed date at the agreed price.

In the premises therefore, a selling hedge in an inverted market, where a loss on the hedge due to a weakening of the basis will be incurred, might nevertheless be a viable option for a business. More consideration of the total situation may be required before a final decision is reached, but a short hedge with futures cannot be dismissed out of hand.

THE SHORT FUTURES HEDGE IN A NORMAL MARKET

The investigation and discussion must now turn to the effect of a selling hedge in a normal market. A selling hedge remains the same in principle, whatever the market condition. The purpose of this discussion is thus to demonstrate how the hedge behaves under normal market conditions.

The only relevant difference between a market in backwardation and one in contango for the purposes of this discussion, is the way the basis moves. In an earlier chapter, this whole phenomenon was fully discussed and it was pointed out then that under both markets conditions, the spot price and the futures price would converge and tend to zero in the futures delivery month. Therein lies the difference of the results of the short hedge.

Under inverse market conditions, the spot price is trading higher than the near futures price. The higher the spot price is over the futures price, the more positive or stronger the basis. A convergence of the two prices therefore inevitably means a weakening of the basis. The basis must become less positive. Under normal market conditions, the converse is true. The spot price will be under the futures price. The basis will therefore be negative or weak. When these two prices converge, they are moving closer together, the basis is thus becoming less negative. The basis is, in other words, strengthening.

The rule on price convergence can thus be phrased in an alternative manner in order to distinguish the situation in a normal market from that in a market in backwardation. It can be said that in a normal market, the basis between the spot price of a commodity and its near futures contract price will strengthen and tend to zero in the near futures delivery month. Conversely, it can be said that in an inverse market, the basis between the spot price and the near futures price of a commodity will weaken and tend to zero in the near futures delivery month.

The effect of these factors on a short hedge in a normal market may best be illustrated by means of an example, iterated as in the previous section.

Consider a mining company that is in the process of opening a new gold mine in Australia. During January, it becomes clear to management that they will only be able to bring their mine into production in May and in the meantime, they are incurring heavy development costs. When they originally planned the development of the mine, they based their calculations on a gold price of not less than $280.00 per fine ounce. At the beginning of January, the spot price of gold is standing at $283.00 per fine troy ounce and the company fears that there may be a further decline in price. That would be a major setback for the new mine. The May gold futures contract on the Chicago Board of Trade is simultaneously trading at $302.50 per fine troy ounce.

Table 6-6. A short hedge in a normal market

Cash Market		Futures Market		Basis
Jan. Long Gold	$283.00	Jan. Short May Gold Futures@	$302.00	19.00 Under

The CBOT contract trades in multiples of 1000 ounces and the mine decides to sell sufficient contracts to cover their expected initial production in May. The company therefore places an order with their broker to sell CBOT May Kilo Gold futures contracts at the market. Assume that they receive a fill at $302.00. Their hedged position is now shown in Table 6-6.

From the prices illustrated in Table 6-6, it is clear that the gold market is in contango. For the purposes of this, and all other iterations based on this example, it will be assumed that the initial basis as illustrated in this table represents a full 4-month carrying charge for gold.

Although the company has not yet produced any gold in January, they will produce and their position is thus long gold. They must therefore employ a short hedge to protect their position.

the imperfect short hedge; the price declines

In the first iteration of the example, a drop in the price of gold will be assumed. For the purposes of this iteration, it will be assumed that gold suffered a decline in price between the beginning of January and the end of April. When the mining company starts selling its first gold production at the end of April, they will receive a price of $275.50 per fine ounce. This is $4.50 per fine ounce lower than their bottom line. However, when the firm receives the fill on the lifting of the hedge, they discover that the short futures positions were covered at $279.75, resulting in a profit on the futures market of $12.75. See Table 6-7 for the full result of the hedge.

The basis strengthened by 14.75 from 19.00 under to only 4.25 under, as indicated in Table 6-7. The net price received on the gold is consequently $297.75 per fine troy ounce ($275.50 actually received + $22.25 profit on the hedge). Of course, if the basis had strengthened more, the profit on the hedge would have been even greater. Had it strengthened less, the profit would likewise have been smaller.

Notice once more the central role played by the move in the basis. The difference between the loss made on the cash market and the profit made on the futures market

Table 6-7. The result of an imperfect short hedge in a normal market after a decline in price

Cash Market		Futures Market		Basis
Feb. Long Gold	$283.00	Jan. Short May Gold Futures@	$302.00	19 Under
April Short Gold	$275.50	April Long May Gold Futures@	$279.75	4.25 Under
Loss:	$7.50	Profit:	$22.25	Change: +14.75

Table 6-8. The result of a short hedge in a normal market after a price rise

Cash Market		Futures Market		Basis
Feb. Long Gold	$283.00	Jan. Short May Gold Futures@	$302.00	19 Under
April Short Gold	$289.50	April Long May Gold Futures@	$293.75	4.25 Under
Profit:	$6.50	Profit:	$8.25	Change: +14.75

equals $14.75, which is, in turn, equal to the amount by which the basis strengthened. Monitoring the basis is thus central to managing risk with commodity futures.

the imperfect short hedge: the price rises

At the end of April, when the gold mining firm wishes to sell the gold, the spot market price it receives is $289.50. At the same time, the firm instructs the broker to lift the hedge. The broker reports back that the short futures positions were closed out at $293.75. The result of the hedge is illustrated in Table 6-8.

The actual selling price of the gold was $297.75 per fine troy ounce ($289.50 received on the spot market + $8.25 profit on the futures).

discussion: the result of the hedge

Again, because of the basic rule that the spot price and the near futures prices will converge and the difference tend to zero in the futures delivery month, it can be stated with confidence that a selling hedge in a normal market will result in a profit on the hedge. There is a condition however. The condition is that the hedge is held until or at least very close to, the futures delivery month. The basis will tend to narrow and widen continuously during the currency of a futures contract and nothing can be said with any certainty concerning the state of the basis before the close approach of the futures delivery month.

Monitoring the hedge basis is therefore an important part of successful hedging practice.

THE SELLING HEDGE USING LONG PUT OPTIONS

The concern is of course, with commodity options. The term 'short' hedge would be somewhat of a misnomer in this case since this hedge is not particularly distinguished by the hedger taking a short position in options. At the start of the section on the selling hedge, it was stated that the purpose of the buying option is to protect the hedger against a rise in the price of the underlying commodity. This remains the purpose when using options.

The foregoing statement requires some further elucidation. Keep in mind that, as is fully discussed elsewhere, a commodity option has a commodity futures contract as its underlying and as such is the only known derivative of a derivative. The commodity option is thus related to the physical commodity twice removed, one might say. Nevertheless, the concern here is to deal with hedging the price of the physical commodity that underlies the futures contract, rather than with hedging the price of the underlying of the option.

It is quite correct of course, to assume that a position in futures contracts can be hedged by means of a commodity option. It is a combination often described as a 'fution' and is greatly favoured by many speculative traders. Technically, such a combination of a futures contract with a hedging option would be called a synthetic option. It can also be used to very good effect by hedgers. Synthetic futures and options will thus be dealt with during the course of this chapter. However, the first question that arises is how options might best be employed for the purpose of establishing a selling hedge.

Since the purpose of a selling hedge is to protect the hedger against a rise in the price of the commodity, the hedging position must be such as to allow a profit to the hedger in the futures market on a rise in the price, to offset the loss in the cash market. This would normally be achieved by taking a short futures position, as was discussed in the previous section. It thus follows that if a short futures position is eschewed in favour of an option, it must be an option to gain a short futures position. A put option is precisely such an option. A put option will upon its exercise result in a short futures position.

The whole purpose of using options rather than futures is to avoid the risk of loss. With an option, the greatest possible loss is the loss of the premium paid on the option. Against this advantage, there is the cost of the premium that the hedger will have to factor into the cost structure of the business. An example will serve to illustrate the situation.

Consider the case of an oil refinery with its main base of operations situated in Antwerp. It is bound by contract to accept certain quantities of pipeline oil on a 3-monthly forward allocation. The company pays the ruling spot price at the time of the allocation, but receives the oil in 3 months time. It then on-sells the oil to refineries and other customers. Its cash market position is therefore continuously long crude oil.

The volatility of the price of crude oil is of concern to the company. The 3-month forward purchase holds serious implications for the company if the oil price drops in the interim. A drop implies that they might have to sell some of their inventory at a loss. In any event, lower oil prices always means lower profits since profit margins remain the same. In addition, because the market is very competitive, the company is well aware of the fact that their selling prices have to be keen in order to maintain its custom. They therefore have to hedge the value of oil. On the other hand, because the company's profit margins are constantly under pressure, it would be a welcome relief if they could realise greater profits by any further rise in the price of oil. They therefore need to hedge against a drop in the price, while not losing the opportunity to gain from a rise in price completely.

In November, the treasurer of the refinery decides to use Brent Crude options on the IPE in London to hedge their requirements to the end of February. The November price was high and the company fears a drop in prices over the next 3 months will force them to sell the inventory at a loss. She bases her hedging strategy on all the foregoing considerations and therefore decides to hedge, using options.

Table 6-9. A selling hedge using a put option

Cash Market	Futures Market		Basis
Nov. Long Brent Crude@ $25.97	Nov. Long Brent Crude Puts	$24.00	1.97 Over
	Nov. Underlying March Futures	$23.75	2.22 Over

The Brent Crude futures contract trades in quantities of 42 000 US gallons, or 1000 barrels of oil per contract. One Brent crude option has one Brent Crude futures contract as its underlier. The treasurer calculates the number of options required for the hedge using the quantity of the allocation. The company's November allocation for February delivery was at a spot price $25.97 per barrel. When the treasurer draws the current prices from the Internet after having received confirmation of the allocation price, she finds that the Brent Crude spot price is $26.30 per barrel. The futures contracts closed on the previous trading day as follows:

January: $25.78 per barrel;
February: $24.71 per barrel; and
March: $23.75 per barrel.

The market is clearly in backwardation and the treasurer realises the implications thereof. She telephones the company's broker and instructs him to buy three IPE March Brent Crude 2400 puts at $1.78 stop. The 2400 strike is the strike closest to the money. At that strike, the put is slightly in the money. The broker later reports that the order was filled at a price of $1.78 per barrel. The hedged position of the company now appears as shown in Table 6-9.

Because of the 'twice removed' nature of an option, there are in fact two relevant bases. The first basis is that between the cash position of the hedger and the strike price of the option. Since the strike of the option is fixed, this basis will only move as a result of the movement of the cash price. The often-discussed trading relationship between spot and near futures does not apply to this particular basis. This basis, being dependent only on the movement of one of the prices involved, can move in any direction at any time. It is as unpredictable as the price itself. The second basis shown in Table 6-9 is the well-traversed basis, about the movement of which a lot is known at this stage.

Because commodity options have a commodity futures contract as its underlier, the profit to be realised at expiration or earlier exercise is determined by the price of the futures contract relative to the strike of the option. It is not determined by the spot price of the commodity. The spot price of the commodity of course influences and governs the price of the futures contract, as has been thoroughly discussed up to now. Nevertheless, the option will be in the money or out of the money depending on the state of the price of the underlying futures contract.

The effectiveness of a hedge with a commodity option is still determined therefore by the movement of the cash/futures basis. Consequently, the condition of the market plays a similar role to the one demonstrated in the previous examples. Given these considerations, the example will be further iterated in terms of the two possible market conditions.

THE SELLING HEDGE LONG PUT OPTIONS IN AN INVERSE MARKET

As was demonstrated in the case of the short hedge using futures contracts, the result is not influenced by the up or down movements of the price. The result of the hedge stays the same. The major factor that influences the effectiveness of the hedge was demonstrated as being the condition of the market. With an options hedge there is the promise of a different result when the price rises or declines. This is due to the inherent feature of long options, namely that one cannot lose more than the premium on the option. This matter will now be investigated further.

the price rises

Assume firstly that the price rises. When the refinery starts shipping its oil during the first half of February, the spot price of Brent Crude has risen to $29.45 per barrel. The company could therefore base their forward sales over the next 3 months on a spot price of $29.45. The March futures contracts are also trading higher at $29.25. The put options are thus out of the money.

The treasurer therefore needs to take no action in order to lift the hedge. She merely allows the put options to expire out of the money. The company forfeits the premium paid on the options. The result of the hedge is set out in Table 6-10.

The $3.48 improvement on the selling price for March is partly offset by the loss of the option premium. However, the result of the hedge is that the net selling price will be $27.67 ($29.45 actual selling price − $1.78 loss on the futures). The result represents an increase in profit on the hedged $25.97 purchase price of $1.70 per barrel (29.45 actual selling price − $25.97 purchase price − $1.78 option premium).

Even though this is a short hedge in an inverse market, there is no loss on the hedge as there would have been had futures been used. The reason is of course that any loss is limited to the premium paid for the option. The basis move does not influence the result

Table 6-10. Result of a selling hedge in an inverse market using options, after a price rise

Cash Market		Futures Market		Basis
Nov. Long Brent Crude@	$25.97	Nov. Long March Puts	$24.00	1.97 Over
Feb. Short Brent Crude@	$29.45	Nov. Premium on Options	$1.78	
Profit:	$3.48	Loss:	$1.78	
		Nov. Underlying March Futures	$23.75	2.22 Over
		Feb. Underlying March Futures	$29.25	0.20 Over
				Change: −2.02

Table 6-11. The result of a selling hedge in an inverse market using long put options, after a price decline

Cash Market		Futures Market		Basis
Nov. Long 3000 Barrels@ $25.97		Nov. Long March Puts	$24.00	1.97 Over
Feb. Short 3000 Barrels@ $21.45		Premium Paid:	$1.78	1.97 Over
Loss:	$4.52	Feb. Short March Futures@	$24.00	0.20 Over
		Feb. Long March Futures@	$21.25	
		Profit:	$2.75	
		Net Profit After Premium:	$0.97	
		Nov. Underlying March Futures	$23.75	2.22 Over
		Feb. Underlying March Futures	$21.25	0.20 Over
				Change: −2.02

of the hedge in a favourable move. In this case, the company is definitely better off by having hedged than by not having done so.

Note that if straight futures contracts had been used, the adverse weakening of the basis would have been $2.02. The weakening would have resulted in a net selling price of $23.95 ($25.97 actual cost − $2.02 basis change, or $29.45 actual selling price − $5.50 loss on futures). This would have been a lower selling price than the purchase price of $25.97 by $2.02, the amount of the basis move.

the price declines

For the purposes of this iteration, the same basic information that was used in the first iteration will be kept intact. Only now, it will be assumed that there was a decline in the price of Brent Crude.

When the company received its oil in February, the spot price of Brent Crude had dropped to $21.45 per barrel. The market was still in backwardation and March futures were trading at $21.25. The options were in the money and the treasurer instructed their futures broker to lift the hedge. The broker lifted the hedge by exercising the puts and by buying an equal number of March futures contracts. The long futures would automatically offset the short futures positions that would be assigned to the company as a result of the exercise of the options. The result of the hedge is illustrated in Table 6-11.

The company's selling price for March, after taking the hedge into consideration, is $24.20 ($21.45 actual selling price + $2.75 profit on the futures). This falls short of the November cost price by $1.77 per barrel ($25.97 cost price − $24.20 actual selling price). Unfortunately, that is not the end of the matter. The premium of the options still has to be considered. When the option premium is brought into the calculation, the net selling price drops to $22.42 ($24.20 net selling price − $1.78 option premium).

This situation does not compare as favourably with a straight futures hedge as the hedge in the previous iteration did. In this particular iteration, a straight futures hedge would have resulted in a net selling price of $23.95 ($25.97 cost price − $2.02 basis change), which is $1.53 better than the net price realised on the hedge with options.

discussion: the result of the hedge

The example with its two iterations suggests that a buying hedge using options can be successful even in an inverse market. However, in the final analysis the success of the strategy depends on the size of the adverse or favourable move.

In both iterations of the example, the price moves were sufficient to overcome the cost structure of the options. Even in the favourable upward move, the price must move by more than the premium of the option before any net advantage is gained.

Given the examples thus far, it is clear that a selling hedge using options will have a greater chance of giving a desirable result when there is a volatile underlying market. Then the odds are better that whatever price moves there are will be substantial moves.

It now remains to be seen what the result of the selling hedge with options will be under normal market conditions.

THE SELLING HEDGE USING LONG PUT OPTIONS IN A NORMAL MARKET

The purpose is again to protect the hedger against a drop in the price of the underlying commodity, but to make use of put options for the hedge rather than futures contracts. Consider the situation of a large dairy farm with its own milk processing plant situated in Kentucky.

In February when the spot price of BFP milk is at $9.25 per 100 lbs., the plant is expecting a large order of BFP standard milk from one of their clients. It is expected that delivery will be required at the end of March. The firm's concern is that the price of milk will drop from present levels, thereby putting pressure on their profit margins.

Clearly, they need to hedge the price of milk in order to maintain their present prices and levels of profit. The board of the farming company had previously directed that preference should be given to using long options when hedges were constructed to manage the company's commodity risks.

Consequently, the treasurer accessed the web site of the CME to determine the previous day's settlement prices of the BFP milk futures contract and options thereon. They would require the equivalent of 400 000 lbs. of BFP milk to meet the anticipated order. The futures contract trades in quantities of 200 000 lbs. and the company would therefore use two option contracts to hedge their position.

The enquiry on the web site indicated that the prices of the futures contracts had settled as follows:

February: $9.65 per 100 lbs.;
March: $10.01 per 100 lbs.; and
April: $10.26 per 100lbs.

Table 6-12. A selling hedge in a normal market using put options

Cash Market	Futures Market		Basis
Feb. 'Long' 400000 lbs.@ $9.25	Feb. Long Two April 1025 Puts	$10.25	1.00 Under
	Feb. Underlying April Futures	$10.27	1.02 Under

This clearly shows that the market was in contango, but not very strongly so. Depending on the exact price of milk and the current interest rate, which taken together establishes the total interest portion of the carrying cost, the carrying charges for BFP milk was around $0.85 per month per 100 lbs. This is the figure that the treasurer uses to base his calculations on. As against that, the deferred futures were trading at a premium of $0.36 (March/February) and $0.25 (April/March), respectively.

Having also accessed that part of the web site that showed the previous day's settlement prices of the options, the treasurer telephoned the company's commodity futures broker. He got hold of her before the market opening and put in an order to buy two CME April BFP milk 1025 puts at $0.43 stop. Later in the morning the broker called back with a fill at $0.43. The company's hedged situation is shown in Table 6-12.

The company is not strictly speaking long the cash milk, because they have not produced it yet. They will however be long since that is essentially the producer's cash position. They are making a sale in the futures market as a placeholder for a sale they know that they will have to make in the future.

The hedge basis, calculated on the spot price used in the quote and the strike price of the puts, is 1.00 under as indicated in Table 6-12. The market does from time to time go into backwardation, a fact of which the treasurer is well aware. Nevertheless, because he intends to hold the hedge to a time as close as possible to the delivery of the futures contract, he knows that the greatest probable 'loss' on this hedge is $1.00, give or take a few cents.

The two possibilities, namely that of a rise in price and that of a decline in price can now be discussed.

the price rises

A rise in price is obviously a favourable price move for the dairy company. The question to be resolved is therefore whether or not a hedge using options on futures will allow the company to profit from a favourable price move. Keep in mind that a perfect hedge allows for no improvement in the hedged position.

Assume that when the company receives the order for milk at the end of March, spot BFP milk is $10.34. At the same time the April BFP milk futures contract is trading at $10.86. The treasurer needs to take no action in order to lift the hedge, because the two put options are not in the money. He merely allows them to expire out of the money. The treasurer then calculates the result of the hedge, which is shown in Table 6-13.

The actual selling price of the milk to the Dairy farm, after taking the option premium into account, was $10.44 ($10.87 actual price received − $0.43 loss on the futures). This

Table 6-13. Result of a selling hedge in a normal market, using put options after a price rise

Cash Market		Futures Market		Basis
Feb. Long 400000 lbs.@	$9.25	Feb. Long Two April 1025 Puts $10.25		1.00 Under
March Short 400000 lbs.@	$10.87	Feb. Premium Paid	$0.43	
Profit:	$1.62	Loss:	$0.43	
		Feb. Underlying April Futures	$10.27	1.02 Under
		Mar. Underlying April Futures	$10.83	0.04 Over
				Change: +1.06

is a $1.19 improvement on the price that the treasurer wanted to hedge. It represents a profit of $1.19 per 100 lbs. over the anticipated price of $9.25 ($10.44 net price received − $9.25 price originally hedged).

The strengthening of the market is favourable for the selling hedge. The selling hedge will always show a profit when the basis strengthens. This would be true no matter whether straight futures contracts or options on futures were used for the hedge. If a straight futures hedge had been used in the above instance, the result would also have been an improvement on the hedged price, but the hedge with the options gave the best result. A futures hedge would have resulted in a net price to the company of $10.31 ($9.25 originally hedged price + $1.06 basis change). The hedge with options is thus definitely of value in the case of a favourable price move occurring.

Nevertheless, the cost of a premium does present a problem. In a hedge using options, the price of the underlying must always first move by at least as much as the amount of the option premium, before it becomes effective as a hedge or before it will allow any advantage in respect of a favourable price move. There are two factors inhibiting the effectiveness of any exchange-traded option as a hedge.

The first factor is that the strike prices are pre-set at certain intervals. If the first strike out of the money is used for the hedge, the hedger enjoys no protection for the difference between the price of the underlying and the strike price of the option. Buying the first option in the money does not solve the problem either. That in the money option will entail paying that much higher a premium.

The second factor is the premium itself. The price of the underlying must move adversely by more than the premium of the option before any protection is given by the option. These two factors operate against the effectiveness of the protection afforded by an option against an adverse price move. Whether that is compensated for by the incurring of less risk is a matter that risk managers must decide for themselves. The risks presented by straight futures hedges are clearly illustrated in the examples and their iterations that were dealt with in the previous sections of this chapter.

the price declines

In the next discussion, the selling hedge will be examined, using options under conditions where the price of the underlying commodity has declined. For this purpose, it will be

Table 6-14. Result of a selling hedge in a normal market using put options, after a price decline

Cash Market			Futures Market		Basis
Feb. Long 400000 lbs.@	$9.25		Feb. Long Two April 1025 Puts	$10.25	1.00 Under
March Short 400000 lbs.@	$8.54		Feb. Premium on Put Options	$0.43	1.00 Under
Loss:	$0.71		March Short Two April Futures	$10.25	0.04 Over
			March Long Two April Futures	$8.50	Change: +1.04
			Profit:	$1.75	
			Feb. Underlying April Futures	$10.27	1.02 Under
			Mar. Underlying April Futures	$8.50	0.04 Over
			Potential Profit:	$1.77	Change: +1.06

assumed that when the dairy company lifts the hedge, the spot price of BFP milk has declined to $8.54 per 100 lbs. The April futures contract is trading at $8.50 per 100 lbs. on the CME.

The put options held by the company are in the money and the treasurer instructs their futures broker to exercise them. At the same time, an order is put in to buy two CME April BFP futures contracts. The two long positions will offset the two short futures positions that will be assigned to the company as a result of the exercise of the options. The broker later reports back that the order was filled at $8.50. The result of the hedge is shown in Table 6-14.

Leaving aside the premium of $0.43 paid on the put options, the price received on the sale of the milk amounts to $10.29 ($8.54 actual price + $1.75 profit on the futures). This compares with the result of a straight futures hedge which would have resulted in a net price of $10.31 ($9.25 hedged price + $1.06 basis change.). The $0.02 difference between the results, even if the option premium is disregarded, is accounted for by the $0.02 difference in the basis move. The difference in the basis moves is because the strike price of the option was $0.02 closer to the spot market price than the actual price of the futures was, thus giving a $0.02 narrower basis at the outset. This again demonstrates the effect of one of the two previously discussed factors that inhibit the effectiveness of exchange-traded options.

Taking account of the premium paid, the net price received on the milk was $9.86 per 100 lbs. ($8.54 actual price received + $1.75 profit on futures − $0.43 premium paid). This still constitutes a $0.61 improvement on the hedged price ($9.86 net receipts after hedge − $9.25 hedged price). The net improvement is also explained by $1.75 profit on the futures − $0.71 loss in the cash market − $0.43 premium on the puts = $0.61.

On the basis that the purpose of a selling hedge is to give protection against an adverse downward move in the price of the underlying, the result in the example was however, totally adequate.

discussion: the result of the hedge

The last two iterations of hedging with options demonstrate that they are effective hedging instruments. They afford protection against an adverse price move, although two inhibiting factors remain. A hedge with futures will likely provide better protection against an adverse move. However, options allow greater opportunity for profit on a favourable move in the price of the underlying instrument. Since the hedger starts from the proposition that the move of the price of the underlying is an unknown, it is impossible to say at the start whether hedging with an option or futures contracts will be the most advantageous.

It is apparent that the discussion of the relative advantages of using options to hedge over using straight futures is an unending one. There are too many variables to which the respective instruments are subject to ever give a final answer. The advantage of the one over the other will always only be manifest after the event. In the end, it is up to management in every business to determine how they favour the one above the other. Some clear guidelines could be laid down by management on using either the one or the other.

Nevertheless, in a hedge with options, a better outcome will be obtained in a more volatile underlying market. On the selling hedge using options, market volatility will improve the odds that the protection afforded by the option against an adverse upward price move will bear fruit. It will also increase the likelihood that the opportunity afforded by options to take advantage of a favourable move will be meaningful.

THE SELLING HEDGE USING SYNTHETIC SHORT FUTURES IN AN INVERTED MARKET

The synthetic futures and synthetic options that will be dealt with here achieve variations in results that should be carefully considered, since they might provide certain benefits that could be specifically sought by management. They are known as synthetics because they are positions created by using combinations of options or options and futures that give the same profit/loss profile as a straight futures position or that of a different option. The advantages and disadvantages of using each of the synthetic instruments can only be demonstrated by comparing the results of their use to the results obtained when the direct instrument is used.

A synthetic short futures position is created by buying a put option and simultaneously selling a call option at the same strike price. The advantage is that, depending on the strikes that are selected, the premium gained by selling the call will partly or completely offset the premium paid for the put. The net cost position should be a small profit on the premiums, a zero cost situation or a relatively small cost to take in the position. The net combined profit/loss profile of this position is the same as that of a short futures position. If the price rises, the put will gain value while, if the price drops, the call will lose value. The comparative advantage or disadvantage of this strategy will now be investigated.

The example of the oil refinery will be revisited to enable some comparisons to be made. The basic facts of the example remain the same. Assume that instead of using put

Table 6-15. A selling hedge using synthetic futures in an inverse market

Cash Market	Futures Market		Basis
Nov. Long Brent Crude $25.97	Nov. Short March Puts	$23.50	2.47 Over
	Nov. Long March Calls	$23.50	
	Profit on Premium:	$0.25	
	Nov. Underlying March Futures	$23.75	2.22 Over

options to hedge the position, as was done in previous iterations of the example, the treasurer decides to make use of synthetic futures.

She has the choice of buying the 2400 slightly ITM puts while selling the OTM 2400 calls, or buying the OTM 2350 put while selling the ITM 2350 calls. She decides to use the second combination as it allows her to start her position at a profit. The ITM options will have a higher price than the OTM options. The income from selling ITM options will thus realise a profit over the amount paid for the OTM options.

She therefore contacts the company's broker and instructs him to buy three IPE March Brent Crude 2350 puts at $1.53 stop and to sell three IPE March Brent Crude 2350 calls at $1.75 stop. Later he reports back that both orders were filled at the stop prices. The hedged position is now as illustrated in Table 6-15.

The synthetic short futures thus established has a profit/loss profiled as if the futures were bought at a price of $23.50. In the case of the previous hedge where put options were used in a normal market, the position left a difference between the actual price of the futures and the strike price of the option of $0.02. In that case, this constituted one of the two factors that inhibited the effectiveness of the hedge. The option only afforded protection from the time the futures price reached the strike price. The company is 'self-insured' for the difference.

In the present case, the synthetic futures seem to suffer from the same disadvantage, but the disadvantage is more apparent than real. The reason is that the net result of taking in the position has already realised a profit of $0.25 per barrel. The cash in the kitty thus bridges the gap between the synthetic futures price and the actual futures price, placing them on a par. The net result of the situation will now be investigated through a number of iterations.

the price rises

The same price assumptions will be made as was made in the first round of iterations when discussing the hedge with options. Therefore, it will be assumed that when the oil refinery started taking orders for fuel in February for delivery in March, the spot price of Brent Crude was $27.45. It will further be assumed that the March futures contract was trading at around $27.00.

Thus, in the present iteration, the put option is out of the money and the short call option is in the money. The short call option cannot be exercised at the behest of the option writer. Since the option has been held up to its expiration, it will not be practical to

Table 6-16. Result of a selling hedge in an inverted market, using synthetic short futures, after a price rise

Cash Market		Futures Market		Basis
Nov. Long Brent Crude	$25.97	Nov. Short March Calls	$23.50	} 2.47 Over
Feb. Short Brent Crude	$27.45	Nov. Long March Puts	$23.50	
Profit:	$1.48	Profit on Premium:	$0.25	0.20 Over
		Feb. Short March Futures	$23.50	Change: −2.27
		Feb. Long March Futures	$27.25	
		Loss on Futures:	$3.75	
		Net Loss After Premium:	$3.50	
		Nov. Underlying March Futures	$23.75	2.22 Over
		Feb. Underlying March Futures	$27.25	0.20 Over
				Change: −2.02

buy the option back. There will not be any sellers. Thus, the broker buys an equivalent number of futures contracts to automatically offset the short futures contracts he knows will be assigned to the company upon expiration of the calls in the money. The OTM put option is allowed to expire.

Assume that the order for long IPE March Brent Crude futures contracts is filled at $27.25. When the put option expires out of the money, it has no value and consequently the premium that was paid on the purchase of the options is forfeited. The profit that was originally realised by selling the more expensive ITM call while buying the less expensive OTM put is kept by the company and is calculated as part of the result of the hedge. The hedge result is shown in Table 6-16.

The result of the hedge is thus that the net price received on the sale of the oil is $23.95 ($27.45 − $3.50 loss on the futures). This is exactly the same result that would have been obtained had futures contracts been used in the hedge ($25.97 hedged price − $2.02 loss on the futures = $23.95). Synthetic futures are thus equally effective in an upward price move of the underlying as straight futures contracts are.

the price declines

All the assumptions will again remain as they were in the second iteration of the example. It is thus assumed that when the cash market purchase of the fuel is made, the spot price of Brent Crude has declined $21.45. The March futures contract was trading around $21.30. The put is thus in the money, but the call option is out of the money.

The treasurer instructs the company's broker to exercise the put options held by the company and at the same time to buy an equal number of futures contracts. The broker fills the order to buy futures contracts at $21.25. The result of the hedge is as shown in Table 6-17. The calls are allowed to expire out of the money.

This iteration again demonstrates that a short or selling hedge consistently results in a loss on the hedge in an inverted market. The net selling price of the oil, after taking the

Table 6-17. Result of a short hedge in an inverted market using synthetic short futures, after a price decline

Cash Market	Futures Market		Basis
Nov. Long Brent Crude@ $25.97	Nov. Long March Puts	$23.50	2.47 Over
Feb. Short Brent Crude@ $21.45	Nov. Short March Calls	$23.50	
Loss: $4.52	Profit on Premium:	$0.25	
	Feb. Short Futures@	$23.50	2.47 Over
	Feb. Long Futures@	$21.25	0.20 Over
	Profit:	$2.25	
	Net Profit After Premium:	$2.50	Change: −2.27
	Nov. Underlying March Futures	$23.75	2.22 Over
	Feb. Underlying March Futures	$21.25	0.20 Over
			Change: −2.02

hedge into account, is $23.95 ($21.45 actual price paid + $2.50 net profit on the futures). The net profit on the futures is calculated by adding the $0.25 profit on the original purchase and sale of the respective options, to the $2.25 profit realised on the short and offsetting long positions of the futures contracts. The result is exactly the same as the one that would have been attained if straight futures had been used: $25.97 budgeted cost − $2.02 basis change = $23.95.

discussion: the result of the hedge

The fact that the net result of this iteration is exactly identical to the previous result is because the basis changes were the same: a weakening of the basis from $2.22 over to $0.20 over. The interposition of the options to achieve a synthetic position thus makes no difference to the overall outcome. If the results are identical, the question then arises what the reason is, if any, that would induce one to use synthetic futures rather than futures or vice versa. The answer concerns a particular company's overall strategy. There is in fact a potential difference between using one rather than the other.

Using the synthetic futures to its full potential involves spending more time and energy on the hedge than is required when using a straight futures hedge. The synthetic option allows a dynamic strategy to be followed because it is made up of two options.

Consider that if, in a hedge with futures contracts, the price of the underlying starts rising, there is very little adjustment that can profitably be made. It is true that one could offset the futures position in order to stop the loss on it, but then the protection against a downward move will not be in place. There is therefore considerable danger in trying to hedge by 'jumping' in and out of futures. Indeed, experience shows that this is a course of action that should be avoided altogether.

On the other hand, in synthetic futures, the short call can be bought back if the price of the underlying is seen to make a substantial upward move. If the call is bought back, most of the profit on the original purchase and sale will be lost, but this must be balanced against the gain on the hedge because of the favourable price move. Furthermore, if the put option is left intact, the protection against an adverse move is maintained.

Another consideration is that, as far as the short call option is concerned, time is in the hedger's favour. Time decay will cause the price of the call to decline thereby making it cheaper to buy back after some time has elapsed. If the futures price trends down again, a call can be shorted above the then marked price. That may re-establish the original profit on the position. The short call and the long put will then no longer be at the same strike, but they don't need to be.

This latter strategy will result in a very effective and extremely profitable hedge on occasions where the price is volatile. However, it will be apparent from the discussion that in order to take advantage of the possibilities afforded by a hedge using synthetic short futures, a firm will have to be prepared to spend both time and effort on monitoring the hedge. This may or may not be acceptable. It is a matter that each business must decide for itself based on its own circumstances.

THE SHORT HEDGE USING SYNTHETIC SHORT FUTURES IN A NORMAL MARKET

The same example as the one previously employed in illustrating the selling hedge with long puts in a normal market will be used. In this iteration, it will be assumed that the company's treasurer decides to hedge with synthetic futures rather than with short puts. In the previous example it was noted that the most advantageous way, and in fact the only correct way of establishing a short synthetic futures position, is by buying the put at the first strike out of the money and by selling the ITM call at the same strike.

In the example of the dairy farm that will also be used in this iteration, it was assumed in the previous iteration that the price of April futures at the time that the hedge is established is $10.27. Given that scenario, the strike to be used is the 1025 strike, since that is the strike of the first put out of the money and the first call strike in the money. Consequently, the treasurer instructs the company's broker in February to buy two CME BFP milk 1025 puts at $0.43 stop and simultaneously to sell two CME BFP milk 1025 calls at $0.45 stop. The orders are filled at the stop prices. The hedged situation now appears in Table 6-18.

Note that although the prices and the contracts are entirely different to the previous example that demonstrated a hedge using synthetic futures in an inverted market, this synthetic futures hedge is again equal to the hedge using straight futures. If the profit on the premium is added to the basis of the synthetic futures, the result is a basis of 1.02 under. This is identical to what the basis on a straight futures hedge would be, as is indicated in Table 6-18.

the price rises

As was the case in the first iteration, it will be assumed that when the milk is sold to the client, the spot price has risen to $10.87 and April futures are trading at around $10.80.

Table 6-18. A selling hedge in a normal market, using synthetic short futures

Cash Market	Futures Market		Basis
Feb. Long 400000 lbs.@　$9.25	Feb. Long Two April 1025 Puts	$10.25	1.00 Under
	Feb. Short Two April 1025 Calls	$10.25	
	Profit on the Premium:	$0.02	
	Feb. Underlying April Futures	$10.27	1.02 Under

The call is in the money and it is automatically exercised against the company upon expiration. Just before expiry, the treasurer gives instructions to the company's broker to buy two April BFP milk futures contracts. They will offset the two short futures contracts that will be assigned to the company upon the expiration of the ITM short calls. Two contracts are consequently bought at a price of $10.83. The long put is allowed to expire out of the money. The result of the hedge is set out in Table 6-19.

The net price received for the milk after taking the result of the hedge into account is $10.31 ($10.87 actual price − $0.56 net loss on the futures market). Predictably, the result is again identical to the result that would have been obtained if the hedge had been established with straight futures contracts: $9.25 budgeted price + $1.06 basis change = $10.31. Another constant that is as expected as it is apparent, is that there has been a profit on the hedge. The profit of course equals the basis change. The basis change in the synthetic futures is in fact equal to the basis change in the futures, namely + 1.06. The basis change of + 1.04 for the synthetic futures, as indicated in Table 6-19, must be increased by the $0.02 profit realised on the premiums at the outset.

the price declines

As was the case in the previous iteration, the basic price information of the first iteration will be maintained. The assumption is therefore that at the end of March, when the order for the milk is received by the dairy, the spot price of BFP milk has declined to $8.54 per

Table 6-19. The result of a selling hedge in a normal market using synthetic short futures, after a rise in price

Cash Market		Futures Market		Basis
Feb. Long 400000 lbs. Milk	$9.25	Feb. Long Two April 1025 Puts	$10.25	1.00 Under
March Short 400000 lbs. Milk	$10.87	Feb. Short Two April 1025 Calls	$10.25	
Profit:	$1.62	Profit on the Premium:	$0.02	
		March: Short Two April Futures	$10.25	1.00 Under
		March: Long Two April Futures	$10.83	0.04 Over
		Loss on Futures:	$0.58	
		Net Loss After Premiums:	$0.56	Change: +1.04
		Feb. Underlying April Futures	$10.27	1.02 Under
		Mar. Underlying April Futures	$10.83	0.04 Over
				Change: +1.06

Table 6-20. The result of a selling hedge in a normal market using synthetic futures, after a price decline.

Cash Market			Futures Market		Basis
Feb. Long 400000 lbs.@		$9.25	Feb. Long Two April 1025 Puts	$10.25	1.00 Under
March Short 400000 lbs.@		$8.54	Feb. Short Two April 1025 Calls	$10.25	
Loss:		$0.71	Profit on the Premium:	$0.02	
			Feb. Short April Futures@	$10.25	1.00 Under
			Feb. Long April Futures@	$8.50	0.04 Over
			Profit on the Futures:	$1.75	
			Net Profit After Premiums:	$1.77	Change: +1.04
			Feb. Underlying April Futures	$10.27	1.02 Under
			Mar. Underlying April Futures	$8.50	0.04 Over
					Change: +1.06

100 lbs. At the same time, April futures are trading at around $8.50 per 100 lbs. The call option is consequently out of the money and is allowed to expire. The put option is however, in the money and it is exercised against the company. Anticipatory to the exercise, the company's broker had been instructed to buy two BFP milk futures, which she managed to do at a price of $8.50. The result of the hedge is set out in Table 6-20.

The net profit on the futures markets amounts to $1.77 per 100 lbs. as indicated in Table 6-20. Taking into account this profit, the net selling price of the milk to the company is $10.31. This is again identical to the result that would have been obtained had the hedge been done with futures contracts instead of with option combinations: $9.25 budgeted cost + $1.06 basis change = $10.31.

discussion: the result of the hedge

All the iterations again demonstrate that once a hedge is in place, the direction of the price move is irrelevant. The result remains the same whether the price of the underlying rises or declines. In the case of a synthetic futures hedge, it is clear that it is just as effective as a hedge with straight futures. In all calculations, the brokerage and exchange fees have been ignored, since they are minutiae in relation to hedging the numbers that are encountered in hedging. Nevertheless, they are an expense that will have to be taken into account.

The only disadvantage that a synthetic futures would therefore have would be that it involves more trading costs. That is because, in order to establish the hedge, two positions have to be taken in options against every one taken in a futures hedge. Furthermore, when a synthetic futures hedge is lifted, additional futures trades are required to offset the futures positions that are assigned. The multiplicities of trades that increase trading costs are therefore the only real difference between the two strategies.

However, the flexibility and real expectation of a far-improved outcome on the hedge, especially in an inverse market where a loss on the hedge is otherwise unavoidable, makes the synthetic futures a better choice. Nevertheless, there is no reason to make use of this more complex and time-consuming instrument if the business does not have any real intention or capacity to take advantage of the flexibility offered by it. Then the additional trading costs, small as they may be, are indeed merely a waste of good money.

THE SELLING HEDGE USING SYNTHETIC LONG PUT OPTIONS

This is the final hedging instrument that will be the subject of discussion in this book. There are other possible combinations of instruments, but the main ones that should primarily be mastered and used are the ones discussed herein. These are the major futures instruments and between them, they should satisfy the hedging needs and preferences of most businesses.

The synthetic long put, like the synthetic short futures, adds a certain flexibility that is lacking in a straight options position. This will become clear as the discussion progresses. Nevertheless, all such advantages come at a price. There will be additional trading costs, but more importantly, it will require more time and resources from the person or persons who are entrusted with the carrying out of hedging strategies in a firm.

A synthetic short put is created by selling a futures contract and buying a call at the first strike out of the money. The short futures position will profit from a fall in price. The long call will profit from a rise in the price of futures, but this gain in value will be neutralised by the loss in value of the short futures position. The 'premium' of the synthetic put equals the premium paid for the long call. Assessing the profit/loss profile of the position at option expiry, it appears that the potential for profit on a fall in price is unlimited while the maximum loss that can be incurred will be the loss of the premium on the long call. This corresponds exactly to the profit/loss profile of a long put. It is also interesting to note that the profit/loss profile corresponds to a put option with the same strike as the strike of the call option.

It will be advantageous to compare the outcome of the following hedges with the outcome of hedges using normel short puts. Therefore, the same examples will be used to demonstrate the former as were used to demonstrate the latter.

For the purposes of this example, it will be assumed that the treasurer of the oil refinery telephones the company's broker and instructs him to sell the required number of IPE March Brent Crude futures contracts at $23.75. The 2400 strike is the first call strike out of the money and the broker is instructed to buy an equal number of IPE March Brent Crude 2400 calls at $1.53. The broker later reports back that all the orders were filled at the limit prices.

The net position of the company now constitutes a synthetic long put. The synthetic long put has a nominal strike of 2400, which is the same strike than the strike of the long put in the first iteration of the example. The cost of the synthetic option's premium is also substantially less than the premium of the long put in the previous iteration. The hedged position of the company now appears as shown in Table 6-21.

Table 6-21. A selling hedge using a synthetic long put option

Cash Market		Futures Market		Basis
Nov. Long 3000 Barrels@	$25.97	Nov. Long Three March Calls	$24.00	1.97 Over
		Nov. Premium on Calls	$1.53	2.22 Over
		Nov. Short Three March Futures@	$23.75	
		Nov. Underlying March Futures	$23.75	2.22 Over

Since the oil market is inverse in the example, the result of the hedge will first be investigated under inverse market conditions.

THE SELLING HEDGE USING SYNTHETIC LONG PUTS IN AN INVERSE MARKET

the price rises

Assume firstly that the price rises. When the oil refinery starts shipping its orders during the first half of February, the spot price of Brent Crude has risen to $27.45 per barrel. The March futures contracts are trading at $27.23 and the call options are thus in the money.

The treasurer immediately instructs the company's broker to lift the hedge by exercising the March Brent Crude calls. The long futures contracts that will be assigned to the company as a result of the exercise of the ITM calls will automatically offset the short futures positions already held by the firm. The result of the hedge is set out in Table 6-22.

Because the price of the underlying futures contract moved favourably, the option is expected to allow some profit. The condition is of course that the price move has been big enough to neutralise the cost of the premium. In this case, there has been no major price shift, but it has nevertheless been sizeable enough at least to allow a net profit of $1.70 per barrel. This equals the $1.70 net profit shown by the hedge where straight long puts were used. As in the case with synthetic futures, it can be said that on a favourable move in the price of the underlying, a hedge using a long put option will be equal to a hedge using a synthetic long put option.

The effect of the hedge is thus to decrease the price received by the refinery from $29.45, being the price that was actually received, to a net received price of $27.67 ($29.45 actual receipt − $1.78 loss after premium).

The next iteration will serve to examine whether the hedge using synthetic options grants as much protection against an adverse price move, as the hedge with straight put options.

Table 6-22. The result of a selling hedge in an inverse market using synthetic puts, after a price rise

Cash Market		Futures Market		Basis
Nov. Long Brent Crude	$25.97	Nov. Long March 2400 calls	$24.00	2.47 Over
Feb. Short Brent Crude	$29.45	Nov. Premium Paid:	$1.53	
Profit:	$3.48	Nov. Short March Futures	$23.75	2.22 Over
		Feb. Long March Futures	$24.00	(Assigned)
		Loss:	$0.25	
		Net Loss After Premium:	$1.78	
		Nov. Underlying March Futures	$23.75	2.22 Over
		Feb. Underlying March Futures	$27.25	0.20 Over
				Change: −2.02

the price declines

For the purposes of this iteration, the same basic information that was used in the first iteration will be kept intact. Only now, it will be assumed that there was a decline in the price of Brent Crude.

When the company placed its order for fuel in the first week of February, the spot price of Brent Crude had dropped to $21.45 per barrel. The market was still in backwardation and March futures were trading at $21.25. The long call options were out of the money and were consequently allowed to expire. The result of the hedge is illustrated in Table 6-23.

The loss in the cash market, which is due to the decline in price under the budgeted figure, can now be offset against the net profit in the futures market. The profit in the futures market is of course, limited by the premium paid on the long calls.

The result of the hedge is that the $21.45 price actually received by the company is augmented by the $0.97 net profit on the futures to realise a net receipt of $22.42 per barrel of crude. The result is identical to the result obtained when a straight long put was used in the hedge.

discussion: the result of the hedge

As was the case with a hedge using straight put options, the success of the strategy depends on the size of the adverse or favourable move. From the examples demonstrated, it appears that there is no difference between making use of a synthetic put or of a straight put. When option prices are perfectly priced, this will be the case. However, it must be pointed out that the results will not necessarily always be exactly the same. Price discrepancies between options of different types and different strikes will occur on the same day. At best it can be said that using synthetic options or using straight options will give a very similar result.

As was the case with synthetic futures, the real difference does not lie in the result that will automatically occur, it lies in the flexibility that a synthetic position affords the user.

Table 6-23. The result of a selling hedge in an inverse market using synthetic puts, after a price decline

Cash Market		Futures Market		Basis
Nov. Long Brent Crude	$25.97	Nov. Long March Calls	$24.00	2.47 Over
Feb. Short Brent Crude	$21.45	Nov. Premium Paid:	$1.53	2.22 Over
Loss:	$4.52	Nov. Short March Futures@	$23.75	0.20 Over
		Feb. Long March Futures@	$21.25	Change: −2.02
		Profit:	$2.50	
		Net Profit After Premium:	$0.97	
		Nov. Underlying March Futures	$23.75	2.22 Over
		Feb. Underlying March Futures	$21.25	0.20 Over
				Change: −2.02

An example will illustrate this. Assume that the price of the underlying futures contract declines below the next option strike. The hedge now benefits from the profit being made on the short futures. If the call option is then sold while a call at the lower strike above the market price of the futures is simultaneously bought, the potential to realise a greater profit on a rise in price is increased. This will result from the strike of the synthetic long put being at a lower level from whereon up, profits might be taken. This strategy can be repeated every time the price drops by a further strike, until it eventually rises, as it might well do if sufficient time to expiry is available. The risk in this strategy is that losses will accumulate because each long call will be sold at a loss as the futures price declines.

THE SELLING HEDGE USING SYNTHETIC LONG PUTS IN A NORMAL MARKET

The purpose of the hedge is still to protect the hedger against a fall in price of the underlying commodity, but to make use of synthetic long put options. In this iteration, it will be assumed that when the treasurer got hold of the company's broker, he put in an order to sell two CME April BFP milk futures at $10.27 stop.

At the same time, the treasurer put in an order to buy two CME April milk 1050 calls at $0.45 stop. He used the 1050 strike, as this was the first strike at which calls were out of the money. Later in the morning the broker called back and reported that all the orders had been filled at the stops. The company's hedged situation is shown in Table 6-24.

The two possibilities, namely that of a rise in price and that of a decline in price can now be discussed.

the price rises

For the purpose of this iteration, it will again be assumed that when the company received the order for the required milk inventory at the end of March, spot BFP milk is $10.34. At

Table 6-24. A selling hedge in a normal market using synthetic put options

Cash Market	Futures Market		Basis
Feb. Long 400000 lbs.@ $9.25	Feb. Long Two April 1025 Calls	$10.50	1.25 Under
	Feb. Premium on Calls:	$0.45	
	Feb. Short Two Milk Futures@	$10.27	1.02 Under
	Feb. Underlying April Futures	$10.27	1.02 Under

the same time the April BFP milk futures contract is trading at $10.86. The treasurer telephones through to the broker and instructs her to lift the hedge.

The two long calls are in the money and the broker proceeds to exercise them. Two long futures positions are consequently assigned to the company at a price of $10.50.

When the fills are reported back to the treasurer, he calculates the result of the hedge as shown in Table 6-25.

The net price realised by the dairy company after all the costs of the hedge have been taken into account, is $10.30 per 100 lbs. The result is not identical to the result of the hedge with long options. In the hedge with long put options, the net selling price achieved was $10.44, which is a $0.14 improvement on the present situation. The difference is explained by the difference in strike prices. In the example where long puts were used, the strike selected for the puts was 1025, since this was the first strike at which puts were out of the money.

In the present case, the treasurer used the same argument in selecting the first call out of the money, because it was the cheaper of the two call options. Unfortunately, that argument fails in practice. The purpose of the present example is also to illustrate that when the strike for a synthetic option is selected, it must be the strike that would have been used had the actual, and not the synthetic option been used.

Assume that 1025 calls had been purchased in the present example as it had in the example with straight puts. The 1025 calls were priced at $0.45. When it was exercised, the long futures would have been assigned at a price of $10.25 and that would have

Table 6-25. Result of a selling hedge in a normal market using synthetic long puts, after a rise in price

Cash Market	Futures Market		Basis
Feb. Long 400000 lbs.@ $9.25	Feb. Short Two April 1050 Calls	$10.50	1.25 Under
March Short 400000 lbs.@ $10.87	Feb. Premium on Calls:	$0.34	
Profit: $1.62	Feb. Short Two April Futures@	$10.27	1.02 Under
	March Long Two April Futures@	$10.50	
	Loss:	$0.23	
	Net Loss After Premium:	$0.57	
	Feb. Underlying April Futures	$10.27	1.02 under
	March Underlying April Futures	$10.83	0.04 over
			Change: +1.06

resulted in only a $0.02 loss on the long and short futures positions. If this is added to the premium paid, it results in a total loss of only $0.47 being incurred, as against the $0.57 loss in the present case. When that loss is subtracted from the price actually received on the milk, it results in a net price of $10.40 being received.

It demonstrates that a better result would have been obtained had the same strike been used for the synthetic put than was used for the straight put. It is also interesting to note that the results of the two hedges would not be the same. This result is an example of price discrepancies that occur in option pricing in the market place.

the price declines

In the following iteration, the result of a hedge using synthetic long puts will be examined under normal market conditions where the price of the underlying commodity has declined. In this iteration, it will be assumed that the treasurer used a better strike selection when he originally bought the calls. The calls will therefore be treated as if they were bought at the 1025 strike rather than the 1050 strike. The only difference that it will make in the present instance, is the higher premium that would have had to be paid.

It will again be assumed that when the dairy company lifts their hedge, the spot price of BFP milk has declined to $8.54 per 100 lbs., and the April futures contract is trading at around $8.50. The call options are consequently out of the money and they are allowed to expire. The short futures positions that were taken up at the outset of the hedge are offset by a purchase of two April futures contracts. The order to buy two April futures contracts is filled at $8.50.

The result of the hedge is shown in Table 6-26.

Taking into account the premium of $0.45 paid on the call options, the actual price received for the milk comes to $9.86 ($8.54 actual price received + $1.32 profit on the futures market). The result is identical to the result obtained with the same hedge using straight long put options.

discussion: the result of the hedge

From the examples discussed, it is clear that using synthetic options in a selling hedge will usually give the same result as a hedge using straight options, although there are exceptions. If used to their full potential, synthetic options have definite advantages over using straight put options in a hedge.

The same comment however applies as was made with reference to the use of synthetic futures. Because a synthetic put involves two positions against the one position required for a straight options hedge, it involves greater trading costs. As has been pointed out, these costs are minimal in relation to the numbers at issue in a hedge and they are further dwarfed by the advantages to be gained.

The advantages to be gained are fully discussed earlier in this chapter. However, these advantages all follow from strategies that the make-up of synthetic options allow. Their use will require more time and resources to be spent on monitoring and managing the

Table 6-26. Result of a selling hedge in a normal market using synthetic long put options, after a price decline

Cash Market		Futures Market		Basis
Feb. Long 400000 lbs.@	$9.25	Feb. Long Two April 1025 Calls	$10.25	1.25 Under
March Short 400000 lbs.@	$8.54	Feb. Premium on Calls:	$0.45	
Loss:	$0.71	Feb. Short Two Milk Futures@	$10.27	1.02 Under
		March Long Two April Futures	$8.50	0.04 Over
		Profit:	$1.77	
		Net Profit After Premium:	$1.32	Change: +1.06
		Feb. Underlying April Futures	$10.27	1.02 Under
		March Underlying April Futures	$8.50	0.04 Over
		Potential Profit:	$1.77	Change: +1.06

hedge. If the business is willing to devote the necessary time and resources to this enterprise, the rewards will be forthcoming and they can add substantial value. However, if there is no intention, capacity or need in the business to make use of these strategies, then using synthetic options will serve no purpose.

COMPARATIVE TABLE ON THE DIFFERENCES BETWEEN A LONG AND A SHORT HEDGE

General overview: the control objective is to compare the basic structures and results of the two types of hedges

	User (Long) Hedge	Producer (Short) Hedge
Market condition		
Normal (contango)	The hedge will show a loss if held to the futures delivery month	The hedge will show a profit if held to the futures delivery month
Inverse (backwardation)	The hedge will show a profit if held to the futures delivery month	The hedge will show a loss to the futures delivery month
Hedging instrument		
Futures contracts	Long futures contracts	Short futures contracts
Options on futures	Long call options	Long put options
Synthetic futures	Synthetic long futures – long one call and short one put	Synthetic short futures – long one put and short one call
Synthetic options	Synthetic long call – long one futures contract and long one put	Synthetic long put – short one futures contract and long one call

CHECKLIST FOR THE REVIEW OF CHAPTER 6

General overview: the overall control objectives of the material dealt with in this chapter are to employ the short hedge with futures instruments to the best advantage of a business

	Key Issues	Illustrative Scope or Approach
6.1	How can the business protect its financial wellbeing from adverse price moves of commodities that it owns, possesses, produces or sells?	The company can protect its commodities values and selling prices by means of a producer's or short hedge in the futures. It is done by: ● Selling a futures contract for an appropriate delivery month ● Buying a put option ● Selling a synthetic futures contract. This is constructed by simultaneously buying a put option and selling a call option at the same strike price ● Buying a synthetic put option. This is constructed by simultaneously selling a futures contract and buying a call option at the strike where a put option will be nearest to the money
6.2	What effect will a rise or a decline in the price of the underlying commodity have on the result of a hedge?	● If the cash position of the business is fully hedged, price moves of the underlying commodity will not affect the outcome of the hedge in any way ● If the futures position is quantitatively smaller than the cash position, a drop in price will result in a loss in the cash market on the unhedged portion, while a rise in price will result in a profit on the unhedged portion ● If the futures position is quantitatively greater than the cash position, a drop in price will result in a profit in the futures on the excess, while a rise in price will result in a loss on the excess
6.3	What effect will it have on the hedge if the underlying market is in backwardation?	A selling hedge in an inverse market will result in a loss on the hedge, if it is held to the futures delivery month. The loss will be equal to the amount by which the basis weakens

continued

	Key Issues	Illustrative Scope or Approach
6.4	What effect will it have on the hedge if the underlying market is in contango?	A selling hedge in a normal market will result in a profit on the hedge, if it is held to the futures delivery month. The profit results from a strengthening of the basis. The maximum profit might exceed the cost of carry only marginally
6.5	What advantage, if any, will the business gain by using options on futures instead of straight futures contracts in a hedge?	• Conventional wisdom has it that options carry less risk than futures. This is certainly true if the profit/loss profiles of the two instruments are compared, but it is not so when they are properly used in a hedge • Its main advantage lies in the facility it creates of allowing a profit to be realised on a favourable price move of the underlying, which is not possible in a true hedge. The condition is that the price of the underlying must move sufficiently to neutralise the cost of acquiring the option • Options allow a variety of hedging strategies to be followed that can enhance the result of the hedge
6.6	What advantage, if any, will the business gain by using synthetic futures instead of straight futures contracts in a hedge?	A hedge with synthetic futures will give the same result as a hedge with simple futures taken at the same time The trading costs for the synthetic futures will be two to two-and-a-half times as much as the trading costs for a simple future hedge The flexibility of synthetic futures will allow certain hedging strategies to be used that are not available with a simple futures hedge
6.7	What advantage, if any, will the business gain by using synthetic options instead of straight options on futures in a hedge?	A hedge using synthetic options will give exactly the same result as a hedge using the straight option at the same strike price taken at the same time The trading costs for a synthetic options hedge will be two to two-and-a-half times as much as a hedge using straight options The flexibility of a synthetic option will allow additional hedging strategies to be used to enhance the result of a hedge

seven

creative commodity risk management

The purpose of this chapter is to give a general discussion of the material discussed in the previous chapters. It will be stressed that a business must be creative in its approach and execution of managing commodity risk. When it comes to managing commodity risk, it will be insufficient merely to keep on following traditional thinking and acting.

However, before creative thinking can be employed, the basics have to be secured. There are right ways and wrong ways to go about the task of managing risk. Every step requires proper analyses and there is room for parallel thinking and innovation along each one. Let it be said from the outset that it is not a task to be undertaken lightly or abruptly. Preparation is necessary. If the right steps are taken in the right logical order and the task is taken seriously, then great advantages will flow therefrom. If the planning and preparation is not done properly, the consequences can be seriously harmful.

There are a number of steps to be taken sequentially. They cannot be spelled out substantively in a book such as this, because the detail of each step will have to be thrashed out within the company itself. However, it will be attempted to indicate the principal steps that need to be taken as well as some guidelines to be followed in their execution. Once these measures have been taken and the necessary procedures are in place, the risk management process can start.

Creativity comes into its own when various strategies and options can be considered and then tailored to meet particular circumstances. Some suggestions will be made, but once again, the onus is on management to be creative in their approach. Nobody knows your business like you do. Nobody will be able to see the opportunities and dangers as well as you can. Therefore, no more than a general train of thought can be suggested here.

COMMODITY RISKS IN BUSINESS

The major types of risk facing a business are usually include market risk, operational risk, credit risk and liquidity risk. This list is not exhaustive. In the UK, the Turnbull report on internal control additionally mentions technological, legal, health, safety and environmental risks (Turnbull report published by ICAEW, 1999, Appendix, p. 13). In practice, these risk types cannot be compartmentalised unconditionally, since there is substantial overlapping. They are, however, useful distinctions for analysis and control purposes. Commodity risk forms part of market risk.

Market risk is variously defined, depending on the type of business involved. In the world of finance it is usually defined as the risk to an institution or business' financial condition resulting from adverse price or volatility moves of the assets contained in its portfolio. Although obviously correct, the definition is more applicable to fund and asset management companies than to businesses in general.

The reference to price moves of assets in a portfolio makes the definition far too restrictive for the purposes of general business. It is suggested that market risk is the risk that a business is exposed to as a result of adverse changes in prices and market conditions for its own goods and services, as well as for such goods and services that it makes use of in the normal course of its business.

It will serve the present purpose just to be reminded of the definition of commodity risk that is proposed in an earlier chapter:

> Commodity risk is the risk to a firm's financial condition resulting from adverse price moves and increases in the price volatility of such tangible or intangible commodities as are produced, held, traded and/or used by it in the course of its business.

The above definition will serve as a guide for further discussion. The definition does create its own imperatives. It targets commodities, the price moves of which influence a firm's financial condition. It stands to reason that if the price moves of a commodity influence the financial condition of a firm, the moves could be either adverse or beneficial. It is only the possibility of adverse moves that cause risk. Beneficial price moves create opportunity. Part of managing risk lies in the facility of eliminating, or at least containing risk, while at the same time not necessarily eliminating opportunity.

This sentiment is echoed by the UK's Turnbull report, paragraph 13, p. 5, where it states that

> a company's objectives, its internal organisation and the environment in which it operates are continually evolving and, as a result, the risks it faces are continually changing. A sound system of internal control therefore depends on a thorough and regular evaluation of the nature and extent of the risks to which the company is exposed. Since profits are, in part, the reward for successful risk-taking in business, the purpose of internal control is to help manage and control risk appropriately rather than to eliminate it.

ANALYSING THE RISK

The first step in risk management is thus to identify and analyse the nature and sources of commodity risks in a business. Identifying such commodities which give rise to financial risk in a particular business is a matter of analysis for every individual firm. Keeping in mind the definition of 'commodity', every firm should examine and record what commodities the firm owns, holds, or uses in some way. The previously discussed considerations that complicate the identification process must then be kept in mind

The result of such an analysis will probably surprise many managers in business. Thereafter, some calculations will show what influence their price moves have on the financial condition of the business. Only when this process has been completed, can the necessary risk management decisions be taken.

identifying the nature of commodity risk in a business

Having investigated what commodity risk is, it remains to discover exactly what the sources and nature of the risks are that threaten a particular business. As was suggested earlier, the first step is to identify the risk. This may seem like a pretty straightforward exercise, but it may involve more analysis than appears at first blush. As will become apparent from the discussion that follows, a number of strategic choices will have to be made in the process of identification and evaluation.

Markets continually trade all types of goods and services. Prices for goods and services are subject to all the forces prevalent in the marketplace at any one time, particularly supply and demand. Consequently, their prices are subject to random variation. It follows that businesses using them face the risk of adverse price movement.

As is also fully discussed in the two preceding chapters, what constitutes an adverse price movement is relative to the activities of the business concerned. For example, what constitutes an adverse price move for a transport operator that uses fuel oil constitutes a favourable price move for the refinery that produces the fuel. Similarly, a favourable move in the price in cotton for a cotton mill would be an adverse move for a clothing manufacturer. As will become apparent below, the above is also an oversimplification of the relative situation of the companies. Such rigorous views on the relative position of a company are traditional, but they are not conducive to finding optimal risk management solutions.

Nevertheless, both parties can manage their risk, and both can neutralise their risk by using the correct techniques. Selecting the correct technique is thus the following step to be taken. However, before the best technique can be selected, a business must decide in the case of each relevant commodity, how managing that particular risk will be approached.

The first decision is therefore a policy decision. The policy decision must be informed, insightful and flexible. However, flexibility must not give rise to vagueness. Having vague policies regarding the management of commodity risk will create more risk in itself. The company must lay down clear guidelines to be followed when managing commodity risks. Clear guidelines can only result from a thorough analysis and a thoughtful consideration of the possibilities and alternatives. Some of these will be discussed below. The discussion deals with the considerations that are appropriate when using futures and options on futures.

positioning the futures hedge

The first strategic choice is what the hedging position of the business will be regarding each of the commodity risks that it is exposed to. The question can be reduced to the question as to whether the company is, or should be a short hedger or a long hedger of the commodity concerned.

Many businesses enjoy the luxury of choice as to whether they want to regard themselves as producers or as users for the purposes of managing the risk regarding any particular commodity. As will be appreciated, each hedge has implications for the hedger that may be advantageous or disadvantageous, depending on other surrounding circumstances.

Consider for example, the clothing manufacturer mentioned above. In the normal course, the business is a user of cotton material and a producer of clothing. The underlying commodity is cotton and the prices of both the materials that they use, and of the clothes that they produce, are substantially influenced by the price of cotton. This will obviously not be the only factor influencing their overheads, but cotton can be singled out for the moment.

If the price of cotton increases, the overhead cost of the business increases. If they want to manage the cost of that overhead, they would be long hedgers of cotton on the futures markets. However, there may be other very important factors that dictate the timing of their purchases of material. For example, inventory orders may be based on a JIT (just in time) program. That could make hedging inventory purchases very difficult.

Whatever the reason, a company might, after close examination decide that hedging the price of their purchases of material would involve a lot of effort, cost or inconvenience and therefore would prefer to hedge its selling price. It is suggested however, that the most important possible consideration of the firm might be that the cotton market is often in backwardation. Consequently, it would be more profitable to use a short hedge in futures. Similarly, if a company found that the underlying market of any commodity is in contango, it must consider the possibility of positioning itself as a long hedger in futures.

If the company used a short hedge it would have to approach the hedge slightly differently from how it would have approached a long hedge. It would then not be hedging the buying price of its purchases, but it would be hedging the selling price of its clothing. If it hedged the buying price, it would have to anticipate its purchases of cotton material and hedge forward accordingly. If it were hedging the selling price of its product, it would be able to hedge after each actual purchase against a drop in the price during the time to sale or delivery of the manufactured goods.

Thus, in the normal course of business hedging the selling price of the product has nearly the same effect as hedging the purchase price of the raw material. If a firm makes its purchases of materials contingent upon considerations other than price, it may face price competition from competitors who bought their materials more cheaply.

Assume that the firm purchases its raw materials at the ruling spot price at the time that it acquires the materials. It then faces the risk that the price of the material may drop after its acquisition, but before the finished product has been sold and delivered. When the finished product comes onto the market it will have to compete with similar products. If the other products can be offered at a discount because the basic costs of materials were lower, the company will have a hard time of it. Such a development obviously debases the value of the firm's product and makes it difficult to survive in the market place against competitors who may have bought their materials slightly later and therefore enjoyed the advantage of a lower purchase price. The answer is to use a short hedge in the futures. The short futures hedge will show a profit that can be used to subsidise the selling price of the finished goods.

On the other hand, if prices of the material are low and the competitive position of the firm is good, then they need to protect themselves against an increase in price of their raw materials. Then a long hedge in the futures will protect the firm's production costs. Either course of action results in the firm remaining price competitive in the marketplace.

Most producers of goods, wholesale and retail merchants as well as import/export firms are in a similar position to the clothing manufacturer in the example. For the purposes of the argument it does not matter whether the product sold or delivered is acquired by the business concerned by means of purchase or manufacture, the hedging principle remains the same. The business concerned will mostly have the choice whether to regard themselves as long or short hedgers in any particular instance. There is an exception to this observation that will be dealt with presently.

The point here is firstly that the positioning alternatives and how they are to be approached for the purposes of hedging must be determined and properly calculated beforehand. As will also be apparent from the example, the business does not have to view itself permanently as either a short hedger or as a long hedger. They can be short hedgers of a particular commodity in one instance and be long hedgers of the same commodity in another.

There are thus a number of factors that a company will have to consider in deciding when to hedge short and when to hedge long when using futures contracts. Nevertheless, what is being suggested is that one of the pivotal factors that must be considered by a business in making this decision, is the condition of the market. If this consideration cannot be conclusive in any particular case, the consequences of a loss on the hedge must be quantified and dealt with. It is a consideration that must never be ignored and swept under the carpet.

There are other factors that must also dictate the nature of the hedge in particular circumstances. As was previously mentioned, circumstances may not always allow a choice of hedge. For example, if a business has given a fixed price quote, it will probably not have the luxury of choice in respect of that particular production. If the material to be used for the production is already in inventory, the firm faces no further risk on the price of the material, except with regard to the carrying charges that will be incurred.

However, if the material still has to be acquired at a deferred date in the future, the risk can only be that the price of the material will rise and thus be more expensive at the time that it must be acquired for the production of the order. The only possibility at that stage is a long hedge. If the market is in backwardation it will be advantageous to use a futures hedge. If it is in contango, then more attention will have to be given to strategy, as will be discussed later in this chapter.

Whenever quotes for any future delivery are called for, the opportunity to choose is at the time of quotation. The following considerations do not apply solely to a manufacturer but to any business that is involved in the sale or delivery of a commodity based product or service. Once a quote has been given the price structure of the quote will have to be hedged by means of a long hedge. This is known at the time the quotation is being prepared. It is also known that commodity futures or options will be used for the hedge. Therefore the prudent course is to look at the futures market at the time of preparation.

If the market is found to be in backwardation, the firm knows that its long hedge will be profitable. The firm therefore has the choice of using the current spot price as the basis of the quote or of using the futures price. Keep in mind that once hedged a rise or a drop in price will not affect the outcome, only the basis move will affect the hedge. It is known that the basis move will be favourable if it is held to the futures delivery month. A sound course of action would probably be to position the price somewhere between the current spot price and the futures price. The point is actually that the suggested procedure will allow the company to give a keen, firm price on its quote.

On the other hand, if on inspection the market is in contango and the futures price is above the present spot price, the only prudent course of action is to use the futures price as the basis of the quotation. It will seldom be the case that the futures price reflects the full cost of carry. The resulting quote will therefore be keener than if the full cost of carry was factored into the quoted price. If the cost of carry is ignored for the purposes of such a quotation, the company will in any event find itself in trouble on the quote. The company knows beforehand that it will not lose more on the hedge than it has provided for by using the futures price as its cost price.

The above discussion focuses on individual hedging decisions. It is clear that the complete hedging and risk management policy of a business should be based on guidelines that will allow different hedging decisions on different occasions. There should be no general hedging stance by a firm. Each hedge should be considered and structured according to the dictates of its own circumstances. It is thus the parameters within which the hedging decisions can be made that should to be indicated in the guidelines.

However, in order to demonstrate the analysis of the business more comprehensively, the example of the clothing manufacturer can be taken further. The business will also be making use of other commodities. These must be identified. Once identified, their individual input must be evaluated. In other words, what effect would an adverse price move in each individual commodity that makes up the overhead cost of a business, have on its financial wellbeing. This will screen those commodity risks that can be accepted from those that need to be hedged.

Assume that after investigation, the company finds that apart from cotton, its use of energy, in the form of natural gas and the cost of money are its greatest price risk factors that require to be hedged. Interest rates can be hedged by means of futures contracts, but since they are not strictly speaking commodities, a discussion on these falls outside the scope of this book. The company thus faces major risk to its operational cost from only two commodities. It must therefore determine its stance with regard to natural gas as well as to cotton.

The basic principles have been discussed above. Natural gas can be hedged from month to month. It depends therefore on what the state of the market is at the start of every period that the firm needs to hedge. Since its energy requirements will be a constant overhead it can anticipate its use for the period ahead and hedge its requirement s for the following month or more at a time.

It will be apparent that once again, the company must try to position itself having regard to the basis move. In a commodity such as natural gas, it would not seem feasible to position the company as a short hedger. However, there may be companies with special circumstances that might allow that position to be taken

It could also happen that for some unforeseen reason the sale and delivery of certain stock is delayed. If such stock has to be held onto it might well be profitable to consider hedging the overhead costs that went into its production on a short hedge. If it is a normal market, the profit on the basis movement will assist in defraying some of the cost of carry. Also, if a drop in price should occur, the goods could be sold at a lower price without incurring any additional loses. In this latter case the cost of energy that went into the production of that particular stock can also be hedged.

SELECTING THE RIGHT HEDGING INSTRUMENT

Having decided in a particular case whether the position that the company should take is a long or a short hedge, the consideration can be moved on the actual hedging instrument to be used.

If the chosen hedge position of the company will result in a profit on the hedge, the choice is simpler. The position can be well managed with a simple hedge using either straight futures contracts or using options on futures. The question is then really whether futures or options on futures should be used.

Keep in mind that if it is possible to hold the hedge until, or very close to the futures delivery month, there will be a profit on the hedge whether the price moves up or down. Under these conditions it is not correct to argue that options carry less risk than futures. That statement on the relative risks of the two instruments is only valid in general terms and specifically when the intended trading is speculative in nature. It is not a valid consideration in a hedge.

The market expectation of a company can also influence the selection of a hedging instrument. However, its view on whether or not the price of a particular commodity is likely to rise or fall should never play a role in the decision to hedge or not to hedge. If the price impact of a particular commodity is severe enough to impact on the financial wellbeing of a company it must be hedged. The cost of being wrong on a view of the market can have too many serious consequences. The chances of being wrong on a particular view of the market are usually pretty good. It is not a sound policy to gamble the financial future of a business on a market expectation.

choosing between futures and options to hedge

The choice between futures and options on futures should centre on the prospect of gain in case of a favourable price move of the underlying commodity. It is in this respect that the market expectation of a company can be brought into play.

The decision between futures and options can thus firstly be based on the company's market expectation. If the responsible people in a company expect the market to move favourably for the company, then it may be important to allow for the opportunity to gain on that move by using options for the hedge. A number of considerations apply in this case.

The first consideration in such a strategy is to price the option. The expected price move must be substantially more than the premium paid for the option, otherwise the costs are wasted. Against the option the hedging route must also be weighed how far out of the money it is. Keep in mind that an option will afford protection against an adverse price move only once the underlying futures price has moved to the strike price and beyond to cover the premium on the option. The breakeven point is thus as high as the premium of the option plus the difference between the current futures price and the strike price.

If the total calculated above is on the high side, another course of action involving options can be considered. The alternative is to buy an option that is slightly in the money and pay the additional price. The latter, namely to buy the first option in the money, can be a viable alternative. The first option in the money may represent better value for money because you may be paying less time value on it. The two options (the first option in the money and the first option out of the money) can be compared by deducting the value of the amount that the ITM option is in the money from its premium. How does its cost then compare with the cost of the other option that is completely out of the money? If its price is now lower than the price of the OTM option, it may be the better option to buy.

Then the price will have to move favourably first by the amount that the option is in the money and then by the cost of the option before it will allow any profit to be had from the price move. The breakeven point to the favourable side will have been increased. The company must therefore give serious consideration to how the premium on the option will be factored into the result of the hedge before embarking on a hedge with options.

An option does of course have the advantage that if the price clearly moves away from it, it can be sold back to the market to recoup some of its costs. Prices unfortunately have the nasty habit of turning around when you expect it least. If the price turns around after the option has been sold, the protection against an adverse move will have been lost. More premium will have to be expended in order to buy another option which may or may not be cheaper than the first one and which may or may not afford protection from the same strike as the first one.

This is too risky a strategy to employ as a hedge. It is strongly suggested that once an option strategy has been made and executed, one stays with it. No more than the premium can be forfeited and that is an element that must be dealt with when the hedging decision is made.

choosing between a futures hedge and a synthetic futures hedge

Once a choice has been made between using futures or options in a particular case, a further choice presents itself. The choice then is between using straight futures or options against using the synthetic version of the instrument. There are a number of elements to consider in making this choice.

In the case of synthetic futures, it has been demonstrated that if the hedge is approached in the same way, the synthetic option gives exactly the same result as the straight futures hedge would have given. It will involve more trading costs simply because more trades will be required to set up a synthetic futures hedge and to lift it.

Although these costs are minimal in comparison with the principal amounts involved, there is no reason to incur them if there is no overriding additional benefit. The major advantage of synthetic futures hedges is that they allow a flexible hedging strategy to be followed. This aspect will be dealt with under the relevant heading below. There is however another advantage that can be gained without taking too much trouble.

It has to be kept in mind that a synthetic futures hedge is really a hedge with options. The short option is used to defray the costs of buying the long option. The long option will give the protection against an adverse price move. Therefore a synthetic long futures will consist of a long call and a short put. The premium collected on the sale of the short put will defray the costs of buying the call option. The inverse holds true in the case of a synthetic short futures position.

When the price of the underlying moves in favour of the long option, time decay works in the hedger's favour. The short option rapidly loses value as the underlying price moves away from it and as its time to expiry becomes shorter. However, when the price moves against the long option and the short option starts gaining value, a loss is incurred. In a straight futures hedge the loss must be endured until the time that the hedge is lifted. Of course the loss on the futures is neutralised by the profit on the cash market. That is not at issue here. If the price move of the underlying causes a loss on the short option however, it need not be endured to the bitter end. Buying it back will offset the short option position.

The latter action will of course result in spending all or most of the money that was originally collected on the sale of the option. Then the hedger will be in the same position as if he had used a straight options hedge in the first place. Keep in mind that a loss-causing move of the underlying vis a vis the short option, will actually be a favourable move for the hedger in the spot market. Getting out of the short option will therefore allow the profit to be taken that option hedges allow.

In a sense therefore, the best of both worlds can be had with a synthetic futures. It can start off as a futures hedge, which means there is neither a premium cost, nor a strike price disadvantage before protection is obtained in the case of an adverse price move. Then it can change into a straight options hedge if the price of the underlying starts moving favourably for the hedger, allowing for a profit to be taken on the move.

A word of caution needs to be sounded at this stage. Although the above is correct in principle and in theory, it may be difficult to realise in practice. It would be unwise to close out the short option at the first indication that the price is moving favourably. Prices move up and down all the time. Sufficient time needs to be given for the situation to mature before any decision can be made. However, then it may be too late because most of the loss on the short option will already have been incurred.

As a general rule, it is suggested that the best course of action is to keep your finger away from the trigger after the hedge has been entered. Accept it as a futures hedge to start off with and do not fidget or fuss about it. Only adjust the hedge when you know the price trend is definite.

The business will in any event never be worse off than if a straight futures hedge had been entered in the first place. If the firm has managed to stay on the right side of the known basis move, a profit on the hedge is ensured whatever else happens.

Nevertheless, there is quite apparently no inherent advantage to the synthetic futures hedge unless a particular strategy is decided upon. Hedging strategy will be discussed later.

choosing between an options hedge and a synthetic options hedge

As far as the choice between straight options and synthetic options are concerned, there may be an advantage in using synthetic options, even if no particular hedging strategy is decided upon.

As is demonstrated in the two previous chapters, the net result of a hedge with synthetic options is virtually identical to the result obtained with straight options. However, it may be that the long option used for creating the net synthetic option position is cheaper than the straight option. This is a matter easily determined by inspection of the two prices. Although this does not influence the net result of the hedge, it may involve less expenditure on option premium at the start.

The second advantage of a synthetic option is that the futures position can be covered (closed out) when the underlying price moves in favour of the option. Remember that the structure of a synthetic option is actually that of a futures position, but the futures position is hedged with an option to neutralise the loss if the price moves adversely in respect of the futures position. If the futures position is covered, the net favourable price move on the long option can be thus realised. A price move that favours the long option will also be a favourable move for the hedger in the cash market. This means that the profit realised on the long option will be additional to the profit realised in the cash market. A synthetic option may therefore start of as a hedge and end up as a means of leveraging a profitable price move of the commodity.

It is suggested that this course of action should not be easily adopted. Great caution should be exercised before the futures position is covered. The purpose of the position is to hedge and not to speculate. As soon as the futures position is exited, the protection on an adverse move is lost. However, it is fast, easy and cheap to take up a new futures position if the price turns around. Nevertheless, jumping in and out of futures positions is not advisable and invites disaster if there is any slip. The main thing is to be aware of the possibility of making such a move.

There are two conditions to be met before exiting the futures position and maintaining the long option position is advisable. The first condition is that it can only be done when there is reasonable certainty that the price is in a favourable trend for the foreseeable future. If the price moves favourable by quite a substantial amount and then turns back in the other direction, it can be extremely advantageous to take up a futures position again leaving a substantial profitable gap between where it was exited and where it is entered the second time.

The second condition is that the futures position must be offset before too great a loss has been incurred on it. If the loss on the futures has been substantial already, there is a great danger that the price is not going to continue in that direction for very much longer or very much further. In that case the manoeuvre holds a lot of danger. The eventual re-established hedge may be a worse hedged position compared with the one originally taken, with losses already suffered to boot.

Again, the best attitude is to leave well enough alone. Decide what to do, if anything, much later in the hedge when things have settled down a bit and a clearer picture of the market may be emerging.

SELECTING THE RIGHT HEDGE MONTH

When futures and options on futures are used, the hedger's major concern must be the basis. It has already been discussed how a business might attempt to position itself on the right side of the basis by assessing its cash position differently, depending on the market. It has also been concluded that that course may often not be open to a business. Then the company must try to protect itself against a basis move by other means. One way of diminishing the impact of a move in the basis on the effect of the hedge, is by considering the hedge month.

It has often been stressed in this book that the predictability of basis moves depends on holding the hedge as close to the futures delivery month as possible, without of course holding it beyond the last trading day of the futures contract. In order to achieve this, the hedger would select the futures delivery month as close as possible to the time that the hedge would have to be lifted. In other words, if the hedger knows, for example, that the company must make a delivery of the cash goods at the beginning of April, April futures would be chosen for the hedge. This of course depends on the contract specifications. In some contracts it may be necessary to use the May contract in the previous example. These are details that need to be discovered during the process of developing hedging guidelines so that the persons responsible for managing commodity risk know what is expected of them and also that management knows what the options are.

The further away the futures delivery month is from the date of the cash transaction that needs to be hedged, the more difficult it is to predict anything about the movement of the basis. Fortunately, the vast majority of futures contracts have 12 delivery months per year, although some have seven. The worst case scenario is that a contract may only have 6 delivery months per year, but there will usually also be a serial month trading. This means that the next calendar month will always be a futures delivery month even though it is not one of the fixed delivery months. The disadvantage is that the serial month does not trade far in advance.

It may thus happen that in a particular contract, a hedger wants to select a month that is not available 6 months in advance when the hedge needs to be established. The practical solution to this problem is quite simple. The hedger will take up a position in the delivery month prior to the month that is actually required. Then, as soon as the serial month that is required for the hedge starts trading, the hedger uses a switch order to switch the presently held futures position from the original month into the month that the hedge needs to be in.

Keep in mind that a futures hedging transaction is really only a 'place-holder' for a cash market transaction that will be done in the future. At the time that the hedge is entered it is thus already essential to know when the future cash market transaction is to be done. If there is any uncertainty about its timing, it will be better to err on the near side than on the far side. It would be better to choose a futures delivery month that is too early than one that is too late. The earlier hedge can usually be more profitably rolled out to a deferred futures month than a deferred month can be rolled back to an earlier delivery month. Because of the basis change there is greater price continuity into the future than in reverse.

FOLLOWING THE BEST STRATEGY

A lot of discussion has already been centred on strategy. It will be attempted here to set out the most commonly used strategies relative to the hedging instruments utilised.

In this chapter the focus is on an attempt to stimulate creative thinking in the approach to managing commodity risk with futures and options. The guidelines contained herein are thus really no more than that. The real innovation must come when management sits down to consider the real-life situation faced by the business.

An important matter to consider is that all strategies should be regarded as opportunistic. In other words, no hedging strategy should be adopted as a matter of policy. All the strategies discussed in this section can be very advantageous under the right circumstances, but if they are used mindlessly they will at best be a waste of time and at worst also a waste of money. Nevertheless, it is important to know about them and to keep them in mind for use when the opportunity presents itself.

It should also be kept in mind that the strategies discussed hereunder are by no means exhaustive. Many other equally good and even better strategies exist. It is a challenge for every business to discover and even develop more strategies that may suit their risk aversion or business needs better.

strategies with futures contracts

Strategies for hedging with futures contracts are limited. The only strategies are to follow the basic rules of trying to get onto the 'right' side of the basis, given the market condition at the time of the hedge, selecting the correct month to hedge in and not taking any other precipitate action. Once a hedge with futures has been entered, there are no adjustments to the position that can profitably be made. The best possible course to follow is to hold the position until the hedge is lifted. The result of the basis move will determine the success of the hedge.

strategies with options

When options are used there is slightly more that can be done after the hedge has been established. When the price of the underlying futures contract rises in favour of the option and it is gaining value, there is no action that can be taken to enhance the outcome.

However, if the price of the underlying is moving away from the underlying, time-decay is working against the option holder. The option is losing value and it might be profitable to sell the option in order to recoup at least some of the costs of purchasing it. This would however not necessarily be a clever move. When the option is sold, the protection against an adverse price move is lost and any reverse in the price trend will result in the losses that it was intended to avert in the first instance.

The downside of the strategy must however be kept in mind. Every time the existing option is sold, it will most probably realise a loss. This is because of the dual action of time decay and the fact that the underlying price is moving away from the strike price of the option. This loss will have to be added to the cost of the next option that is bought. Although it is true that, on condition some time has elapsed between the previous purchase and the next one, the next option might be cheaper than the previous one, this difference will probably not compensate for the loss on the sale of the previous option.

Additionally, there will be trading costs. Although the trading costs are not great per transaction, the multiplying effect of continually selling and buying options will present a growing trading cost element. All these factors together spell out a rising cost situation to the hedger which may not be offset by any real gain on the hedge. The price of the underlying may just continue heading in the same direction for the whole period of the hedge.

The above criticism of the strategy is not given with a view to dissuading hedgers from its use, but rather to warn against using it as a matter of course. It is an extremely powerful profit enhancing strategy if used with circumspection and restraint.

There are two further main strategies that are available with options. They are both spread strategies, but with entirely different approaches. The first one to be discussed is an option bull/bear spread. The purpose of an option bull/bear spread is to neutralise the cost of the basic option hedge. A number of other option spreads are available, but they are mostly of advantage in speculative trading. The first one to be discussed is known by two names – one name being applied when calls are used and the other when puts are used. The names are 'bull call spreads' and 'bear put spreads', respectively. By whatever name, the principle of the spread remains the same.

The structure of the spread is in principle, simply that an option at the strike nearer the money is bought, while an option of the same type at a strike further away from the money is sold. If the purchase and sale is done at the same time, the premium paid on the long option will be greater than the premium received on the short option. There will therefore be a net cost in taking up the position, but the net cost will be substantially less than the outright purchase of the nearer the money option.

The ratio underlying the spread is that if the price of the underlying moves favourably for the long option, it will come into the money first and will gain more value than the short option will lose. If the position expires with the price of the underlying between the two strikes, the ITM long option will show a profit and the OTM short option will expire, leaving the premium received as a net gain. If the position expires with both options in the money, futures positions will be assigned upon their expiry ITM. If the structure is carefully followed, it will be observed that, no matter whether calls or puts had been used, the short futures will be assigned at the higher of the two strikes and the long futures will be assigned at the lower strike. The profit will therefore be equal to the difference in the strike prices. On the other hand, should the underlying price move away from the options and they both expire OTM, the loss on the spread position will be less than it would have been on a simple options position.

The problem with using the spread as a hedge is that it caps the profit in the futures market. Once the spread position has been taken, the maximum profit is limited to the difference between the two strikes. Keep in mind that a price move that puts the options in the money, amounts to an adverse price move in the cash market for the hedger. Capping the profit in the futures market may thus be inadvisable where the price keeps on moving in the same direction. After the price has gone through the strike of the short option, the hedger is basically no longer hedged.

That does not mean that the strategy is entirely inappropriate for a hedger, but it does mean that it should be approached differently. It is suggested that a spread position is never taken as a hedge to start off with. Start the hedge as a simple options position. If the price moves in the option's favour let it move and leave it alone. If the price is above the strike of the option, and all market indications make it clear that the price of the commodity is going to reverse its trend, the selling of an option at the nearest strike out of the money becomes a serious consideration for the hedger. If there is a serious prospect that the steam has gone out of the existing price trend, the strategy obviously has the advantage that its capping of the possible profit has no real significance. Also, because the underlying price will be close to the strike of the option to be sold, a better premium may well be realised and the cost of the original option may be neutralised to a greater extent than it would have been if the position had been taken originally. This latter effect obviously depends on a number of variables and is postulated as no more than a possibility.

If the price then trends the other way and the options both expire out of the money, the hedger will have gained more profit from the favourable price move on the cash market. The price will not have had to move by as much to neutralise the cost of the option as it will have been already neutralised to an extent by the sale of the option at the higher strike.

The final alternative option hedging strategy to be discussed is the buying of a strangle. A strangle is a spread position that consists of two long options (per position), one of each type. The two options are said to 'strangle' the price of the underlying because the put option will always be above the price of the underlying futures while the call will always be below the price. Both options are thus in the money. Consider the same scenario as is in the previous spread. Instead of selling an option of the same type at the first strike out of the money, an option of the opposite type is now bought at a strike in the money.

Please note the wording of the previous sentence. The second option that is bought is bought at a strike in the money, not necessarily the first strike in the money. It is imperative that the spread does not expire with the last option out of the money. That would be a disastrous result, because of the additional costs incurred. It would therefore be better to buy the option at an even further into the money strike, just to be certain that that option will not expire out of the money.

The purpose of this spread is obviously not to minimise cost, but rather to ensure a profit on the hedge. It is therefore a strategy to be considered especially when the basis move is against the hedge. The hedge would start off as a normal options hedge. If the futures price moves away from the strike of the option no action is taken. However, if the original option goes into the money and it then appears that the trend of the underlying price is reversing or the market gets locked into a sideways movement, the second in the money option can be bought. The longer the time left to expiration, the less safe the action would be.

In the premises of the strategy, the price of the futures on expiration will thus be either somewhere between the strikes of the two options, or it will be such that only the last bought option is in the money. Thus the purpose is to have either both options to expire in the money or only the last option to expire in the money. If the two options both expire in the money, the profit will be the difference between the strikes of the two options less the premiums paid. It does not matter where exactly the futures price actually ends up – if it is between the strikes, the profit will be the same.

The purchasing of the second option thus locks in the profit. When this action is contemplated, the locked in profit can be calculated. Be sure to do the calculation before any action is taken. If the price has not moved substantially in favour of the first option there is unlikely to be a profit at all. The point is therefore to make 100% sure that there is a profit to be locked in, otherwise you might just be locking in a loss.

If the position expires with the first option OTM, then the second option must necessarily be ITM. The second option will now be further in the money and the profit on it will get bigger and bigger the further the price moves in its favour. The only cost to be factored against the profit is still the premiums paid on the two options. The important point to understand is that, whatever happens, given the parameters discussed, the profit on the hedge can be greater, but never less than the profit that was locked in when the second option was bought.

This latter strategy might thus have the result of a profit on the hedge as well as a profit on the cash market, even against an unfavourable basis move. However, the situation must be carefully considered and calculated before any precipitate action is taken.

strategies with synthetic futures

In the previous section on choosing between a straight futures position and a synthetic futures position, a basic strategy with synthetic futures was discussed. That strategy can be described as a strategy of option conversion. The synthetic futures position is converted into a straight options hedge by losing the short option when the price moves in its direction and away from the long option.

The main drawback of that strategy is that it may result in a high net cost, depending on the amount by which the short option has appreciated by the time it is decided to repurchase it. Because the move of the futures price is placing the short option further and further into the money, it will be in the money when it is repurchased. This means that its premium will reflect the amount by which it is in the money, over and above any time value the option may have. The profit that was realised when the synthetic futures position was taken may be small compared with the increase in price. There is fortunately, an alternative to consider.

Instead of purchasing an identical offsetting option, an option of the same type can be purchased at the first strike out of the money. This option will be cheaper than the in the money option. In addition, the profit on the synthetic futures will be retained. Thus, the lower price of the OTM option will be further diminished by that profit. The net situation is then that if the futures price remains between the strike of the short option and that of the newly acquired option of the same type, the hedger will be in a losing situation on the futures. However, this should leave him reasonably flat overall, as it represents a situation where he will be making a profit on the cash market.

Should both the short and the new long options eventually expire in the money, the loss on the futures cannot exceed the difference between the strikes of the two options, less the net premiums paid. In fact on the overall position, no matter where the futures price ends up at expiry, the total loss, if there is a loss, can never be greater than the difference between the strike prices, less the premiums paid. The position can still end in a profit if the futures price turns around and the long option ends up in the money. The hedger's situation will then be what it would have been in a simple straight options hedge. The profit on the long option will be offset only by the net premiums paid.

strategies with synthetic options

A synthetic option consists of a futures contract with a hedging option. The structure of a synthetic option is such that if the futures price moves in the options favour and thus adversely for the cash market situation of the hedger, it will always be the futures contract that gains in value. There is no need to adjust the futures situation in any way as there is no advantage to be gained. What may be contemplated however, is to adjust the position of the hedging option. The option is referred to as a hedging option because its purpose is to neutralise the loss on the futures contract if the price moves adversely for the futures contract. The option is at the first strike out of the money, taken from the point of view of the synthetic. In other words, if a synthetic put option is being constructed, then the option that must be bought is the option at the first strike where a put will be out of the money. This is so notwithstanding the fact that it will be a call option that is bought to hedge the loss on the futures contract.

It may be advantageous, on condition that the price has moved favourably for the futures contract by a wide enough margin, to sell the original option and to substitute it with another option at a strike nearer the money. This will ensure that whatever profit has been accumulated on the futures contract is basically locked in, should the price turn around. The price will of course be locked in from the strike of the new option and beyond. This will not enhance the profit being made on the favourable move. But it will certainly ensure a greater profit should the underlying price move favourably for the cash market position of the hedger. In that case it can deliver a profit on the futures.

The profit that will be locked in to the futures market will be the difference between the price that the futures contract was bought or sold, as the case may be, and the strike price of the adjusted option, less all the costs incurred, including the option premiums paid. This too is a calculation that can and must be made before the option position is adjusted. It must not be adjusted unless a profit is locked in, or the original net cost of the synthetic option is not at least substantially reduced.

THE CHALLENGE TO MANAGEMENT

The successful management of commodity risk presents some special challenges to management. The challenge mainly stems from the fact that the knowledge, experience and information required to manage the risk is not centred in one department or in one or two people. Risks, such as interest rate risk, credit risk and currency risk can usually be handled within the financial department and can quite readily be monitored by the internal control function of the company. Not so with commodity risk. Some of the challenges that need to be faced are discussed in this section.

To start off with, the availability of so many strategies to manipulate and enhance the performance of a hedge with futures and options on futures, demonstrates the flexibility and hence the reason for the popularity of these instruments. A business will be selling itself short if it does not include futures and their options in its arsenal of risk management weapons.

It will also be obvious, that apart from the terrific advantages that this sort of flexibility bestows on a business, it also demands a firm commitment to the process of hedging. Monitoring the markets must be done constantly and consistently as part of somebody's responsibility. Hedging decisions must be considered and made continuously. When the system is properly ensconced as part of the culture of the firm, it will likely be found that the activity is not so onerous after all. The benefits will be such that it would become inconceivable to be without it.

It will thus be one of the first duties of management to see that the company's culture and structure allows for the proper management of commodity risk. This book is not a book on management and thus a discussion of appropriate management techniques and structures falls outside its scope. Nevertheless, risk management does make demands on the structure and on the management style of a business. The present purpose is thus to discuss a few of the more pertinent management issues that are raised by the challenge of managing commodity risk.

the guidelines

Management's first responsibility will be to lay down guidelines for managing commodity risks. The issues raised hereafter and definitely many others, are among the most pressing challenges that management will face.

Laying down guidelines will be one of the most difficult tasks, but without it no success will really be possible. The absence of guidelines will create risk because management will actually lose control over the management of commodity risk. This is not far fetched because this is has led to major financial disasters in the not so distant past.

Employees who are entrusted with hedging positions have in these cases easily exceeded reasonable limits, became over-confident and started taking greater speculative positions as their expertise and confidence grew. This has especially proven to be the case where the risk takers in the company have their compensation linked to the performance of their portfolios.

A hedger should never be primarily concerned with the profits made on the portfolio of derivatives used for hedging. The whole purpose of a hedge is to neutralise losses. A loss on the derivative therefore does not represent an overall loss to the company. The correct approach would be to judge performance on the overall result achieved by the hedger. Did it succeed in what it was supposed to do? Then the value added by the hedger can be judged according to its true value.

culture

Managing commodity risk is not a function merely of the financial department that can be left with them and forgotten about. The knowledge and inputs from a wide spectrum needs to be brought together in order to manage commodity risk properly. Managing commodity risk is thus a function that may be executed by the financial department, but it is a function that they will not be able to fulfil properly without the active co-operation of the whole company.

No function of business can be successfully carried out if there is not a culture to support the activity. Thus in the case of commodity risk, there should be a general awareness that commodity price risk is a risk that management actively seeks to control.

There must be general information available on identifying commodity risk in a business since lower echelon employees often identify problems with the commodities that they deal with on a daily basis, long before it comes to the attention of management. In this manner commodity risks may be proactively identified and dealt with.

The employees that are most likely to identify these risks are those employees that are engaged in the buying department, inventory control, orders, production, sales and despatch. They are likely to be the first to hear about small and large developments in the marketplace. They are working at the coal face so they are the first to pick up on imminent changes in prices, adjustments in the policies of suppliers, buyers, competitors, amendments in product specs and hundreds of other factors that will influence the commodity risk of a business directly and substantially.

human resources

The main challenge to the human resource function in a firm is proper training. Various levels of skill are required at different levels of functionality.

For example, it is not necessary that the sales rep knows how to construct a long hedge, but she does need to know that if customers are discussing a change in their buying policies, it may create commodity risk in her firm. She needs to know that that there is a proper channel for reporting that information so that proper notice of the implications will be taken.

In order to assist in creating a risk management culture within the business, human resources will have to ensure that training and information is available to all personnel. Key persons in the company that have vital knowledge in relation to commodity risk must be identified and properly trained. It will be necessary to make people in the buying, inventory control and sales departments aware of their required input. Similarly, the persons responsible for production need to share their knowledge of the commodities used, their grades, alternatives and so on, with the people in finance so that the correct hedges can be constructed.

This implies that people in finance will have to be trained to know a lot more about the nuts and bolts of the manufacturing process and what exactly goes into it, than would otherwise be the case. They also need to know a lot more about how the marketing arm works, what sells the product and what the customers require. Then again, the people in these latter departments need to be trained to know more about commodity risk management so that they obtain greater insight into the valuable role that they can play in its successful implementation.

The most important training exercise however, is the training of management and managers. Commodity risk management, as does any risk management, starts at the top. In the case of commodity risk, the responsibility permeates through to the whole organisation. Human resources have the responsibility to see that every department that has a relevance to managing commodity risk acquires the required level of knowledge and expertise.

channels of communication

It is management's job to see to it that there are proper channels of communication wherein information about commodity risk can flow to and from the commodity risk management hub in the company. It is suggested that because of the special requirements of managing commodity risk, such a 'hub' is required in a company of any size.

The hub is a central communication point where relevant information is gathered and from where management's requirements are communicated to all departments. It is also suggested that there should be regular meetings of people directly responsible for risk management to discuss the information and all related issues. This is to ensure that there is input from all departments within a business when commodity risk management decisions are taken and policies laid down.

internal control

Internal control has a very vital function in the whole process. Systems must be developed to keep track of the use of derivatives and exposure. Futures and options create leveraged risk. They are also off-balance sheet instruments. Special measures will thus be required to record and monitor these positions.

Furthermore, it will be internal control's special task to see that those responsible for managing the risk do not actually take speculative positions under the guise of hedging. They will also have to ensure that position limits and the correct hedging instrument for the job is used. The guidelines decided upon by management will have to spell out these details.

Finally, internal control will have to monitor the effectiveness of the commodity risk management system. Thus, they will have to form part of the process during its design, its implementation and its execution. By implication, those responsible for internal control in a business will also have to achieve a high level of knowledge of and competence in managing commodity risk. Once achieved, that knowledge and expertise will have to be continually refreshed upgraded and maintained.

CHECKLIST FOR THE REVIEW OF CHAPTER 7

General overview: the overall control objectives of the material dealt with in this chapter are to address the issues raised by the exigencies of managing commodity risk in the best possible way and to encourage creative solutions.

	Key Issues	Illustrative Scope or Approach
7.1	Does the business have clear guidelines on its commodity risk management policy?	• The guidelines must not only contain generalities and caveats based on its risk aversion. It must state what commodities are to be hedged and under what circumstances

continued

Key Issues	Illustrative Scope or Approach
	• The derivative instruments that may be used must be stated • The maximum exposure of the business to derivatives in general or to particular instruments should be circumscribed • Management's attitude to speculative transactions should be unequivocally stated • Approved hedge enhancing strategies should be spelled out • Clear responsibilities should be allocated for hedging • If remuneration of responsible employees is to be linked to performance, it is the performance of the hedges that should be evaluated and not the profits or losses in derivatives
7.2 Does the business have an ongoing system of information gathering and review of its commodity risk management guidelines?	• The only certain thing in business is that everything will change. In order to manage commodity risk properly, informed inputs would be required from responsible people in a number of departments • In many businesses it might be necessary to formalise this structure into a committee with regular meetings • Channels of communication need to be created, allowing commodity risk management information to flow in all directions in the business
7.3 Does the business have the right human resources to get the job done properly?	• It will not always be possible or advisable merely to nail the responsibility for commodity risk management onto an existing job description • A training program must be designed for employees to create awareness of the need for commodity risk management and what their role might be • Higher level training and knowledge should exist at middle and senior management levels • Training and expertise must be ensured up to board level

continued

	Key Issues	Illustrative Scope or Approach
7.4	Has the business provided for the management of commodity risk in the budget?	Like any activity, risk management costs money. If the budget is inadequate, the exercise can be about as harmful as it can be beneficial. It is not only the direct costs of additional personnel, equipment and other facilities that might be required, it is the funds that must be available to put up as margin and the costs following on that
7.5	Has the business developed internal control measures to monitor and evaluate the commodity risk management function?	Derivatives are off-balance sheet instruments. Proper control systems must be in place or they must be developed in order to keep control of the overall exposure to derivatives. This will not present a problem if they are consistently used as hedges, but over-exposure will show if it is being used speculatively Systems must be developed and put in place that will monitor and control adherence to the guidelines laid down by management Parameters must be put in place against which the performance of the risk management function can be measured. This will also be invaluable in reviewing guidelines and in fine-tuning the procedures followed by the business

index